Social Engineering in IT Security
Tools, Tactics, and Techniques

Sharon Conheady

Mc
Graw
Hill
Education

New York   Chicago   San Francisco
Athens   London   Madrid   Mexico City
Milan   New Delhi   Singapore   Sydney   Toronto

Cataloging-in-Publication Data is on file with the Library of Congress

McGraw-Hill Education books are available at special quantity discounts to use as premiums and sales promotions, or for use in corporate training programs. To contact a representative, please visit the Contact Us pages at www.mhprofessional.com.

Social Engineering in IT Security: Tools, Tactics, and Techniques

1234567890 DOC DOC 10987654

ISBN   978-0-07-181846-9
MHID   0-07-181846-4

Sponsoring Editor	**Technical Editor**	**Composition**
Brandi Shailer	Eireann Leverett	Cenveo Publisher Services
Editorial Supervisor	**Copy Editor**	**Illustration**
Janet Walden	LeeAnn Pickrell	Cenveo Publisher Services
Project Manager	**Proofreader**	**Art Director, Cover**
Vasundhara Sawhney,	Madhu Prasher	Jeff Weeks
Cenveo® Publisher Services		
	Indexer	**Cover Designer**
Acquisitions Coordinator	Jack Lewis	Jeff Weeks
Amanda Russell		
	Production Supervisor	
	James Kussow	

To Dad, for the left side of my brain, and to Mom, for the right side of my brain.

To Paul for writing me a computer game back in the day. Best £13 I ever spent.

To Gina and Holly. Some people stand on the shoulders of giants... I stand on the shoulders of midgets but it is just as good.

To Michaela aka Lulu P. for words, from Whitby to Nashville.

To anyone I have ever social engineered, I'm sorry. I hope you are more security aware as a result.

—Sharon Conheady, June 2014

About the Author

Sharon Conheady is a director at First Defence Information Security where she specializes in social engineering. She has social engineered her way into dozens of organizations across the UK and abroad, including company offices, sports stadiums, government facilities, and more. Sharon has presented on social engineering at security conferences, including DEF CON, DeepSec, Recon, CONFidence, and InfoSec, and regularly leads training seminars on how to perform ethical social engineering tests and how to defend against social engineers. She graduated summa cum laude with a first class degree and gold medal in Computer Science, Linguistics, and French from Trinity College Dublin and an MSc in Information Security from Westminster University.

About the Technical Reviewer

Eireann Leverett is slightly less famous than his moustache and once placed second in an Eireann Leverett impersonation contest (truly!). He studied psychology and philosophy at Antioch College, artificial intelligence and software engineering at the University of Edinburgh (BEng), and advanced computer science at Cambridge University (MPhil). He works at IOActive as a senior security researcher, performing penetration tests and writing whitepapers on the security of industrial systems. When he is not hacking power plants and oil rigs for his clients, he is an avid collector of books and ephemera. The subjects that interest him include con artists, card and dice cheats, pickpockets, sideshows, circus, and magic.

Contents at a Glance

Contents

Foreword

I can still remember the first time I even heard about Sharon Conheady from a friend in the UK. He said, "Hey do you know Sharon, she does what you do, but she is much smaller and waaaayyyyyy cuter than you."

Of course I had to know who this person was. A short time later, Sharon and I started a conversation online and before long she was on my podcast and was one of the only women I knew actively doing social engineering. We interviewed her about being a social engineer in the UK and how different the laws are there than here in the United States.

The crew and I at www.social-engineer.org run a contest every year at DEF CON in Las Vegas and one year we invited Sharon to give a speech on what it's like to work as a woman in this field. The room was packed and she captivated the audience with her stories.

There is no doubt in my mind that Sharon is one of a kind. She has a perpetual smile, a lovely personality, and the brains to match. I enjoyed reading this book and seeing her personality and sense of humor (notice I spelled that correctly, Sharon) shine through the pages. I have written two books and I know it is a labor—there's the research, then the work, and then the worries if people will like it.

For me, I really liked Chapter 4, and I am sure you will, too. It covered how to start planning your social engineering test. I have seen so many people fail at social engineering because they lack proper planning, so it was excellent to see Sharon devote an entire chapter to that.

Sharon describes the topic of Chapter 8 as dreadful, but as a working social engineer myself, I know it is imperative to discuss the writing of the report. Sharon does a wonderful job describing how to accomplish this professionally and yet get the points across to your customers.

My favorite though is Chapter 3; I just enjoy the psychology behind it all. Sharon identifies these topics and gives you, the reader, a good basis to understand why these attacks work.

All of this is just my opinion, so don't take my word for it—read this book for yourself. Whether you are a security enthusiast, a corporate security officer, someone looking to get into the field, an educator, in law enforcement, or anyone in between, knowing what types of attacks are out there is the first step to staying protected.

If I could form the social engineering dream team, Sharon would be on that team. Having this book on your shelf is like her there giving you some of her time to hone your social engineering skills. Enjoy it. Read it. Learn from it.

All the best,
Christopher J. Hadnagy
Chief Human Hacker
Social-Engineer, Inc
www.social-engineer.com

Acknowledgments

I couldn't have written this book without the input of my good friend and technical reviewer, Eireann Leverett. I met Eireann when I was presenting at a security conference in Luxembourg. I put a photo of Victor Lustig in my slide deck, and when Eireann's eyes lit up on seeing it, I knew we were kindred spirits. Both Eireann and I are fascinated by deception in all its forms, from social engineering to magic, freaks, and geeks, and circus performers. I knew he would be the perfect person to review my book. Thanks Eireann. Every time we talk I end up with a new list of research topics. I have a feeling that will continue even after this book has been published. I am looking forward to many more conversations about con artists, crooks, and random weird stuff.

I am grateful also to my publishing team at McGraw-Hill Professional. Thanks for finding me, convincing me to write a book, and supporting me through the process.

I owe a final thanks to the person who gave me my break into the world of security testing. Thanks to Sarah Lloyd for recruiting me for your penetration testing team. I can't help feeling that you saw my potential as a social engineer in my interview, for better or for worse.

Introduction

Earth: mostly harmless, as Douglas Adams would have it. This book is about a small part that is not mostly harmless: social engineering. Social engineering attacks are becoming ever more popular and can have disastrous consequences. Social engineering tests can help organizations understand their susceptibility to malicious social engineers and can give staff practice at identifying social engineering techniques. However, performing a social engineering test is not as straightforward as it may first appear. This book describes the background to social engineering and why it works, and it presents a methodology for how to perform an ethical social engineering test.

Who Should Read This Book

This book is for security professionals who are interested in performing ethical social engineering tests and for anybody who is interested in how social engineering works. By understanding the steps that social engineers take, readers will hopefully be better able to defend against them.

What This Book Covers

This book presents a methodology that can be used to perform an ethical social engineering test. It also covers the background of social engineering, the legal and ethical issues involved, why social engineering works, hardware and software tools that can be used for social engineering, and finally what the future of social engineering may hold.

Chapter 1 provides an introduction to social engineering and explains many of the concepts that are expanded on later in the book, as well as documents the evolution of social engineering from the con artists of old to current social engineering attacks.

Social engineering testing is a gray area from a legal and ethical point of view. All too many security practitioners offer social engineering tests without considering the impact of their tests on their targets and without researching the legality of their actions. Chapter 2 discusses the ethical and legal aspects of performing a social engineering test, including what to include from a contractual point of view and the all-important Get Out of Jail Free card, along with several case studies from the press and whether they would constitute a legal and ethical social engineering test.

Chapter 3 looks at why social engineering works from a victim's point of view and what it is about human nature that has made us susceptible to social engineers and other scammers since time immemorial. As human beings, our nature is to trust and respect other individuals, especially if they convey some kind of authority. Most of us tend to be helpful toward other people, and if there is an added motivation for being helpful, all the better. There is also a distinct lack of responsibility when it comes to social engineering, whether it's because people don't think it's a danger or they are just too lazy to do anything about it. Underlying all of this is a lack of awareness—how can people defend against social engineering if they don't even realize it is a problem?

The next section of the book describes the social engineering testing methodology. Chapter 4 discusses how to plan a social engineering test, including performing a threat assessment, scoping the test and setting goals, project planning, and defining the rules of engagement. A good social engineering test is based on a plan that the testers can refer back to throughout the entire process.

Chapter 5 talks about research and reconnaissance, including what to look for when visiting the location you are targeting for onsite social engineering tests and how to perform research from open source resources. The success of the social engineering test relies heavily on the quality of the research and reconnaissance done beforehand.

Chapter 6 discusses how to create a believable scenario. To do this, social engineers need to create a character and a situation in which it would be plausible for the said character to make a request. There are many exercises available that help you create and practice social engineering scenarios, a couple of which are described in the chapter.

Chapter 7 is about executing the test—often easier said than done! There is a lot to think about when you are actually executing your test, not least how to exit the attack. This point is where the test succeeds or fails (depending on your point of view). This chapter discusses executing both onsite and remote tests, what to do when you are inside, and challenges you may face on the test.

Chapter 8 covers possibly the most dreaded part of the social engineering test: writing the report. It is a discussion of what should or should not be included in the final deliverable.

In Chapter 9, we look at the tools of the trade, both software and hardware. Social engineers can appropriate hundreds of tools to help their tests or attacks succeed, whether it's tools for information gathering or tools that can be used during the execution of the test.

Although there is no 100 percent defense against social engineering, you can take certain steps to make it more difficult for social engineers to target you successfully. Chapter 10 describes some of the measures you can take to reduce your chances of being the victim of a successful social engineering attack. You may not necessarily know that you have been targeted by a social engineer; therefore, this chapter includes a checklist to help identify whether you have been targeted. Finally, it looks at how to respond to a social engineering attack, both during and after the attack occurs.

Chapter 11 is a discourse on the future of social engineering. What we have seen or at least detected so far is, for the most part, pretty basic social engineering and has shown a lack of imagination and creativity compared to what we will see in future. This is about to change. We live in an increasingly connected world where it is becoming easier than ever before for social engineers to build profiles on their targets and create believable attacks that are more likely to succeed. In this chapter, we look at some of this new technology and the implications it has for social engineering.

1 Introduction to Social Engineering

They say a little knowledge is a dangerous thing, but it's not one half so bad as a lot of ignorance.
—Terry Pratchett

Welcome to the twisted and deceitful world of social engineering where nothing is as it seems. What you are about to read can be used for good or for evil. The choice is yours to make. Social engineering involves convincing people to perform actions they would not normally do. This usually involves revealing certain information or bypassing certain security controls, giving the social engineer access to sensitive information or facilities. It can be as simple as slipping in through a door that someone has left open or as sophisticated as setting up a long-term scam where the social engineer becomes an internal employee at her target organization and then steals information from the company.

Because computer security is becoming more sophisticated, hackers are increasingly combining their technical expertise with social engineering skills as a means of getting what they want. Social engineering can help ease along a technical attack, making it quicker and easier to execute. Many of the technical attacks we hear about include an element of social engineering. More often than not, however, the attack goes unreported. Sometimes people don't even realize they have been social engineered. A good social engineering attack is hard to detect, after all—although after reading this book, you will have a much greater chance of doing so! Victims may only identify the technical aspect of the attack and may not realize that it included a social engineering component. When they do recognize that they have fallen for a social engineering attack, victims are sometimes too embarrassed to report the attack, fearing it could make them appear gullible and they might lose credibility by doing so. Some people, some security professionals included, are under the misguided impression that only unwitting victims who are all too ready to be duped are at risk from social engineers. But even the most security savvy among us can fall victim to social engineering attacks.

Social engineering attacks can have disastrous consequences, both for a victim's finances and reputation. An organization can have the best technical security controls in the world, but these controls may not protect it against a determined and skilful social engineer. Education and awareness are key to preventing social engineering attacks. Social engineering testing can play a big role in this, by identifying weaknesses in an organization's security program and by giving its staff the opportunity to identify social engineering techniques in practice.

The objectives of this book are twofold. First, it presents a methodology that you can use to perform an ethical social engineering test. Second, by considering the different stages of the social engineering process, you will understand the steps that a social engineer will work through and hopefully be better able to defend against social engineering attacks as a result. My intentions in writing this book are neither to tell readers how to perform malicious social engineering attacks nor to encourage them to do so. Rather, it is to inform readers of the different stages of the social engineering process so they can better defend against malicious social engineering attacks. Like the quote at the beginning of the chapter from one of my favorite authors and creator of the Discworld, Terry Pratchett, I would rather people have a little knowledge, in this case about what the bad guys are up to and how they do it, rather than a lot of ignorance on the topic.

Different Types of Social Engineering

There are many types of social engineering attacks, but they can be broadly split into *physical* social engineering, when the attacker attempts to gain physical access to a sensitive office or location, and remote social engineering, when the attacker attempts to gain access to information or resources remotely, for example, over the phone or via email. Some social engineering attacks combine the two; for example, the physical breach may follow a series of remote social engineering attempts. Often social engineering is combined with a technical attack, making for an extremely effective and dangerous assault. The types of social engineering attacks are reflected in the various social engineering tests you can perform.

Physical Social Engineering

In a *physical* social engineering attack, the social engineer attempts to gain access to a physical location. He may do this via various methods, including

- Impersonation or false pretenses, for example, pretending to be a member of staff or a third party who has authorized access to the location
- Tailgating (following someone through an entrance without the person knowing) or piggybacking (following someone through an entrance with that person's knowledge or permission)
- Taking advantage of weaknesses in the physical security system, for example, disabling CCTV systems so security guards can't see the breach as it is happening or bypassing a fingerprint scanner using various methods

This book describes plenty of examples of physical social engineering attacks. For now, let's take a look at two types of attacks: dumpster diving and distraction attacks.

Dumpster Diving

Dumpster diving involves going through the dumpsters or trash cans of the target organization to discover potentially sensitive information or information that can be used to further an attack—anything from printed-out snippets of code to discarded computers or electronic media. Dumpsters, both internal and external, provide rich pickings for social engineers. Even the rubbish you discard at your home can be used by social engineers, so it is important to discard sensitive information appropriately. Chapter 5 includes details on dumpster diving, including the types of information social engineers look for and what equipment they bring on the dive.

Distraction Attacks

In physical social engineering attacks in particular, social engineers may use a distraction to divert attention from the real attack. Social engineers working in groups may create a commotion that keeps the security guards busy while their accomplices sneak into the building. The classic social engineering movie *Sneakers* has a great example of this. An apparently very agitated Robert Redford arrives at reception and asks if his wife has left a cake for him for the surprise party on the second floor. At the same time, Redford's colleague is disguised as a delivery man who is trying to drop off an unscheduled delivery of cleaning products. The receptionist is getting increasingly flustered. A car horn beeps and Redford, implying that it is his wife, goes out and returns holding a cake and some balloons, again supposedly for the party on the second floor. Both Redford and his colleague get upset with the receptionist. Between the two of them, they create such a furor that when Redford shouts, "Just push the goddamned buzzer, will you?" the receptionist buzzes him straight through.

Thieves often use distractions during robberies. I witnessed a distraction theft in Barcelona when a guy stopped a driver to ask her for directions. While she was leaning out the car window and pointing out the directions on the map, his accomplice reached in the other car window and grabbed the woman's handbag. She didn't notice a thing. Distraction theft is also common at ATMs where thieves target unsuspecting patrons as they withdraw their money. One thief distracts the victim, for instance, by dropping something or spilling a drink on the victim, while another thief grabs the victim's cash and/or bank card. A popular distraction in the UK is to drop some money on the ground, say a £20 note, and then tell the victim that he dropped it. While the victim is either picking up the money or denying that it is his, an accomplice makes off with his cash or bank card. One of the thieves will have most likely shoulder surfed the PIN code as the victim entered it, so the victim stands to lose a lot of money rather quickly.

A *ten attack* is a type of distraction attack that is frequently seen in the movies. It involves using an attractive person (someone you would rate a ten out of ten, thus the name) to distract the security guard while the accomplices sneak into the building. Someone told me that they once created the diversion for a ten attack in a most interesting manner; this person had broken both legs and was in a wheelchair and pretended to have difficulties getting into the building. While the security guards and receptionists were distracted, the other social engineers slipped in unnoticed.

Remote Social Engineering

Any communications system can be used by social engineers, whether it's telephone, email, social networking systems, instant messaging, or even fax machines, which rather unbelievably can still work wonders for social engineers (try sending a fax to your target organization in advance so they are expecting you, for example). *Remote* social engineering may involve direct, real-time communication with the target (over the phone or via instant messaging, for example) or communication that doesn't require an immediate response (email), which gives social engineers more time to plan their next steps.

Social Engineering by Email

Social engineering emails take many forms. The social engineer tries to build rapport as a precursor to the actual breach, or she tries to elicit information or spread malware by tricking the email recipient into opening a malicious attachment or visiting a malicious website. Two of the most common forms of social engineering over email are phishing and 419 scams.

Phishing emails typically take the form of fake notifications purporting to be from a well-known organization (often banks, payment systems, and auction sites), asking for the recipient's personal information including user credentials, credit card numbers, or banking information. Phishing attacks are, essentially, a *bait-and-hook* scam in which the email is the bait, used to lure unsuspecting victims in before hooking information from them. The social engineering really takes place during the bait, which should be enticing enough to convince the intended victims to open the message and follow the instructions within it. The hook is the method whereby the social engineer gets information from their victims, either a link to a malicious website or a telephone number that the victim is asked to call, for example.

Phishing messages used to be easy to identify, thanks to bad grammar and spelling, poorly formatted emails, and obviously fake links. However, they are becoming more sophisticated and more convincing because they have been increasingly personalized with more background research. Phishing attacks that are customized and targeted at particular individuals are known as *spear phishing*. When targeted toward rich or powerful targets, they are sometimes called *whale phishing*. And phishing is not limited to email. You can get phishing messages via social networks, SMS (*SMiShing*), or voicemail (*vishing*).

The classic *Nigerian 419* or *advance-fee fraud scam* is named after the article of the Nigerian penal code under which the perpetrator can be prosecuted. The fraudster poses as or represents a distressed but reputable person who for one reason or another needs some money to help her out of a jam; of course, the victim will supposedly be rewarded many times over for his generosity—although the reward never quite arrives due to one complication or another, which usually requires more money to solve. The scam combines emotion (feeling sorry for the person who has made the request because her family has died, she has been wrongfully imprisoned, she is being persecuted, and so on) with the potential to make a quick and hefty profit while feeling good about helping somebody out, appealing to good Samaritans and business people alike. Basically, the scammer tries to convince the intended victim to advance her some money in return for sharing in the profit later on.

Social Engineering by Phone

In social engineering attacks via the telephone, the social engineer attempts to get the victim to disclose sensitive information or to perform an action such as visiting a malicious website or granting the social engineer access to a certain system. The caller generally assumes a false identity and may use various techniques to convince the victim, such as being overly friendly, acting in an authoritative manner, or applying pressure. The caller may purport to be from tech support or an anti-virus organization, a financial institution, or even a charity. In many business cultures, challenging someone's identity is not socially acceptable and may be seen as impolite, so getting away with assuming a false identity may be easier than you think.

Mumble Attack   *Mumble attacks* are telephone social engineering attacks that are generally targeted at call center agents. The social engineer poses as a speech-impaired customer or as a person calling on behalf of the speech-impaired customer. Victims of the attack are often made to feel awkward or embarrassed and release information as a result.

Online information brokers used mumble attacks to dupe employees of Verizon Wireless into disclosing thousands of private cell phone records, which the brokers then sold. They called Verizon customer service purporting to be from the organization's "special needs group" (a nonexistent department) and requested account information. They claimed to be making the request on behalf of a voice-impaired customer who was unable to make the request. If the Verizon customer service agent asked to speak directly to the customer, the social engineer would then impersonate a voice-impaired individual by using a mechanical device to distort his or her voice.

I often use a "mumble attack lite" during my social engineering tests. Irish people are known for speaking very quickly. As an Irish person, I sometimes take advantage of this trait. Let's face it—you can ask someone to repeat themselves only so many times before you begin to feel awkward. I've used this to my advantage on social engineering tests in foreign countries, where eventually my targets have given up on trying to understand me and just comply with my request. Magicians sometimes use mishearing people or getting people's names wrong as misdirection for their magic tricks. There is a great quote from "The Last Nazi" episode of the TV series, *The Unit*, when Jonas tells Bridget, "You muffle the name, 99 to 1, they'll come back at you and deliver it to you."

Combination Attacks

Many security breaches combine attacks to achieve their goals, whether combining remote and physical social engineering, such as the Boy Who Cries Wolf attack or the road apple attack, described next, or a combination of social engineering and the more traditional technical attacks.

Boy Who Cries Wolf Attack

When was the last time you responded to a car alarm? Did you contact the police, investigate the alarm, or look for the car's owner? We hear car alarms every day, but few, if any, of us do anything about them. Because we hear them so much, we have become conditioned into not responding.

Like in the classic fable, in a Boy Who Cried Wolf attack, a series of false alarms are set off prior to the real attack, so that by the time the real attack actually happens, no one thinks it is an attack so they don't bother responding. In a way, they have been social engineered into thinking the attack isn't real. The University of British Columbia fell victim to a Boy Who Cried Wolf–style attack in 2008, when thieves made off with 15 art objects worth $2 million from their Museum of Anthropology. A few hours before the break-in, a couple of the museum's surveillance cameras mysteriously went offline. Campus security received a call from someone purporting to be from the alarm company telling them there was a problem with the system and asking them to ignore any alarms that were triggered, which they did. That night, when the lone security guard on duty at the museum went out to have a cigarette, the thieves broke in and stole the pieces.

In the classic comedy heist movie, *How to Steal a Million*, Audrey Hepburn and Peter O'Toole execute a fantastic Boy Who Cried Wolf attack. The glamorous perpetrators hide in a utility closet of a museum and proceed to set off the hi-tech burglar alarm repeatedly. Annoyed by the continual disruption, the security guards eventually disable the system, clearing the way for Hepburn and O'Toole to make off with the goods.

Road Apples

As well as being a bit of a countryside phenomenon, a road apple is a physical object, usually a storage device, such as a USB drive, memory card, or CD, that a social engineer leaves in the vicinity of his target organization in the hope that one of the organization's staff members will pick it up and plug it into their computer, unknowingly running a malicious program—or, in the case of an ethical social engineering test, a benign program that might do something like redirect the user to a training and awareness website.

A good road apple piques the intended victim's curiosity or otherwise convinces him or her to plug it into the computer. It might be marked "salary information," "naked images," or "redundancy information," for example—anything that a victim might find interesting. Some clever fraudsters in North Dakota created road apples in the form of traffic violation notices, placing them on cars. Recipients of the notices were then requested to visit a website where they could identify their vehicle and pay the fine. When they visited the website, they were prompted to install a toolbar to view images of their vehicles. Instead, they downloaded malware, leading to the compromise of their machines.

The name road apple is appropriate, because if you "bite a road apple," you are well and truly in the sh!t. Think of road apples as classic bait-and-hook scams, much like phishing, except that the bait is a physical device. The original road apple was the

Trojan Horse from Greek mythology. Nowadays we just update the big wooden horse to something a little more contemporary.

Chapter 7 gives some tips on how to create an effective road apple for your social engineering test.

The History and Evolution of Social Engineering

The first references to the term *social engineering* date back to the late nineteenth century when "the social question," that is, the fate of blue-collar workers, was frequently debated by philanthropic industrialists. Jacob C. van Marken, a Dutch industrialist at the time, coined the term *sociale ingenieurs* (social engineers) in an essay published in the *Delftsche Corps-Almanak* in 1894. van Marken postulated that modern employers needed the assistance of social engineers in managing the human aspects of the industrial plant, just as they needed mechanical engineers to manage the mechanical aspects of the plant. Such social engineers would manage "specifically human problems."

In the early twentieth century, the term began to shift from industry to politics and then to social science, where it encompassed behavioral control, societal transformation, and nationalist politics, to varying degrees. Even Sigmund Freud's nephew, Edward Bernays, considered that it was necessary to manipulate society, which would otherwise be irrational and dangerous. Bernays noted that the propaganda used in the war had been extremely effective in influencing the public's opinion. He put the propaganda model to full use in peacetime, developing the field of public relations, which is essentially a type of social engineering. Social engineering was not a well-liked discipline and was frequently controversial. Not much has changed in this respect as it shifted from social sciences to technology.

The Golden Age of Con Artistry

The con artists from the late 1800s and early 1900s were the natural predecessors of today's social engineers, albeit they executed their scams with much more style and flair than we tend to see today. This was the golden age of con artistry. In fact, according to historian Karen Halttunen, police estimated that nearly one out of ten professional criminals in New York in the 1860s was a confidence man! These tricksters had a repertoire of colorful scams with equally colorful names—the gold brick, the sick engineer, the Spanish prisoner, Jamaican switch, the golden wire, and the badger game, among others.[1] The most successful scams were elegantly simple, such as the glim dropper scam described in the following sidebar. Many of these scams will seem familiar as they are the precursors of many of today's social engineering attacks. Just add some technology into the mix and voilà—a modern social engineering scam!

---

[1]Many of these cons are beautifully described in David Maurer's 1940 book, *The Big Con: The Story of the Confidence Man*. Maurer was a linguistics professor who interviewed hundreds of con artists in the 1930s and became an expert in the language used by the underworld at the time.

The Glim Dropper

The premise of the *glim dropper* con is that you take something worthless (often something personal or fake jewelry) and make your victim an offer on it should it come into their possession. Then, usually with the aid of an accomplice, you arrange to sell the item to the victim for a lower price. The victim knows he can make a profit so he gladly accepts, but the original offer never rematerializes.

When this scam first appeared, the worthless item, the "glim," was a glass eye. The scam required several accomplices, one of whom had to be a one-eyed man. The one-eyed man went into a shop where he pretended to have lost his glass eye. (I don't have a glass eye and I'm not entirely sure how easy it would be to lose a glass eyeball, but that's beside the point.) The one-eyed man would offer the shopkeeper a $1,000 reward for the return of the eye, leaving his contact information. The following day, an accomplice entered the shop and found the glass eye. The shopkeeper, spotting the opportunity to make a quick profit, would sometimes offer to return the eye to its original owner, but the accomplice would insist on returning it in person. Rather than lose the generous reward, the shopkeeper would offer a lesser amount, say $100, for the eye. If the accomplice was confident enough, he would bargain upward from there, sometimes as high as $250 if he was lucky. Of course, the one-eyed man never returned to collect his glass eye and could never be contacted again.

The scam sounds pretty dated, doesn't it? But like many of these older cons, with a new twist it can still work today. An eBay user, BadgerMatt, wrote on Reddit about how he tricked a buyer who refused to pay into handing over the money using the glim dropper con in 2011. The buyer had purchased sports tickets from him for $600 but refused to pay because she had overbid and claimed her husband wouldn't let her buy them. BadgerMatt created a new eBay account, which he dubbed Payback, and emailed the non-paying buyer, telling her that he noticed she won the tickets, which he had meant to bid for, and offered her $1,000 for them. She said she would sell them for $1,100, despite not having actually purchased the tickets. So she contacted the original seller account BadgerMatt and agreed to purchase the tickets on condition that he drop them off for her that very night, which he obligingly did (and demanded an extra $20 for the hassle of driving over at midnight). The following day, she contacted Payback to check that they were still on for the exchange. Payback told her he could no longer make the game so the exchange was off. BadgerMatt got his $600 and an extra few bucks thanks to social engineering the buyer using the glim dropper.

William Thompson: The Original Confidence Man

The term *confidence man* was first coined by the *New York Herald* in 1849 during their coverage of the arrest of William Thompson, a swindler operating on the streets of Manhattan. Thompson, a well-dressed man with a polite manner, would approach strangers and start a conversation as if he knew them. Eventually he would ask his victim or mark, "Sir, do I have your confidence in me to trust me with your watch until tomorrow?" The mark, supposing Thompson to be an old friend, would agree and hand over his watch to the trickster. Needless to say, Thompson disappeared and the victim would see neither Thompson nor his valuable watch again.

Thompson tricked several New Yorkers out of their expensive watches before a victim from whom Thompson had absconded with his $110 pocket watch, recognized him on the street and had him arrested. The trial made newspaper headlines across the country when he was arrested in 1849 and again in 1855. Although Thompson was by no means the first con artist, he was reportedly the first to use the word "confidence" to his victims, resulting in the term *confidence man*, or *con man* for short.

Victor "The Count" Lustig (1890–1947)

Thompson's confidence scam pales in comparison with the sheer audacity of Victor Lustig's Eiffel Tower scam. Lustig was born in what is now the Czech Republic in 1890. He became a successful con man and was wanted by the police in several European countries. He relocated to the United States and decided to give himself the title of "Count" as he thought it sounded important. While in the US, he perpetrated many scams, including swindling none other than Al Capone himself out of $1,000. Lustig convinced Capone to invest $50,000 in a scam he was planning. He promised the notorious gangster that he would double his money within 60 days. When the 60 days were up, he returned to Capone and confessed that the scam had fallen through. Lustig returned Capone's investment to him and the gangster was so impressed that he gave the Count a $1,000 reward, which was supposedly what Lustig had been playing for all along.

On his return to Europe, Lustig played out one of his most famous and daring capers. It was widely reported by the press that the Eiffel Tower was in need of repair. Some people were campaigning for the tower to be torn down. Lustig appointed himself "Deputy Director-General of the Ministry of Mail and Telegraphs" and contacted five of the most prominent scrap metal dealers in Paris. He requested that the dealers meet with him in the suite of a prestigious Parisian hotel, Hôtel de Crillon, to discuss a confidential business matter. He explained to the dealers that it would be too expensive to repair the Eiffel Tower so they were going to dismantle it for scrap metal and sell it to the highest bidder. He reminded the potential buyers that the Eiffel Tower was never meant to be a permanent structure and quoted Alexander Dumas, who had called it "a loathsome construction." He asked them to keep the controversial meeting secret or risk public outcry. His scenario was well played out and well researched; the scrap metal dealers swallowed it hook, line, and sinker.

Lustig spoke to each of the dealers and selected the one who he felt was most likely to fall for his scam, one Monsieur André Poisson. Lustig drew up a fake contract handing over ownership of the Eiffel Tower, cashed the check he received from Poisson and fled to Austria. Lustig scanned the newspapers every day for reports of the scam, but Poisson never reported it, most likely out of embarrassment.

A short time later, Lustig felt confident enough to go back to Paris to pull the stunt again. This time, the victim reported his $100,000 loss to the police and the story hit the press, prompting Lustig to return to America.

It's Just Another Case of History Repeating Itself

Lustig's Eiffel Tower scam was similar in many ways to the social engineering scams we see today. He took advantage of current events (the state of the economy and proposed plans to dismantle the Eiffel Tower) to create a plausible back story for his scam. He impersonated someone of authority—a fictional government official—sending forged letters on letterhead. It was an extremely good deal for buyers—like many scams, maybe a bit too good to be true, but his victims bit the bullet and fell for the scam regardless. Finally, Lustig sold the Eiffel Tower twice over because the first victim was supposedly too embarrassed to go to the police, just as many victims are today, allowing crooks to get away with their scams and continue to prey on other victims.

Many fraudsters have since sold popular landmarks. It's not as unusual as you might expect. In 1947, George C. Parker regularly sold New York landmarks to unsuspecting tourists. He sold the Brooklyn Bridge twice a week, telling buyers they could charge people a toll to cross the bridge. More recently, in 2010, a British truck driver, Anthony Lee, was sentenced to five years' imprisonment for trying to sell one of London's most prestigious properties, the Ritz Hotel and Casino. Lee contacted a director from property-source.com, a specialist in finding property for private clients, purporting to be a "close friend and associate" of the reclusive billionaire Barclay brothers who own the Ritz Hotel. He explained that he was going to buy the Ritz for £200 million and planned to sell it immediately for "the bargain price of £250 million," offering to split the £50 million difference with the director if she could find a buyer. At the time, the Ritz was valued at between £450 and £600 million, so as with the Eiffel Tower scam, it was another case of the deal being too good to be true. The buyers put down a £1 million deposit to secure the deal. Lee claimed he received a better offer, but the deposit was nonrefundable. He was later found guilty of obtaining the £1 million by deception and sentenced to five years in prison.

Over the course of his career, Lustig had 45 known aliases and counted nearly 50 arrests in the US alone. In 1935, Lustig was finally sentenced to 20 years in Alcatraz because of a counterfeit dollar scheme he had running. Ironically, he was protected by order of another prisoner—Al Capone! He died from pneumonia in prison having served 12 years of his sentence. Before he died, Lustig wrote his "Ten Commandments for Aspiring Con Men." They apply just as easily to social engineers today[2]:

1. Be a patient listener (it is this, not fast talking, that gets a con man his coups).
2. Never look bored.
3. Wait for the other person to reveal any political opinions, then agree with them.
4. Let the other person reveal religious views, then have the same ones.

---

[2]Kathryn Lindskoog, *Fakes, Frauds & Other Malarkey* (Zondervan Publishing House, 1992). I'm not sure about number 5 on the list if it's part of an ethical social engineering test...

5. Hint at sex talk, but don't follow it up unless the other fellow shows a strong interest.
6. Never discuss illness, unless some special concern is shown.
7. Never pry into a person's personal circumstances (they'll tell you all eventually).
8. Never boast. Just let your importance be quietly obvious.
9. Never be untidy.
10. Never get drunk.

Social Engineering in the 1920s: Charles Ponzi

A Ponzi scheme is a pyramid scheme scam that pays early investors returns from the investments of later investors. Although Charles Ponzi did not actually invent the Ponzi scheme, he practiced it so extensively and so successfully that the scam came to be named after him.

Ponzi arrived in the United States from Italy in 1903. He drifted from job to job, often getting into trouble for cheating or stealing from customers and even for smuggling illegal immigrants across the border. Ponzi noticed that you could buy international postal reply coupons in Italy and redeem them at a profit in the US because of the difference in currency values. He set up a very official-sounding business in Boston, which he called the "Securities Exchange Company" to take advantage of this arbitrage. He sought investors for his company, promising them a hefty profit on their investment of 50 percent within 45 days or a full 100 percent within 90 days. He paid returns to early investors with later investors' money, pocketing much of the money himself, although most investors chose to reinvest the money rather than taking their profits. People began to line up to give cash to this apparent financial wizard. Ponzi reportedly had over 40,000 investors and by mid-1920 was making $250,000 a day!

It wasn't to last. Newspapers and banks started to investigate him and rumors of Ponzi's criminal past began to emerge. Investors panicked and started to withdraw their money, causing the scheme to crash and six banks to crumble in the process. Ponzi's victims collectively lost an estimated $20 million, with the story making headlines across the world. Ponzi served three-and-a-half years in jail and had frequent brushes with the law for the rest of his life. He ended his days in poverty, living in Brazil where he got occasional work as a translator. Ponzi died a pauper in a charity hospital in 1949. Ponzi schemes are still all-too-common today, as Robert Allen Stanford's $7 billion scheme[3] and Bernie Madoff's even bigger $50 billion scheme have shown.

Social Engineering in the 1940s: The War Magician

Magicians are often very accomplished social engineers. They are masters of deception, manipulation, and misdirection. No history of deception would be complete without a nod to Jasper Maskelyne, also known as The War Magician. Maskelyne was a third-

---

[3]Stanford is a former US billionaire who is currently serving a 110-year federal prison sentence for running an international Ponzi scheme which involved selling fraudulent certificates of deposit from his offshore bank in Antigua.

generation magician in the United Kingdom. He worked as a stage magician in the 1930s and '40s. When World War II broke out, he joined the camouflage department in the military, where he claimed to be responsible for some incredible feats of large-scale deception against the Axis forces.

The story goes that Maskelyne created the illusion of a German battleship on the river Thames to convince the British military that it could use an illusionist on the battlefield. He used a small balloon model and a system of mirrors to conjure up the illusion of a 61-foot-long juggernaut! The military was convinced and put Maskelyne's skills to use. What better way to fight the Nazis than through magic and illusion!

Maskelyne was put to work for MI9 in Cairo, where he created devices that were intended to help soldiers to escape if captured, such as playing cards that contained maps, shoelaces with hidden wire that could saw through bars, and real currency hidden in board games. His MI9 team reportedly smuggled almost 2,000 such devices into German Prisoner of War camps.

During his time in Egypt, Alexandra harbor was a ripe target for Axis forces, owing to its proximity to the Suez Canal. In a feat that beggars belief, Maskelyne managed to hide the entire harbor from aerial bombers. He set up a full-scale dummy harbor three miles away from the real one using canvas ships and plywood buildings. He duplicated the light grid and harbor lighthouse. When the Luftwaffe came to attack, Maskelyne switched the lights off at the real Alexandra Harbor and switched them on at the fake harbor instead. The Germans fell for it. They believed they had actually engaged in battle and won. Maskelyne encouraged the illusion by pretending to fight back with fake shells and setting up the real harbor to look as if it had been attacked, with fake rubble made of papier-mâché and canvases that were painted to look like bomb craters deployed around the harbor. Maskelyne went on to hide the Suez Canal and to allegedly mastermind Operation Bertram, to mislead the Germans about where and when the Battle of Alamein was to take place.

Maskelyne described some of his achievements in his book, *Magic: Top Secret* (S. Paul, 1949). Some of his stories have been confirmed; others have been questioned by skeptics. They are all entertaining. Maskelyne was undoubtedly a great social engineer; whether he put his skills to use against the Axis Forces or against a susceptible public.

Social Engineering in the 1950s: Frank Abagnale

Frank William Abagnale, Jr. is one of the world's best-known social engineers, thanks largely to the Hollywood blockbuster based on his biography of the same title, *Catch Me If You Can*. Abagnale was a career con artist between the ages of 16 and 21, specializing in impersonation and check forgery. He exceled in using social engineering techniques. Abagnale posed as a pilot for Pan Am Airlines to get free flights (although he never actually flew any planes) when he was just 16 years old. In the five short years before he was arrested, Abagnale assumed no less than eight different identities, from teaching assistant to attorney, airline pilot to doctor. He cashed $2.5 million in fake checks in every US state and in 26 foreign countries.

Abagnale served 5 years of his 12-year sentence. Despite two attempts to escape, he was paroled on the condition that he would help the FBI to uncover other check forgers. He has since made a very successful career as a security consultant, with a reported net worth of over $10 million!

Social Engineering in the 1970s–1990s: Kevin Mitnick

Kevin Mitnick was at one point the most-wanted computer criminal in the US. Like Abagnale before him, he used social engineering from an early age. When he was just 12 years old, the young Mitnick discovered a way to get free transport on the LA bus network, which used a punch-card ticketing system at the time. He social engineered a bus driver into telling him where he could purchase the same kind of punch that bus drivers used for the transfer passes by telling the driver that he needed one for a school project. He bought his own ticket punch and collected unused transfers from the trash, which he punched himself whenever he needed a free bus ride.

When Mitnick was still in high school, some friends dared him to hack into a system called The Ark, which was used at Digital Equipment Corporation (DEC) as a development platform. Mitnick called the system manager claiming to be a member of the project team and convinced the guy to give him access to the system and select a new password. It took him less than five minutes. Mitnick did several stints in juvenile prison for various hacking-related offenses.

From the 1970s until his final arrest in 1995, Mitnick hacked into multiple organizations, including Pacific Bell, Sun Microsystems, Nokia, and Motorola, among others. Mitnick attributed much of his success to what he called *social engineering*, which he explained in his book *The Art of Deception: Controlling the Human Element of Security* as "Social engineering uses influence and persuasion to deceive people by convincing them that the social engineer is someone he is not or by manipulation. As a result, the social engineer is able to take advantage of people to obtain information with or without the use of technology."[4]

Mitnick served five years in jail, including eight months spent in solitary confinement. He now runs a security consulting firm, Mitnick Security Consulting LLC.

Social Engineering Since 2000

Just as the turn of the twentieth century was a golden age for con artists, the turn of the millennium has been a golden age for social engineers. Social engineering attacks have become more sophisticated and widespread in recent years. The rise of social media has provided a great resource for social engineers looking to create a believable attack. We live in an increasingly connected society where everyone is a potential target for social engineers. Many organizations have been victimized by social engineers. The next section looks at the different types of social engineers who exist today.

---

[4]Kevin Mitnick, *The Art of Deception: Controlling the Human Element of Security*, Wiley, 2003.

Where Are All the Ladies?

There has been no shortage of female con artists, imposters, and social engineers throughout the ages, although we don't tend to hear as much about them for some reason. But as Beyoncé said, "Who runs the world? Girls!"

Barbara Erni in the 1700s

Barbara Erni, also known as Golden Boos, was a con artist from Liechtenstein who robbed inns across Western Europe throughout the 1700s. Erni would arrive at an inn in possession of a large trunk that she would request be locked away in the most secure room in the house as it contained valuable treasure. The valuable treasure was, in fact, a dwarf. At night, the dwarf would climb out of the trunk and pilfer the room. Erni ran the scam for decades without being caught. Finally, the law caught up with her, and she was beheaded in 1785. Golden Boos was the last person to be executed in Liechtenstein before they abolished the death penalty more than 200 years later in 1989.

The "man in a suitcase" scam is still going strong. A couple of people were arrested on an airport bus in Ireland in 2008 after passengers reported hearing noises from the baggage hold. Police found a 17-year-old youth inside a suitcase; he had a laptop and a camera in his possession, taken from the bag of another passenger. A follow-up search revealed a haul of suspected stolen goods to the value of €10,000 (approximately $14,000).

The Fox Sisters in the 1800s

The young Fox sisters of Hydesville, New York, were the unlikely founders of modern spiritualism in the mid-1800s. Soon after the Fox family moved into their new home in 1848, they began to hear mysterious rapping sounds, which the sisters claimed were messages from the spirit world and clear evidence of life after death. Two of the sisters, Margaret and Kate, discovered a way to communicate with the "spirit" that inhabited their home through a system of clapping their hands and snapping their fingers, which would, in turn, elicit more rapping sounds. They eventually learned that their resident spirit was that of a murdered peddler, Charles B. Rosna, whose remains were buried in their cellar. (In fact, some bones were found in the cellar, but not until over half a century later in 1904.) The Fox sisters became national celebrities and inspired a wave of spiritualism in the US and Europe. In 1888, Margaret revealed that they had faked it all by tying an apple to a string and bumping it on the floor or by cracking their knuckles and joints (including their toes). Spiritualism continues to fascinate people to this day, in spite of its dubious origins by the social engineering siblings.

Big Bertha Heyman in the 1800s

Around the same time as the Fox sisters, Prussian-born Bertha Heyman, also known as "Big Bertha," was busy defrauding (mostly) men in New York City. Bertha was dubbed the "Confidence Queen" and was described as "one of the smartest confidence women in America." Her ruse involved pretending to be a woman of considerable means who was unable, for one reason or another, to access her fortune. To this effect, she stayed in luxurious hotels, had an entourage of servants, and wore expensive clothes. She convinced various individuals to lend her significant sums of money, including an attorney, a train conductor, a businessman, a Wall Street broker, and even her jailer when she was behind bars! She lived it up while she was in prison, using her charm on public officials to convince them to allow her to go on carriage drives and visits to the theater. They called her "The Princess."

In his 1886 book, *Professional Criminals of America*, which profiled some 400 of the nation's leading criminals at that time, Thomas Byrnes said of Heyman: "When plotting her schemes she would glibly talk about her dear friends, always men well known for their wealth and social position. She possesses a wonderful knowledge of human nature, and can deceive those who consider themselves particularly shrewd in business matters."

Dina Wein Reis in the 1900s

Former New York socialite and con artist Dina Wein Reis scammed her victims for over a decade in her guise as the CEO of a retail distribution company. She would contact companies pretending to be looking to hire someone to replace her, and she would convince them to ship her merchandise from their current company, promising them access to lucrative markets through her completely fabricated and nonexistent "National Distribution Program." She would sell the merchandise to a middleman who then sold it on to the end retailers. This practice is known as *product diversion*. Wein Reiss was reported to have swindled companies across the United States out of at least $20 million. She was arrested for conspiracy and wire fraud in 2008. She agreed to pay $7 million in restitution to her victims and was given a five-year prison sentence of which she would serve 31 months.

Esther Reed in the 2000s

High-school dropout Esther Reed is best known for faking her way into several Ivy League universities using false identities. Reed attended Harvard under the name of a friend's sister for several years and even made it on to their debating team. She assumed the identity of a missing person, Brooke Henson, and was admitted to Columbia University. Her ruse began to unravel when police contacted Brooke's family to let them know she had been found. When the police visited her, Reed told them that she did not want to be reunited with her family as she had been a victim of domestic abuse. The police became suspicious (among other reasons, a police

(continued)

investigator on the original missing-person case said that Brooke could never have gotten into Columbia) and requested a DNA test. Reed went on the run. She was finally arrested in 2008 and was sentenced to 51 months in prison followed by 3 years of probation, and was ordered to pay $125,916 in restitution. Reed's brother was quoted as telling the police that she could argue either side of an argument and that, "She could convince you it was daylight outside in the middle of the night." Her story is being made into a movie, *The Girl Who Conned the Ivy League*.

Who Are the Social Engineers Today?

We are all social engineers to some extent. Any situation in which you interact with other people has an element of social engineering in it—that's how society functions. Some roles require more social engineering than others, such as sales and marketing professionals, politicians and headhunters, among others. There are some people, however, who will always use social engineering maliciously for their own ends.

Malicious social engineers tend to fall into three categories:

- Opportunists with little preparation and little to no budget
- Well-funded attackers with lots of preparation
- Trusted insiders

They vary in terms of the level of skill they have, the amount of preparation and resources they assign to their attacks, and the level of risk they are willing to take. Some malicious social engineers may fall into a combination of these categories. For example, a trusted insider could be someone recruited from within an organization, or someone who spends a lot of money and preparation to get a job within that organization with the intention of using social engineering techniques to access sensitive information or resources.

Opportunists with Little Preparation

Many organizations are targeted at some stage by opportunists or petty criminals who are looking to make a quick buck. This type of attacker tends to utilize an unsophisticated attack scenario and does not invest in the attack either financially or by preparing. An example could be a thief looking to steal valuables from an organization's building (although he may steal laptops, it's usually for their resale value rather than the information on them), or a scammer who sends out a customized blanket phishing email. It may even be a prankster playing a joke for her own or other people's amusement. When prankster DJs fooled the Duchess of Cambridge's maternity hospital into disclosing information about the pregnant duchess, the only preparation they did was to obtain the telephone number for the hospital. This prank is discussed further in Chapter 2 from an ethical and legal point of view.

Such attackers can nevertheless be dangerous from an information security or financial point of view. As well as the potential loss of physical assets, organizations risk information on assets lost becoming public. In 2005, T-Mobile had a security breach in which the contents of socialite Paris Hilton's cell phone were published online, including her address book containing other celebrities' contact details, her personal notes, and intimate photos. This story hit the headlines in a big way. A teenager was subsequently prosecuted and sent to jail for 11 months. Reports vary on how the teenager got access to Hilton's handset, but they all include some element of social engineering. One report claims he social engineered a T-Mobile store worker into telling him a password for the firm's internal computer system. Another report claims he social engineered a T-Mobile employee into opening an email infected with a virus that allowed him to access its system. Either way, it impacted T-Mobile's reputation.

Organized External Attackers

The second category of social engineers are organized attackers who want to obtain sensitive information, make a significant financial windfall from the attack, or cause disruption to a particular target. Examples of this kind of attack include corporate espionage, organized crime, and politically motivated attacks, for example, certain environmentalist groups trying to disrupt oil or gas conferences.

These adversaries are often well funded and can afford more sophisticated attacks that take place over a longer period of time. For example, in January 2010 Google announced on its blog that it had been targeted by a highly sophisticated operation, eventually dubbed Operation Aurora by McAfee. The attackers identified employees at Google with access to proprietary data and then looked at who their friends were on social media. Rather than targeting Google employees directly, they compromised the social networking accounts of their friends and sent the Google staff messages with malicious links. These attacks were aimed at least 33 corporations, in addition to Google, including Adobe Systems, Juniper Networks, and Rackspace, who all publicly confirmed they had been targeted. The primary goal of the attack, according to McAfee, was to gain access to and potentially modify source code repositories at the targeted organizations. The attacks were reported to have originated in China and resulted in Google reviewing its Chinese business operations. Operation Aurora was clearly a very sophisticated and targeted attack that involved a lot of preparation and research, rather than just sheer opportunism like the previous T-Mobile example.

Internal Attackers

Insider threats to information security are a serious problem for organizations. Even the NSA is not immune to insider security breaches, as former employee Edward Snowden demonstrated when he leaked information about the NSA PRISM program, making headlines around the world. Insiders working for an organization already have a great deal of information about how the organization operates. They know where sensitive information is kept and the processes and procedures for how to access it. They already have authorized access to internal systems and to the building itself. Insiders know where the soft spots are.

An insider attack can be undertaken by insiders in various roles:

- Someone who has physical access to the building with authorized access to IT systems, such as a disgruntled employee
- Someone who has physical access to the building but no access to IT systems, such as a cleaner
- Someone who has physical access to the building but limited access to IT systems, such as a third-party contractor
- Someone who has already gained unauthorized remote access to the IT systems

Introduction to Social Engineering Testing

Social engineering is a huge problem for organizations today. Performing a social engineering test is an extremely worthwhile exercise to improve defenses against malicious social engineers. A social engineering test can

- Test the effectiveness of physical and logical security controls and provide recommendations on how to improve them
- Test the level of and even improve security awareness among staff
- Give staff practice at identifying the techniques that social engineers may use and at learning how to deal with social engineering situations

However, knowing how to conduct a social engineering test can be difficult, as a number of challenges are involved. How do you create an effective scenario? What are you allowed to do from a legal perspective? How do you report on a social engineering test? This book will teach readers how to perform an ethical social engineering test using a repeatable social engineering test methodology.

The Social Engineering Test Methodology

The social engineering test should be approached like any business project and the methodology is largely reflective of that used for penetration tests. The social engineering methodology has five phases, as shown in Figure 1-1. It starts with project planning and target identification, moving through to research and reconnaissance, scenario creation, and finally to attack execution and reporting. This methodology can be tailored for each test and no two social engineering assignments are the same. The purpose of the methodology is to design social engineering tests that are systematic, repeatable, and consider the legal and ethical implications of the actions taken.

In the planning and target identification phase, you work with your client to identify who or what you will or will not test, when you will run the test, and how you will go about it. The objective of this phase is to define a project plan with clear goals that have been authorized by the appropriate people. It includes the following activities:

- Threat assessment
- Scoping the test and setting goals

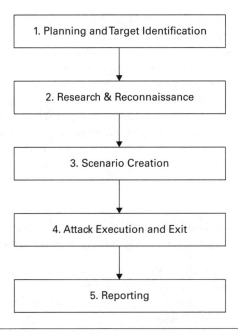

FIGURE 1-1   The social engineering testing methodology

- Project planning
- Defining the rules of engagement

The research and reconnaissance phase involves gathering as much information as possible about your target in the time you have allowed within your budget for this phase. If you are doing a physical test, you visit the location you are targeting to gather information about it. What time do people arrive for work? Are there any unofficial entrances, fire escapes, and so forth? For remote tests, the research and reconnaissance phase involves gathering information from publicly available sources such as corporate websites, social networks, and newspapers.

You use the information you have gathered through your research and reconnaissance activities to create a plausible attack scenario, in the scenario creation phase. In this phase, you design the back story that gives you a reason for requesting the information or access that you are seeking. Your scenario will be used to convince your target to comply with your request. To create a good scenario, you brainstorm potential scenarios and choose the one that is both achievable and most likely to succeed. You develop the scenario further and practice, practice, practice until it is time to execute the test.

Executing the test is the most exciting phase of the social engineering test methodology. The execution phase for a remote attack in which there is no real-time interaction (such as a phishing test) is relatively straightforward—you lay the bait and wait for your victim to respond. It gets more complicated as soon as you start having direct real-time interaction with your target, for example, over the phone or in person. You play out your scenario to attempt to gain access to the information or resources that you are targeting. Then you attempt to exit the execution phase without alerting your target that they have been social engineered.

Reporting on your social engineering exploits can seem rather dull after the excitement of the test itself, but it has to be done. The report is the deliverable that your client receives from the project. Your report is likely to consist of two sections: the executive summary and the technical details (methodology used, timeline, findings, and recommendations). As you are writing your report, keep the audience for each section in mind.

How Much Information or Levels of Access Should Be Provided for the Social Engineering Test?

When you are planning a social engineering test, you will need to decide how much information the testers will receive and what level of access they will have to perform the test. First, like a penetration test, a social engineering test can be performed with varying levels of knowledge about the target, from a black-box test where the testers know nothing about their targets to a white-box test where the testers have a deep understanding of how the target organization works. Usually, social engineering tests are performed as gray-box tests, with some information, such as contact details or floor plans, provided in advance in the interest of saving time and money.

Second, the level of access the social engineering testers will have depends on what role the social engineers will play. Social engineering tests can be done from a variety of perspectives, including

- That of an outsider who is a stranger to the target organization
- That of a third party who has limited access to the organization
- That of an internal employee

Keep in mind, however, that even internal employees have varying levels of access within an organization.

Your social engineering testers will work with you to decide which is the most appropriate perspective to perform the test from and what kind of information should be provided in advance. Chapter 4 covers planning the social engineering test.

Final Thoughts

Defending against malicious social engineers is becoming more difficult. Their attacks are becoming more targeted and more believable, which is exactly why we need to understand how social engineers operate. We need to educate ourselves and our colleagues and start thinking like social engineers. We need to get into the mindset of social engineers, understand what drives them, and how they can use our information against us. We can't predict every attack. And we can't issue patches for social engineering. But by thinking like a social engineer, we can detect where some of our vulnerabilities lie and better defend them.

You can be the person who stops the social engineering attack from being successful. You can refuse to give information over the phone; you can opt to not visit that link; you can question the person who followed you into the office. To defend against social engineers, you need to understand how they operate. Consider the following questions:

- What would be a social engineer's motivation for targeting your company?
- What would a social engineer want to steal?
- What would the social engineer's likely budget and skill set be?
- How might the social engineer get in?

Now read on while keeping these questions in mind.

2

The Legal and Ethical Aspects of Social Engineering Tests

There are two types of people in this world, good and bad. The good sleep better, but the bad seem to enjoy the waking hours much more.
—Woody Allen

Social engineering testing is a legal and ethical minefield. There are quite a few limitations that quickly become apparent once you begin your social engineering test or even embark on your social engineering career. You must keep two questions in mind throughout each stage of the social engineering test:

- Is it legal?
- Is it ethical?

The legal aspects of a social engineering test can be complicated, and you would be wise to take advice from a lawyer who is not only local to the jurisdiction you are operating in but also specializes in this area of the law. Laws affecting social engineering tests can vary widely from one jurisdiction to the next. Whereas carrying lock picks and using them as part of your test may be lawful in one country, it may be illegal in another, so be sure to get legal advice on this before engaging in any lock-picking scenarios. Likewise, data protection laws differ from region to region and can greatly impact your test scenarios; again, do your research on what is legal or illegal before you begin. This does not mean performing a quick Google search on applicable laws. You *must* speak to a qualified lawyer who specializes in this area to understand fully the rules, risks, and potential consequences of your activities before engaging in testing in a new jurisdiction. Your social engineering contract needs to take into account applicable laws or regulations that might impact your test. Many testers view the contract as something to get out of the way before doing a test. The contract, however, is your protection in case of legal entanglement.

But the legal complications can seem trivial compared to the ethical dilemmas you may face throughout the course of a social engineering test. Is it ever possible to execute a fully ethical social engineering test?

All security testing involves ethical questions at some level; social engineering testing even more so, as it involves people as well as machines—people whom you

Disclaimer: This chapter outlines a number of the legal and ethical issues that I have encountered in my career as a social engineer. It is not intended as and should not be relied on as legal advice. Prior to engaging in social engineering activities in any jurisdiction, you should consult with a qualified legal professional to ensure that you have a full understanding of the legal risks involved in your activities and any measures that you need to take to ensure that those activities are carried out in a lawful manner.

may feel bad about misleading and who may be angry that they have been duped and who may take legal action (civil or criminal) as a result. People have different boundaries when it comes to social engineering, both in terms of what they feel comfortable doing themselves as a tester and in what they feel comfortable doing to other individuals as their targets. Social engineers are likely to have broader boundaries than most people (otherwise they would never get the job done), but they should have tighter boundaries than a criminal. Some people have no qualms about using crutches or a wheelchair to deceive someone into holding a door open for them; for others, this is a step too far. Some people find it difficult to lie to others, believing this crosses their ethical boundaries. Some individuals may be surprised to discover they actually have any ethics at all once they start social engineering. The ethics of social engineering is highly personal.

The more social engineering tests you perform, the more ethical and legal quandaries you will come up against. Because a number of ethical, legal, and potentially embarrassing issues may arise for you and your client, this chapter outlines some of the more common situations that occur in social engineering testing. It does not tell you what is right or wrong from an ethical standpoint—that is up to each individual social engineer and is defined by the scope of each social engineering test.

It would be great to see more people performing social engineering testing ethically and responsibly. There are many stories about social engineering tests gone wrong and people ending up on the wrong side of the law because they haven't thought through their social engineering scenarios. We'll look at several examples later in this chapter. If you approach your test responsibly and have a comprehensive contract in place, you can avoid these issues.

Malicious Social Engineers vs. Ethical Social Engineers

We all have a tendency to glamorize the social engineering exploits we hear about in the media, especially when it comes to the con artists of old. Often we admire them for getting one up on the organizations or systems that they compromise, especially when it's a clever scheme. Hollywood loves a good con artist story. *Catch Me If You Can*, the movie based on the exploits of Frank Abagnale Jr., one of the most successful con artists of all time, was a box office hit and is one of my favorite movies.

I am intrigued when I read about a social engineering scam, and I sometimes find myself envious of the freedom malicious social engineers and con artists have when executing their attacks. However, most of these attacks are malicious and often illegal in nature and are perpetrated by individuals with a different set of ethics and moral code than those of security professionals performing social engineering tests for a living. No matter how much we romanticize or glamorize the criminals of the past, or indeed the present, they were nevertheless criminals and their victims paid, in some cases, with their lives.

A malicious social engineer tries to get unauthorized access to information or resources using any means possible. An ethical social engineer may have the same objective but has more boundaries and (one would hope) a different intent, and she occasionally gets lucky enough to perform a test that doesn't cross any of these lines. Being an ethical social engineer can, at times, be quite restrictive. Malicious social engineers do not necessarily operate within the confines of the law. They almost certainly do not have the same moral or ethical dilemmas that an ethical social engineer will have.

Take, for example, the tragic and sudden death of singer-songwriter Amy Winehouse. Within hours of her death, scammers had posted hundreds of malicious links to the story of her death. To give another example, 419 scammers have no problems telling recipients of their emails that their entire family has died in a plane crash or some similar sob story, such as the very moving account Mrs. Elizabeth Maxwell provides in the sidebar. Fortunately, not many ethical social engineers will resort to such dubious tactics during the course of a social engineering test.

419 Scam Email Example

Subject: From Mrs Elizabeth and Daughter
PLEASE LET ALL YOUR CORRESPONDENCE AND REPLY BE ON MY PERSONAL AND ONLY EMAIL ADDRESS.
maxwell.elizbeth@yahoo.com.hk

Dear Beloved Friend

This business proposal to you is strictly confidential, with due respect.

Sorry at this perceived confusion or stress may have receiving this letter from me, Since we have not known ourselves or met previously. Despite that, I am constrained to write you this letter because of the urgency of it. By way of self introduction, I am Mrs.Elizbeth Maxwell, the wife of late Brigadier - Gen.Ben Maxwell former ECOMOG ARMY COMMANDER West African peacekeeping force in Liberia who died in the Liberia civil disturbance [War]. My daughter and I is trapped in obnoxious custom and traditional norms.

(continued)

We have suffered maltreatment and untold hardship in the hands of my late husband's family, simply because I did not bear a male child [heir apparent] for my late husband. By tradition, all that my late husband had, [wealth] belongs to his brothers/family. And myself is to be remarried by his immediate younger brother which I vehemently refused. They have taken all that I suffered with my husband to acquire including treasures, houses and his bank particular seized by them.

I wanted to escape to your country with my only child on exile, but again they conspired and stole my international passport and other traveling documents to further frustrate me.

Thank God, two weeks ago, I received Key Text Code from a Security Company IN EUROPE that my late husband deposited U.S $30 Million cash with this company. It has therefore, become very necessary and urgent to contact someone, a foreigner like you to help me receive/secure these funds overseas in a reliable bank Account (presumably an empty Bank Account, if available) and to help invest it on our behalf as well,while we find a way of getting out to meet with you in your country. These funds are kept on an "OPEN BENEFICIARY MANDATE" with the Security Company in EUROPE to avoid detection, seizure or diversion.

I have had several telephone discussions with the Officer incharge of the security company in EUROPE, who has express willingness to help me on meeting the company's demands.

This is why I have contacted you to help save me and my only child to receive these funds on our behalf. But, you would need to give me sufficient assurance that if you help me, you would not divert the funds. Me and my child have resolved to give you 40% of the total sum and 10% set aside for any expenses that occure by you will be refunded back to you. For this is all me and my child have got to live on.

Please, I have reposed my confidence in you and hope you will not disappoint me. I look forward to your urgent response, including your full mailling address indicate your private phone/mobile numbers and also your fax number for easier communication.

Please note that this project is 100% risk free but you must keep it very secret and confidential with strong assurance that you will not let me down at all.

NB: The secret codes and the Pin Number for this fund are safely kept with me which I can give you as soon as you express desire to help me.

Stay blessed.
MRS ELIZBETH MAXWELL

PLEASE LET ALL YOUR CORRESPONDENCE AND REPLY BE ON MY PERSONAL AND ONLY EMAIL ADDRESS.
maxwell.elizbeth@yahoo.com.hk

On a practical note, malicious social engineers do not work under the same contractual obligations in terms of timing, deadlines, and budgets. Working as an ethical social engineer, when our client pays us for a ten-day social engineering test, then ten days is what our client gets. If the test must be completed by the end of the month so our client can report to an audit committee, so be it.

Malicious social engineers sometimes have the financial resources to set up incredibly elaborate and complex long-term social engineering scams with huge payouts. (This is sometimes known as the *long con*, as opposed to the *short con*, which is more opportunistic in nature and involves swindling victims for the money they currently have on their person only.) Consider the wire scam plot from the movie *The Sting*, where a group of con artists set up a fake betting shop to con unsuspecting pundits out of their cash. This true-to-life con was documented in David Maurer's book *The Big Con: The Story of the Confidence Man* (Anchor 1999, first published in 1940). In an ethical social engineering test, this setup could potentially work very well; however, it would be a costly endeavor that your client would have to be willing to pay for.

If you look at the following social engineering headlines and consider them from a legal and ethical perspective, the limitations of ethical social engineering testing fast become apparent:

- Radio DJs and Kate Middleton prank call
- The epic hacking of Mat Honan
- Condé Nast transfers $8 million to phisher

Radio DJs and Kate Middleton Prank Call

In an extreme case of social engineering inadvertently going wrong, Australian DJs Michael Christian and Mel Greig played a prank call on the hospital where the Duchess of Cambridge, Kate Middleton, was being treated for acute morning sickness during her pregnancy in December 2012. As documented in the transcript in the sidebar, the DJs impersonated the Queen and Prince Charles, speaking with incredibly fake British accents and asking after the Duchess's health. They were transferred by the nurse who answered the call to the nurse who was responsible for Kate's wellbeing. Incredibly, they succeeded in obtaining confidential information on the Duchess's condition. The story hit the international news in a big way, to the point where the DJs involved had to go into hiding. Tragically, the nurse who had transferred the call—we can only assume in her desperation following the incident—committed suicide shortly thereafter. This is an extreme example of the consequence that can ensue when a con goes wrong.

The DJs in this case presumably did not have any malicious intent. They had performed many prank calls previous to this, for the entertainment of their listeners. The British Crown Prosecution Service found no evidence to support a charge of manslaughter. Although there was some evidence to warrant further investigation under the UK Data Protection Act 1998, the Malicious Communications Act 1988, and

Transcript of Prank Call About the Duchess of Cambridge

Michael Christian: Here's the thing. We've been handed a phone number and we have been told that this phone number is the hospital where Kate Middleton is currently staying. We thought we'd give it a call. We don't want to cause any trouble, we don't want to stress her out because she is doing it tough. But I reckon we could maybe get her on the radio tonight.

Mel Greig: Look, I don't know. I mean everybody will be trying this.

Christian: Well, this is why I've thought of a plan. We can't just ring up and go "Hi it's MC and Mel from the Summer30, can we chat to Kate?" Hang up. Not gonna happen. You are going to be the Queen...

Greig: This is awesome.

Christian: I'm going to be Prince Charles.

Greig (Queen voice): Hello, I'm the Queen.

Christian: Ben and Em (off microphone) so you're involved in this as well, we thought that maybe you could be the royal corgis, if you're OK with that?

[Barking noises]

Em (over intercom): Sure we'll pop on in, in a sec.

Christian: I'm going to dial this number.

Greig: This is fun, I mean (adopts Queen voice), this is fun.

Christian: So you're going to be the Queen.

Greig: Hello, I'm the Queen.

Christian (in a Prince Charles voice): Hello. Prince Charles over here, mummy.

Greig: Oh, you're Prince Charles, I like your ears.

Christian: Let's give this hospital a call and see if we can get Kate Middleton or maybe even Prince Wills on the phone tonight. So the number is going in ... oh Jeez, I hope this happens.

(Phone rings)

Nurse 1: Hello, good morning, King Edward VII Hospital.

Greig (Queen voice): Oh hello there, could I please speak to Kate please, my granddaughter.

Nurse 1: Oh yes, just hold on ma'am.

Greig: Thank you.

Christian: Are they putting us through?

Greig: Yes.

(Laughter)

Christian: If this has worked, it's the easiest prank call we have ever made. Your accent sucked, by the way, I just want you to know.

(Laughter)

Greig: I'm not used to playing 80-year-olds. (Phone connects) Kate, my darling, are you there?

Nurse 2: Good morning, ma'am, this is the nurses' station, how may I help you?

Greig: Hello, I'm just after my granddaughter Kate. I wanted to see how her little tummy bug is going.

Nurse 2: She's sleeping at the moment and has had an uneventful night, and sleep is good for her, as we speak. She's been given some fluids to re-hydrate her because she was quite dehydrated when she came in. But she's stable at the moment.

Greig: OK. Well, I'll just feed my little corgis then (barking in the background). So when is a good time to come and visit her? Because I'm the Queen so I'll need a lift down there. Charles! When can you take me to the hospital, Charles?

Christian (pretending to be Prince Charles): When will it be all right to come down and see her? Maybe in the morning or something? If that's OK?

Nurse 2: I would suggest that any time after nine o'clock would be suitable, because the doctor will be in in the morning and we'll just be getting her freshened up in the morning. I would think any time after nine.

Christian: Wonderful. Is Wills still there or has he gone home? I haven't spoken to him yet.

Nurse 2: He went home at about half past nine last night. Actually, probably about nine o' clock last night.

Christian: OK, Lovely. But they're all OK, everything's all right?

Nurse 2: Yes, she's quite stable at the moment. She hasn't had any retching with me since I've been on duty. And she has been sleeping on and off.

Christian: Wonderful.

Nurse 2: I think it's difficult sleeping in a strange bed as well.

Christian: Yes, of course, it's hardly the palace, is it!

Greig: It's nothing like the palace is it, Charles? Oh, when are you going to walk those bloody corgis?

Christian: Mumsy, I'll go and take the dogs outside.

Greig: I need to go and visit Kate in the morning. My dear, thank you so much.

Nurse 2: You're very welcome.

Greig: Thank you, bye.

Christian: Goodbye.

(Hangs up)

(Laughter)

Greig: She was giving us real information!

Christian (as Prince Charles): Mumsy, I think that they believed everything we said.

the Communications Act 2003, they decided that no further investigation was required because any potential prosecution would not be in the public interest.

Could we make such a prank call as an ethical and legal social engineering test? From an ethical point of view, such an approach would not be respectful of our intended target. When it comes to social engineering, we must always keep in mind that we are testing people, not just machines. We never know how people are going to react. That's why we need to think through each potential scenario and consider how it might affect those who are duped by the social engineer. Where possible, we should avoid leaving our victims feeling humiliated or angry. In social engineering, there is always going to be a victim, but we can try to minimize the damage done.From a legal point of view, there may be restrictions regarding whose information you are entitled to access. It is extremely unlikely that you would be permitted to access information (particularly healthcare information) belonging to the royal family or, indeed, any celebrities. In many cases, you wouldn't be allowed to access any real information. Instead, a fictitious account may be set up that you can attempt to access without raising any data protection or privacy concerns.

The Epic Hacking of Mat Honan

When *Wired* journalist Mat Honan was hacked in the summer of 2012, it was widely reported by the press. His Google and Twitter accounts were hijacked as well as his AppleID account, which was used to remotely erase all of the data on his iPhone, iPad, and MacBook, including photos of his baby daughter. Unfortunately, Honan had neglected to make backups. Racist and offensive messages were broadcasted from his Twitter account, and, for a short while, the hackers also had control of the official Gizmodo Twitter account, where Honan used to work.

Phobia, one of the hackers claiming to have been involved in the hack, contacted Honan on his new Twitter account and explained how and why they executed the attack. They simply wanted access to Honan's three-character Twitter handle, "Mat." It wasn't personal.

> *I honestly didn't have any heat towards you before this. I just liked your username like I said before.*

After identifying Honan's Twitter account, the hackers found it linked to his personal website, where they found his Gmail address. Phobia went to Google's account recovery page and entered Honan's Gmail address, which allowed him to view the alternate email that Honan had set up for account recovery. This information was partially obscured, but there was enough information to continue the attack, showing that Honan held an Apple-run email account and, therefore, had an AppleID account.

> *m****n@me.com*

To access Honan's AppleID account via Apple's tech support call center, Phobia needed two further pieces of information: Honan's billing address and the last four digits of his credit card number.

His billing address was easily obtained by doing a simple *whois* lookup on Honan's personal web domain, which they had found on his Twitter account.

To obtain the last four digits of Honan's credit card number, Phobia called Amazon, claiming to be Mat Honan and requested to add a credit card number to the account. To do this, Phobia needed the following three pieces of information, which he already had:

- The name of the account holder—obviously Mat Honan
- The email address of the account holder—published on his personal website
- The billing address of the account holder—obtained via a whois lookup of his personal website

Shortly after, Phobia called Amazon a second time, again posing as Honan and claiming he had lost access to his account. On providing the billing address and credit card number associated with the account (which Phobia had previously updated and, therefore, knew), Amazon allowed Phobia to add a new email address to the account. Phobia then visited the Amazon website and requested a password reset to the new email account. He was then able to view a list of all the credit cards on file for Honan's account. Phobia was not able to see the complete numbers, just the last four digits, but this is all he needed to gain access to the AppleID account.

Could we execute a similar attack as a legal and ethical social engineering test? Probably not. This scenario involved social engineering both Amazon and Apple, so you would need to have permission from both companies—an extremely unlikely situation. Performing such a social engineering test with the consent of one company but without the consent of the other would be unethical, not to mention legally questionable.

In an ethical social engineering test, you are unlikely to be allowed to pick customers at random and try to access their accounts. As in a penetration test, you will probably have to set up test accounts that you can then attempt to access. You certainly couldn't erase data in the course of the test. So although this was a sophisticated and effective social engineering attack, it would most likely not pass muster as a legal and ethical social engineering test.

Condé Nast Transfers $8 Million to Spear Phisher

In November 2010, Andy Surface, a construction worker from Alvin, Texas, emailed a fake invoice to Condé Nast, the publishers of magazines such as *Vogue* and *The New Yorker*, for $8 million. Condé Nast paid the invoice. The email was from a fake company whose name sounded very much like the publisher's printing company.

Surface had allegedly incorporated a business called Quad/Graph with the county clerk's office and opened a business bank account under this name. Condé Nast's printers are called Quad Graphics. Surface emailed an electronic payment authorization PDF form to Condé Nast, requesting that future payments to Quad Graphics be made into the Quad/Graph account. Accounting departments receive requests to change payment accounts for perfectly valid reasons on a regular basis. Condé Nast accepted the email, signed the form, and faxed it back to a fax number specified in the email, allowing its bank to make payments to the fraudulent account. It is unknown how Surface knew about the electronic authorization PDF form.

The scam was finally revealed after a six-week stretch when the real publishing company contacted Condé Nast to inquire about outstanding payments. Federal authorities froze the fraudulent bank account before Surface was able to withdraw the money.

Surface eventually formally renounced any claim to his ill-gotten gains, saying that he himself was "the real victim" of the scam. In the *Houston Chronicle*, Surface claimed that the scam was actually perpetrated by an "old man that got my phone number off Craigslist and stole my identity."

He called me last year, he said he was a Seattle businessman who had 20 businesses was looking for folks to invest... He said to go down there (to the bank) and set up the accounts. I had no idea this guy was a scam. I had never even heard of these companies.... I'm just an old working boy that got fooled. I put my cowboy boots on, I wear Wrangler jeans.... You think it's something you're doing right, and it turns out to be a disaster.

Houston Press reported that a relative said Surface spent inordinate amounts of time on a computer and wouldn't let anyone see what he was doing. "I assumed it was just porn," the relative said...

A court filing in Manhattan federal court sought forfeiture of the funds on the basis that they were derived from proceeds traceable to wire fraud, in violation of Title 18, United States Code, Section 1344, as well as traceable to money laundering transactions, in violation of Title 18, United States Code, Section 1956. To date, Surface does not appear to have faced criminal charges for this incident, although *Forbes* reported that he pleaded no contest on a separate charge of "terroristic threat of family/household" in December 2010.

Could this situation be performed as a legal and ethical social engineering test? In the Surface scenario, there was an obvious attempt (whether by Surface or the mysterious "old man") to obtain property under false pretenses, so it was a clear case of fraud. In addition, Quad Graphics could have sued the perpetrator for attempting to pass himself off as the legitimate company. Then there was the fraud on the County Clerk's office and bank in setting up the bank account. However, any legal or ethical issues that arise in a similar context could potentially be addressed where appropriate disclosures and consents are obtained in advance. This may include disclosures or consents from the bank with which the account has been set up and/or any local government entities, depending on applicable laws. For example, let's assume that Condé Nast is the client. If Condé Nast consents in advance to the exercise, in this case, there is no malicious or fraudulent intent.

Is It Legal? Is It Ethical? The Legal and Ethical Aspects of Social Engineering

Whatever country or state you perform your social engineering test in, I strongly recommend that you get legal advice from a local lawyer who specializes in this field on what you can or cannot do in your test. This field is highly technical, and the applicable laws and regulations are equally technical. Much of the time, whether or not your activity would be considered illegal comes down to your intent. As an ethical social engineer, you are not performing these dubious activities to gain an illegal profit. By having a comprehensive contract in place and being well versed in the applicable laws in the appropriate jurisdiction, you can avoid any doubt in this area.

The Social Engineering Contract

The *social engineering contract* is a binding agreement between you and your target organization, allowing you to perform potentially illegal activities on behalf of your clients. The social engineering contract must be signed by you and an authorized signatory for your client organization in order to make it legally binding, turning your potentially illegal activities into legal ones. Typical issues that your contract should address include

- A description of the social engineering test and the types of activities involved.
- The time window during which you are authorized to perform the test.
- Any limitations on when you can perform the testing. Can you test outside of business hours or on weekends? For example, some call centers contract out to a third party for out of hours calls—testing the third party may be out of scope.
- Any restrictions in place for the test:
    - Physical locations, for instance, in a food production plant, are you allowed on the plant floor?
    - IT systems—are there any you are not allowed to target?
- Depending on your test scenario, written permission for any of the following activities:
    - Using trademarks or logos to forge documents
    - Removing assets or documents from the premises
    - Lock picking

In some cases, you may wish to have the scenario you are planning to use approved by your client organization. If you get it in writing, you may avoid any legal difficulties that may arise later. Some organizations insist on being party to the proposed scenario; others prefer it to be a complete surprise. In the latter case, your Get Out of Jail Free card (discussed in the next section) will be critical. If you want to err on the side of caution, discuss the ethical and legal impact of your test scenarios with a representative from the company's HR department. The social engineering test may involve deceiving or manipulating employees, and it is the duty of the HR department to uphold the rights of the organization's employees.

Note that certain activities will always be unlawful, regardless of whether your client purports to consent to you engaging in such activities in the context of a contract. That is why speaking to a lawyer to confirm applicable laws and, where possible, to ensure that your contract complies with such laws is so important.

The Get Out of Jail Free Card

The social engineering contract should also be accompanied by what's known in the industry as a *Get Out of Jail Free* card, in other words, a letter of indemnity that you can present should you be apprehended during the course of your test. This letter should contain the following information:

- An explanation of what you are doing along with examples of the potential activities you are proposing to engage in, particularly in the case of a "surprise" operation that has not been specifically approved in advance.
- The dates during which you will be performing the test.

- Two contact names and numbers for individuals within the company who have commissioned or know about the test.
- A statement by the organization acknowledging that you will be carrying out the relevant activities, specifying that it has consented to such activities and agreeing to release and indemnify you from any and all liability arising in connection with such activities. (Typically, the organization will seek to exclude fraud or negligence from the scope of such release or indemnity.)
- Your name and the name of any team members who are involved in the test.

I learned to always have two points of contact when a team member was apprehended during the course of a test and the only point of contact turned out to be on holiday for two weeks. This led to a tricky situation where the targeted organization had difficulty verifying whether the test was legitimate. Eventually the organization was able to contact the individual who was away, but they were none too happy about being disturbed while on holiday!

In terms of contact details, I usually include a request to the reader to verify independently the contact details of my point of contact rather than using the information on my Get Out of Jail Free card, which can always be spoofed! As a final precaution, I have my target organization print the letter on its letterhead to increase its authenticity. You may wish also to get a document such as a copy of board consent to confirm that the signatory has authority to sign on behalf of your client organization.

> **Tip** It is recommended that you retain contractual documentation and, in particular, your Get Out of Jail Free card, for a period of at least 12 years following the completion of the test. This period may vary depending on your organization's processes and local privacy or data retention regulations. This is another reason to contact a lawyer before performing your test.

Using a Fake Get Out of Jail Free Card

Some social engineers like to first use a fake Get Out of Jail Free card if they are caught, to add another level to the social engineering test. The problem with this is that it may create a Boy Who Cries Wolf scenario where the real Get Out of Jail Free card may be rejected, leading to a potentially awkward situation.

Laws You May Break

In the course of performing a social engineering test, you may carry out activities that, in the absence of appropriate consents, could potentially contravene the following laws:

- Forgery and trademark infringement
- Computer misuse
- Data protection and privacy
- Breaking and entering

- Bribery and corruption
- Impersonation or pretexting
- Theft of physical assets, information, or identities
- Malicious damage

The following sections describe some of the situations that may push these legal, and ethical, boundaries.

> **Tip**   If something would be illegal or unethical as part of a social engineering test, is there any way to simulate or "gamify" it instead? Consider this as you read through the potential issues in the sections that follow. I give some ideas for how to do this in Table 2-1, later in the chapter.

Forgery and Trademark Infringement (Including Logos)

Social engineers often forge documents to further their attacks, whether it's forging ID cards, spoofing emails, or sending faxes to announce their arrival. However, if you are going to forge a document under a real company name or make use of any company logos, you must have explicit authorization to do so. Logos are generally protected by trademark and, potentially, copyright law.

In a truly ethical social engineering scenario in which a social engineer wants to test if she can gain physical access to a building with an invalid entry card, she could ask the organization to issue her an deactivated entry card prior to the test and then she could use this to try to gain entry.

Legal ramifications could also rule out forging documents such as invoices that look like they are from a supplier or other existing third party to your target organization. If you are going to forge documents or make use of trademarks during the course of your test, note this in your contract and make sure it's explicitly authorized by your target organization.

Again, as mentioned already in this chapter, you should also confirm the applicable legal portion to ensure that you are not breaking any mandatory laws that are not waivable by the client. For example, it is generally illegal to forge legal documents such as passports, identity papers, birth certificates, social security cards, or drivers licenses no matter what the circumstances, so avoid this at all costs.

Computer Misuse

If your social engineering test has any technical aspects, which is often the case, there is always potential for computer misuse. As for a normal technical penetration test, you must obtain the appropriate legal authorizations for your activities from all the parties involved. You will need to obtain written authorization from someone who is responsible for the systems you are testing to allow you to perform potentially illegal activities on the network. Any kind of penetration testing without authorization can be considered hacking.

Data Protection and Privacy: Recording Your Social Engineering Attempts

As a social engineer, I have a treasure chest of different tools that rival James Bond's, from yellow jackets to hidden cameras. Many of the tools I have are recording devices. I use such devices to record either the social engineering attempt as evidence or to recall what has happened or specific pieces of information. A hidden camera pointed at someone inputting the secret code into a keypad can be useful. It may also be illegal. Generally, you must have the permission of all parties to record any kind of interaction. Journalists frequently covertly record conversations, with the justification that the content is in the public's interest and should, therefore, be disclosed. Companies may have different rights to record, and this may filter down to social engineering testing. Again, it depends on the jurisdiction in which you are operating, and as I've indicated previously, you should always confirm the applicable laws with a local lawyer.

Data Protection and Privacy: Obtaining Sensitive or Personal Information

Consider how you are going to obtain personal or sensitive information during your social engineering test. Will it be through social media, telephone, email, or other false pretenses? Once you have obtained this information, how are you going to store it? Will it comply with data protection regulations in the area where you have performed the test?

Always remember what the aim of the social engineering test is. Is it to obtain a certain individual's personal information or is it to show gaps in the processes that allow you to obtain sensitive and/or valuable information pertaining to your target organization? Consider how each piece of information you are attempting to obtain is relevant to your target organization and to the social engineering test. Although tracking an employee from your target organization down on Facebook and finding out what his hobbies are can be fun, you must consider how this is relevant to the organization as a whole.

In one social engineering test, I obtained physical access to a financial organization and found lots of personal information around the office, from employees' personal bank statements, to university course work and results, tax letters, and even the passports belonging not only to one of the executives but also to both of his daughters. His daughters didn't sign up for the social engineering test. Would it be ethical to make a copy of these documents? What about taking them offsite? Although a malicious social engineer may well take advantage of such a situation, I decided to do neither. The girls weren't employees of the organization and were not privy to the social engineering test. Furthermore, the aim of the test was to gather sensitive information about the organization—not about the children of employees of the organization.

Is it ethical or even legal for an organization to give you permission to social engineer its staff? If it's within the confines of the work environment, and the company in question has informed its staff that this kind of test may take place, it appears straightforward and is likely to be legal and ethical from the company's point of view. For example, if someone allows you to enter the building without checking your credentials—a clear fail—you've uncovered a weakness for your client. If you phone the call center and obtain certain sensitive information—again, a clear fail— you're operating within the confines of the test.

But what if it's outside of the work environment? What about obtaining personal information from an individual at the pub on a Friday night, information that later allows you to compromise the organization? What if a staff member takes his laptop with him when he leaves in the evening, stops off to buy some dinner on his way home, and leaves the laptop in his car. Is it legal or ethical to break into the staff member's car to obtain the laptop, even if your target organization has asked you to do this? The answer to this particular question may vary depending on whether it's a personal or a company-owned vehicle. What if you attempt to compromise an organization through contacting its staff via their personal social networking accounts?

The answers to these questions vary from person to person and situation to situation, even in the ethical social engineering sphere. For example, I wouldn't break into someone's car to remove a work laptop or work-related information. Think about how that person would feel if you were to do so. He may not feel safe in the future, and I would hate for that to be as a result of my social engineering test. Neither would I contact staff on their personal social networking accounts, as this is outside the work domain and is their personal life. However, I know of ethical social engineers who have done both very successfully. The ethical boundaries are different for everyone. Never get involved in a social engineering test where you have to go beyond your ethical boundaries.

Lock Picking

Lock picking is an extremely useful skill for social engineers and learning it is fun. You may find yourself in a situation where you can slip into a building by lock picking a backdoor. Lock picking a filing cabinet in HR may lead to a gold mine of sensitive documents. Perhaps the objective of your test is to access the server room in a particular building, and you are skilled enough to pick the lock on the server room door—although sometimes sheer brute force works. In one particular physical test, we were able to walk in through the car park and shove the door for the server room so hard that it opened....

The difficulty here is that you probably shouldn't break things in the course of your social engineering test. If you force a door open, will other potentially malicious individuals then be able to use it to gain access to your organization or sensitive areas within it? If you pick a filing cabinet and your lock-picking skills aren't up to scratch, you could jam it—a form of denial of service—leaving it inaccessible for staff who really need to use it; or you could break the lock, leaving it open and accessible to both authorized staff and any unauthorized individuals who happen to be passing by.

From a legal perspective, you may or may not be allowed to carry lock picks in the country or region in which you are operating. In the UK, carrying lock picks may count as "going equipped" to commit a crime and can land you on the wrong side of the law. You need a valid reason to carry lock picks in a public place, and being a hobbyist probably doesn't count! The jury is out on whether performing as an escape artist is a valid reason. The ethical social engineering case has never, to my knowledge, been tested in a court of law, but I wouldn't want to be the first one to find out.

In the US, laws vary from state to state. In most states, whether it is illegal generally comes down to whether there is reasonable cause to believe that you had some intent to break the law. In California, locksmiths must be licensed by the state. The Open Organisation of Lockpickers (TOOOL), whose mission is to advance the general public knowledge about locks and lock picking, is a superb resource on the subject and has an overview of lock-picking laws from state to state within the US, as shown in Figure 2-1.

Leaving aside any specific legal rules relating to lock picking, the damage caused by such activities could potentially be the subject of a legal action. To that extent, if you intend to engage in this activity, you should reference it specifically in your Get Out of Jail Free card and ensure that your indemnity/release is broad enough to cover any liability arising from the damage that ensues. As mentioned, such indemnity/ release will frequently exclude damage caused by your negligence or fraudulent behavior. In that context, remember that although your Get Out of Jail Free card is

Picks are legal by statute, state must prove criminal intent

Picks are legal due to lack of any statute

Picks are legal, but other related laws should be noted

Posession of picks can be considered evidence of criminal intent

Lockpicks are considered restricted under current law

FIGURE 2-1 TOOOLs lock-picking laws in the United States from http://toool.us/ laws.html

a critical protection, it is not a license to act with complete disregard for your client's premises and possessions. With or without your Get Out of Jail Free card, you owe your client a duty of care to act within the limits of reasonableness.

> **Note**　You carry lock picks at your own risk—if you wish to use them as part of your social engineering test, get it written into your contract.

Bribery and Corruption

Financial bribes can be quite effective. Almost everyone has a price. In 2013, sources revealed that Bosch, the German technology firm, had paid a Dyson engineer £11,500 (almost US$20,000) to leak details of its revolutionary high-speed brushless motors. The mole worked for Dyson for over two years. Dyson had spent over 15 years and £100 million (approximately US$167 million) developing the motors in question. Once an employee has accepted a financial bribe, can his or her employer ever fully trust that person again?

On a practical note, if you offer someone in your target organization a bribe of, say, $2,000, who pays the $2,000? Can you expense it back to your client?

From a legal perspective, anti-bribery and corruption laws are currently receiving much attention. In the UK, for example, the Bribery Act 2010 created four new criminal offences:

- Offering a bribe
- Accepting a bribe
- Bribing a foreign official
- Failing to prevent bribery (for commercial organizations)

Individuals found guilty face a maximum of ten years in prison, and the punishment for businesses is an unlimited fine. Companies can be prosecuted for failing to stop staff or people associated with them from *bribing another person on their behalf*. Would a social engineer bribing someone as part of a test count as bribing another person on the company's behalf? Perhaps.

This legislation has extraterritorial reach (extending its applicability beyond the territory of the UK) and has resulted in a renewed focus in many jurisdictions on their anti-bribery and corruption legislation. The result is that internationally this is an evolving and frequently highly regulated area.

Unauthorized Impersonation of Individuals or Organizations, or Pretexting

In January 2012, a social engineer tricked a Citibank call center agent into issuing him a debit card under Microsoft co-founder Paul Allen's account. Allegedly, the social engineer, Brandon Price, a US Army deserter from Pittsburgh, Pennsylvania, called a Citibank call center impersonating Paul Allen. He changed the bank account's address to his own and then stated that he had misplaced his debit card at his residence but

What Kind of Bribes, if Any, Are Appropriate?

With all the ethical and legal complications in mind, what kind of bribes might be considered acceptable during an ethical social engineering test? How about something small like a chocolate bar or flowers? Chocolates proved to be a key weapon when diamond thief Carlos Hector Flomenbaum stole over €21 million (nearly US$30 million) of diamonds from a diamond vault in Antwerp. You will hear more about him in the next chapter.

Reciprocity is a hugely effective social engineering technique. The social engineer gives something to his target so he will feel obliged to reciprocate by giving the social engineer something in return. In his book *Influence: The Psychology of Persuasion* (HarperBusiness, 2006), psychologist Robert Cialdini notes that we tend to comply with requests when the person who has made the request has given or *promised something of value*. So as an ethical social engineer, rather than actually giving something to your target individual, you could perhaps offer her the chance to win something of value, like entering her into a drawing to win the holiday of her dreams if she complies with your request to provide information. From the target's point of view, it seems like you have offered this chance to many individuals, so you are not trying to bribe that person in particular. Added to this, winning the prize is not guaranteed.

did not want to report it stolen. He ordered a new debit card that was subsequently overnighted to him via UPS. Price used the card to make a payment on a loan before trying a failed wire transfer and in-store purchase, attempting a total of over $15,000 worth of transactions. Could this work as an ethical social engineering test? It raises a number of issues.

You would probably need to have permission from Paul Allen himself—or any other individual you choose to target—to attempt to access that person's debit card details. In reality, this means you would have to set up a test debit card user and then attempt to steal these details. Alternatively, you could attempt to "steal" your own details (although that would assume you have an account with the organization you are testing) or "steal" a debit card belonging to an individual from your target organization who has given you permission to do so, but I have yet to meet a client who is quite that trusting!

Incidentally, you can get into a lot of trouble for accessing information belonging to celebrities or other individuals in the public eye. You may need extra permission from your client to attempt this.

Most social engineering tests involve some kind of impersonation, whether it is of a real or fake individual or organization. However, there may be legal and/or ethical restrictions on who you can impersonate. For example, although we see it in movies all the time, impersonating a police officer is illegal in almost every country.[1] The offense of impersonating a police officer may include the following actions:

- Verbally identifying yourself as a police officer
- Carrying or showing fake badges or warrant cards
- Wearing fake uniforms
- Operating fake vehicles, which may also extend to equipment used by law enforcement officers, such as red or blue flashing lights

However, posing as a police officer is quite effective as a malicious social engineering technique, as Verizon found when thieves dressed as police officers stole more than $4 million worth of equipment from a data center in London. The London Metropolitan police said in a statement "It is believed three to five male suspects, dressed as police officers, gained entry to the property at approximately 9 P.M. by claiming to a member of staff that they were investigating reports of people on the roof of the building...."

It may also be illegal or unethical to impersonate certain individuals. In the UK, a colleague got into trouble in their early days of social engineering by impersonating a fire officer and learned never to impersonate a public official again.

However, pretending to be someone who doesn't exist may not be illegal, in other words, you can't impersonate a real person but you may be allowed to impersonate a fictitious one. In an excellent example of this, Provide Security ran an experiment that it presented at Black Hat in 2010 in a talk entitled "Getting in Bed with Robin Sage." They found a photo of an attractive "emo chick" who they thought would appeal to security professionals on an adult website and used this photo to set up a fake social networking profile under the alias Robin Sage on Facebook (as shown in Figure 2-2), LinkedIn, Twitter, and other social networking sites. Provide Security used this profile to contact nearly 300 people in the security industry. The company confirmed that using a stranger's photo for the social network accounts was legal, as long as there was no personally identifiable information used.

There were numerous clues that revealed the Robin Sage profile was fake. For example, Robin Sage is the name of a US Army Special Forces exercise, so anyone who bothered searching her name may have noticed that this was a bit suspicious. Her occupational title of "cyber threat analyst" at the Naval Network Warfare Command does not really exist. Also, she was listed as being 25 years of age with 10 years' work experience.

In spite of this, hundreds of people from the security industry, including individuals from the military and intelligence community, accepted her friend requests. Robin obtained incredible amounts of information, including the coordinates of army personnel

---

[1]You are almost certainly wondering if it is illegal to impersonate a police officer, how do strippers get away with it? The answer is, they don't always! Stuart Kennedy, a genetics student at Aberdeen University and part-time stripper, has been arrested several times and has spent over 100 hours in police custody. In one case, he was arrested while driving home from a nightclub. He claimed he had been forced to flee fully clothed in his police uniform after being threatened by an angry boyfriend....

FIGURE 2-2   Robin Sage's Facebook profile set up by Provide Security

in Afghanistan and Iraq as well as job opportunities, dinner invites, and tickets to security conferences.

It gets more complicated still: what about pretending to be someone who doesn't exist working for an organization that does exist? For example, posing as an employee from your target organization's current auditors, you request certain sensitive information. Technically, if you are going to pretend to be operating on behalf of a real organization, you will need the organization's permission to do so, so you would need permission from the auditors. This rules out impersonating an existing supplier or other third party, such as pretending to be a cleaner from the cleaning agency used by your target organization, unless you have the agency's permission.

On an ethical note, I got quite far with one organization who I noticed did a lot of work with various charities. I pretended to be calling from a fake charity and set up a meeting to come in and talk to them. I couldn't go through with it. I figured that charities shouldn't get a bad name because of my social engineering exploits—and there I found I had ethical boundaries! You may find your ethical boundaries once you are asked to cross them. This line can vary greatly from person to person—what may be acceptable to one tester may not be acceptable to another. I know of several testers who have successfully used the charity scenario, but I just wasn't able to do it. Guilty feelings are an indicator of ethical boundaries.

Laws Against Impersonation or Pretexting   Using impersonation to obtain private information is sometimes referred to as pretexting and, depending on what kind of information you are attempting to access, may be illegal. In the US, pretexting of telephone records is a federal felony with fines of up to $250,000 and 10 years in prison for individuals or fines of up to $500,000 for companies. This legislation was brought into effect after the HP spying scandal where the then chairperson, Patricia Dunn, hired private investigators to investigate board-level leaks to reporters. Some of these private investigators impersonated HP directors to gain access to their cell phone billing records. The controversy led to Dunn's resignation and in part to the US Congress passing a law specifically prohibiting pretexting.

In the UK, the concept of *blagging* was thrust into the spotlight following the *News of the World* phone-hacking scandal, which led to the British newspaper shutting down after more than 160 years' of publication. Private investigators and journalists employed by the paper were alleged to have intercepted and, in some cases, deleted voicemails belonging to murdered schoolgirl Milly Dowler, British service personnel killed in action, and various celebrities, politicians, and members of the British royal family among others.

Blagging in the UK is a breach of section 55 of the Data Protection Act 1998, which concerns the unlawful obtaining of personal data and says that a person must not knowingly or recklessly obtain or disclose personal data or information without the consent of the data controller.

Using impersonation or pretexting to such a degree can be taxing—even as part of an ethical social engineering test. One of the information brokers sentenced following this scandal was Daniel Sumners, a self-confessed blagger, who used pretexting to elicit confidential information from banks, medical record holders, HM Revenue & Customs (HMRC), the Driver & Vehicle Licensing Agency (DVLA), Criminal Records Bureau, and Interpol. When he was arrested, Sumners admitted he knew what he was doing was illegal and later said, "I'm glad this has happened because now it has been spotted. I can't do it anymore."

Using Social Networking for Social Engineering

Using social networking for social engineering is very effective and used to great success by malicious social engineers. *USA Today* reported on financial firm, Terremark's network compromise in 2010. Attackers gained access to a Terremark employee's (let's call him Bob) Facebook account. They accessed Bob's contact list of friends and manually reviewed messages and postings on his profile. They noticed a message saying that Bob had been at a picnic with some of his friends over the weekend. When they saw this news, they sent individual messages to around a dozen of Bob's closest Facebook friends, including a fellow employee at Terremark - we'll call her Alice. The message read, "Hey Alice, look at the pics I took of us last weekend at the picnic. Bob."

The link in the message led to a malicious executable file, which, when Alice clicked it expecting to see the photos, installed a keystroke logger on her machine. Once an hour, the program sent a text file of Alice's keystrokes to a Gmail account controlled by the attackers. When Alice logged into Terremark's virtual private network, the attackers noted her username and password. They then used Alice's login credentials to access Terremark's network, which they had access to for a matter of weeks.

The attackers gained control of two servers before they were detected. A friend of Bob who had also received the original message mentioned to him that the picnic photos he had sent had failed to render. Bob got suspicious and a technician uncovered the network compromise.

If we are trying to perform a social engineering test as ethically and legally as possible, then we must consider the bounds of the social media terms and conditions. In my experience, I have mostly used social media for reconnaissance. On a typical social engineering test, I can think of dozens of ways to exploit my targets via social media, most of which must be ruled out due to legal or ethical complications.

Take the scenario where your client asks you to set up a fake Facebook profile with the objective of befriending its staff and eliciting sensitive information. What are the legal and ethical implications of doing this?

You Are in Breach of Facebook's Terms and Conditions   Among the Facebook terms and conditions (as detailed in the sidebar) that may impact your social engineering scenarios are

- *You will not solicit login information or access an account belonging to someone else.* Therefore you cannot attempt to trick your target into divulging his or her login details, even if you suspect the target uses the same login details for his or her workplace.
- *You will not use Facebook to do anything unlawful, misleading, malicious, or discriminatory.* Social engineering is, by its very nature, misleading. It is difficult to think of a test situation on a social network where you would not be misleading your target individual.
- *You will not provide any false personal information on Facebook, or create an account for anyone other than yourself without permission.* Technically, you can only set up an account under your real name. You cannot set up accounts under anybody else's name without their permission. There goes the scenario where you create an account belonging to one of your target's friends or co-workers.

Such activities are not necessarily illegal, but they are in breach of the terms and conditions of use.

Excerpt from Facebook's Terms and Conditions

A social engineering test could potentially breach many of these terms, particularly those that are highlighted:

3. Safety

We do our best to keep Facebook safe, but we cannot guarantee it. We need your help to keep Facebook safe, which includes the following commitments by you:

1. You will not post unauthorized commercial communications (such as spam) on Facebook.
2. You will not collect users' content or information, or otherwise access Facebook, using automated means (such as harvesting bots, robots, spiders, or scrapers) without our prior permission.

3. You will not engage in unlawful multi-level marketing, such as a pyramid scheme, on Facebook.
4. You will not upload viruses or other malicious code.
5. **You will not solicit login information or access an account belonging to someone else.**
6. You will not bully, intimidate, or harass any user.
7. You will not post content that: is hate speech, threatening, or pornographic; incites violence; or contains nudity or graphic or gratuitous violence.
8. You will not develop or operate a third-party application containing alcohol-related, dating or other mature content (including advertisements) without appropriate age-based restrictions.
9. You will follow our Promotions Guidelines and all applicable laws if you publicize or offer any contest, giveaway, or sweepstakes ("promotion") on Facebook.
10. **You will not use Facebook to do anything unlawful, misleading, malicious, or discriminatory.**
11. You will not do anything that could disable, overburden, or impair the proper working or appearance of Facebook, such as a denial of service attack or interference with page rendering or other Facebook functionality.
12. You will not facilitate or encourage any violations of this Statement or our policies.

4. Registration and Account Security

Facebook users provide their real names and information, and we need your help to keep it that way. Here are some commitments you make to us relating to registering and maintaining the security of your account:

1. **You will not provide any false personal information on Facebook, or create an account for anyone other than yourself without permission.**
2. You will not create more than one personal account.
3. If we disable your account, you will not create another one without our permission.
4. You will not use your personal timeline for your own commercial gain (such as selling your status update to an advertiser).
5. You will not use Facebook if you are under 13.
6. You will not use Facebook if you are a convicted sex offender.
7. You will keep your contact information accurate and up-to-date.
8. You will not share your password (or in the case of developers, your secret key), let anyone else access your account, or do anything else that might jeopardize the security of your account.
9. You will not transfer your account (including any Page or application you administer) to anyone without first getting our written permission.
10. If you select a username or similar identifier for your account or Page, we reserve the right to remove or reclaim it if we believe it is appropriate (such as when a trademark owner complains about a username that does not closely relate to a user's actual name).

Are You Entitled to Look at Employees' Information?   If an employee's profile is publicly available for everyone to see, then information posted to her social networking pages would appear to be fair game. However, if you need to friend the employee to look at her information, the situation is a little more complicated. It is misleading and contradicts the terms and conditions of many social networking sites. Is it ethical to befriend people so you can see their personal information? How would they feel about it if they found out they had been duped? How do you "unfriend" them after the test? You will have to delete your account permanently (as opposed to deactivating it, in which case some information may still be visible to others). Remember that some social networks may still retain information from your fake account.

Can You Try to Get Employees to Reveal Sensitive Information on Their Social Networking Account?   Doing this may count as some kind of incitement or conspiracy, depending on the circumstances. You may be conspiring with the employee to steal their employer's information. Alternatively, you may be inciting the employee to break the law, again depending on the circumstances. It also raises the issue of the sensitive information being made available for others—potentially including malicious social engineers—to see.

Even if we decide to use only information that falls within a business context, that, in itself, presents some further dilemmas. It is straightforward if your targets post company-related information on their accounts, mention who they work for, if they are going on a work trip, their salary details, and so forth. However, does it count as a business context if you use their pet names or their mother's maiden name in password guessing?

Various countries, especially in the EU, have strict privacy and data protection laws. Any information that can be traced back to an individual can be considered private unless it has voluntarily been made public by its owner. As a result, in my social engineering career, I have mostly used social media for passive reconnaissance rather than actually executing an attack.

Even then it can lead to some unintended outcomes. Imagine the scenario where you use information posted on an employee's profile as part of your compromise of the company the employee works for. You present the report to your target organization; it identifies the employee in question and fires them. The now ex-employee sues the company and demands to know how the company was able to find their personal information. The company mentions your social engineering report, and you get in trouble for having performed a potentially unethical or even illegal test, maybe even being sued in turn.

Theft of Assets and Information

In one of the bolder social engineering examples reported by the media, Czech thieves actually dismantled and stole a 10-ton bridge to sell for scrap metal. The group used a crane to dismantle the pedestrian bridge along with about 650 feet of railway track. When the police questioned them about what they were doing, they showed forged documents that said they were working on a new bicycle path.

Although you are highly unlikely to be asked to remove a bridge as part of your ethical social engineering test, this situation does raise the following questions: can you take the property offsite and can you cause a denial of service?

Can You Take Property Offsite?   When you plan to remove assets or information, you should obtain written consent from an authorized signatory in advance of removing anything. Even so, you must be careful. A USB key left in the office may be the private property of an employee, who may be angry if you take it. It gets more complicated still if you consider cases where employees store personal data on corporate systems. Imagine if an employee is pursuing a part-time MBA and has used her company laptop to work on her thesis. If this laptop were to be removed as part of a social engineering test, it could be quite traumatic for the employee.

If you do take sensitive data or assets offsite, or gain electronic access to them, you may have to meet data protection requirements when storing them. Sometimes you are better off placing a sticker on the object you could have removed and photographing it, rather than actually taking the object offsite.

Denial of Service   The thieves in the bridge-stealing example effectively caused a denial of service attack against the Czech bridge. People (users) looking to cross the bridge were no longer able to do so after this attack.

Organizations often automatically unlock all their doors when a fire alarm is sounded. If, as a social engineer, you held a match to a fire alarm, causing the alarm to go off and all the workers to exit the building, you are effectively stopping the staff from working and performing a denial of service attack against your target organization. To get around this, instead of setting off fire alarms, I find out when the next scheduled fire alarm test is and then go into the building when I am sure there is little chance of a real fire taking place! Be careful of causing a denial of service.

Theft via Dumpster Diving

Social engineers can reap great rewards through *dumpster diving*, the practice of searching for valuable assets or information in individual's or organization's trash. Laws on dumpster diving can vary widely from region to region, with dumpster diving potentially being classified as theft, depending on where the dumpster is located. In 2009, an eco-activist in Belgium was accused of theft and burglary and sentenced to 28 days of prison for taking food from a dumpster at a supermarket. In the United Kingdom, for example, property in a bin remains the property of the person who owned it until the council (or sanitation company) collects it. After it has been collected, it becomes the property of that body. Corporate dumps tend to be locked, which complicates the scenario.

If you do intend to perform dumpster diving as part of your reconnaissance mission or at any stage during the social engineering attack, you are advised to seek the permission of your target organization.

Legal and Ethical Options

As ethical social engineers, we tread a fine line between legal and illegal, ethical and unethical activities. Because of this, many of the social engineering tests we do tend toward proof of concept (PoC) or "gamifying" the test; for example, instead of taking an item offsite, we leave something onsite to prove we've been there. It's up to each social engineer to decide how far he or she wishes to take the test in legal and ethical terms—the test does need to be somewhat realistic, after all.

Table 2-1 provides some proof of concept or gamified options that you can use as part of your social engineering test, bypassing some of the legal or ethical concerns you or your client may have about various activities.

TABLE 2-1   Ethical and Legal Options for Your Social Engineering Test

Legally or Ethically Dubious Option	PoC/Gamified Option
Taking information or physical assets offsite	Leaving something (for example, a calling card) onsite to prove you've been there
Gaining physical access using an invalid entry card obtained via social engineering or theft	Gaining physical access using an invalid entry card provided by the client
Accessing sensitive information	Having the client set up some fake information (for instance, a fake helpdesk ticket) that the staff believes to be real and that you can then attempt to access
Accessing personal information	Having the client set up a fake account that the staff believes to be real and that you can attempt to access, or, alternatively, having the client set up an account under your own name and attempting to access it
Bribing your target with money or something of value	Offering your target something inconsequential and low value like a chocolate bar, a pen, or the potential to win something
Setting off a fire alarm to clear the building and unlock doors, giving you access to the building	Using social engineering to find out when the next scheduled fire alarm test is and attempting to gain access then
Forging documents or impersonating a real person or organization	Forging documents or impersonating a made-up organization or person

Legal Do's and Don'ts

Here are some do's and don'ts to keep your social engineering tests legal.

Do:
- Get a signed contract and Get Out of Jail Free card before embarking on your social engineering test.
- Carry your Get Out of Jail Free card with you at all times during the test.
- Seek permission (ideally in writing) for any activities that might otherwise be illegal or unethical, for instance, dumpster diving or penetration testing.
- Keep any sensitive information or physical assets that you take offsite secure.
- Consult a lawyer in every locale in which you will be performing the social engineering test. Remember that the laws will vary from country to country.

Don't:
- Attempt any social engineering activities without a valid contract and Get Out of Jail Free card in place.
- Attempt any penetration testing activities without authorization.
- Impersonate real people or organizations without their permission.
- Impersonate law enforcement or public officials. Ever.
- Cause an intentional denial of service or damage to your target organization.
- Record people without their permission.
- Offer financial or valuable bribes.
- Target employees outside of their workplace unless the relevant employee has clearly and expressly authorized it (and you will still need to exercise caution).
- Attempt to obtain personal non-work-related information from employees.
- Breach the terms and conditions of social networks.
- Trick people into revealing information on social networks or other public forums.
- Break the law!

Free Pizza and Social Engineering in Your Personal Life

I am often asked how social engineering impacts the rest of my life and whether I practice much social engineering on my friends and family. Switching off the social engineering persona can be difficult, although some of the traits can be useful in your outside life.

It used to be that any Google search on social engineering returned dozens of links on how to get free pizzas. Social engineering is not about getting free pizza, unless your client happens to be Pizza Hut and they have asked you to test their sales processes!

At the end of the day, if you social engineer a pizza out of Pizza Hut, burger from McDonalds, or whatever it may be, unless you pay for it, you're stealing it.

How to get a **pizza** for **FREE (Social Engineering)** - YouTube
www.youtube.com/watch?v=z68gZJwdAAg
Mar 2, 2007 - Uploaded by Bagatov1953
In this video we show you how to get a **pizza** for free. All you need are some **Social Engineering** (human ...

The Broken - Get **Free Pizza** - YouTube
www.youtube.com/watch?v=dBSDfo5g2tw
Oct 13, 2006 - Uploaded by ikickallass
The point of **social engineering** is to trick the other people. If you didn't trick them then why would they give you a ...

How to Get **Free Pizza (Social Engineering)** on Vimeo
vimeo.com/2207259
Nov 10, 2008
Shot this a while ago as part of an International Baccalaureate school project. The purpose of this video is to ...

As ethical social engineers, we don't want to encourage unethical behavior within the community. Scams such as the one described in Figure 2-3 are all too common, with many social engineers proud to boast of their exploits.

Remember—once you are a social engineer, you deceive, manipulate, and trick people for a living ... but you also educate them. Unfortunately this means that some people, possibly including clients, may view you as a professional con artist. People may suspect that you are constantly trying to trick them; even others within the security community may expect you to have questionable ethics. It's not unusual for people sitting beside me at security conferences to check that they still have their wallets!

Even when he was on his best behavior in prison, Frank Abagnale claimed that people always suspected him. The better his behavior, the more convinced the prison guards became that he was up to no good. His application for parole was refused several times. On one occasion, a member of the review committee even told him that his record was perfect and that was a problem! In his book *The Art of the Steal* (Crown Business, 2002), Abagnale says, "Everything I did was always assumed to

---

□by **giga-byte** » Wed Nov 02, 2005 4:37 pm

what me and my friends do is, go into starbucks, order 2 cups of coffee. Then when they are done my friends go in and take them, then i go in and say "where is my coffee" they usualy be like, oh crap those guys took it, and we act like we are all mad and stuff and like we gonna beat someone up but they calm us down and say the ywill make new ones and they give them to us. Works 100% of the time, also works with in n out.

FIGURE 2-3 A social engineer boasts of his exploits. What a lot of work and risk to go to to save the cost of a cup of coffee!

have an ulterior motive. That's what happens when you have a reputation, and the reputation is that of a master con man."

Final Thoughts

The ethics of social engineering is highly personal; something that seems okay for one social engineer may cross the boundaries of another social engineer. The more social engineering tests you do, the more you will recognize where your boundaries lie.

Remember to always heed this advice:

- Before you start, make sure you have a valid contract that has been signed by an authorized signatory for your target organization.
- Carry your Get Out of Jail Free card with you at all times.
- Ensure you are aware of any legislation that may affect your test.

Always keep in mind the goal of your test and think about the impact of what you are doing on the person you are doing it to. Do your best to simulate a real-world attack within legal and ethical constraints.

3 Why Social Engineering Works

All truths are easy to understand once they are discovered; the point is to discover them.
—Galileo

Effective social engineers are experts in human nature. They know how to prey on weaknesses to manipulate or deceive their victims. The average person's instincts and reactions are fairly predictable. People are trusting and curious, like free stuff, and, above all, are usually unaware that they are being targeted. From a security professional's point of view, fighting against this can be difficult. One of the best ways to change people's mentality when it comes to security is to run a social engineering test that targets them in a safe and controlled environment.

People are the weakest link in any security program. Social engineering fundamentally works because of human weaknesses. To defend against social engineering, we must understand what it is about human nature that has allowed us to fall for social engineering tricks and other scams for as long as we can remember. There are many social engineering techniques and many reasons why they work. Each social engineering attack is different. We learn to defend against one technique and then fall victim to another. In this chapter, I discuss the following six key reasons why social engineering works:

- Misplaced trust
- Respect for authority
- Desire to be helpful
- Motivations to comply with the social engineer
- Lack of personal responsibility
- Lack of awareness of social engineering scams and other cons

Most social engineering attacks could be prevented if people verified and validated the social engineer's identity or requests properly. Condé Nast would not have transferred $8 million to a phisher if it had performed adequate due diligence. Security professionals would not have accepted Robin Sage's friend requests if they had done some background checks. But for various reasons—perhaps because people do not have time or feel they do not have time to verify requests—social engineers and other confidence tricksters get past our defenses.

We trust that people are who they say they are. We respect and rarely question those in positions of authority, who often encourage this unquestioning support. We naturally want to help our fellow human beings, particularly in the workplace. We may have various motivations for helping the social engineer, possibly financial, or maybe we just want to get ahead at work. Social engineers get away with a lot because so few people want to take responsibility for validating their requests. We don't like confrontations, or we are just too busy to bother confronting suspicious individuals. Social engineering works because people don't realize that it is a threat—and no one expects to be targeted. How can people defend against social engineering when they don't even know what it is?

Misplaced Trust in the Social Engineer

The main reason any social engineering attack or other scam works is because people are trusting. Our human nature is to trust other people. The society we live in works on trust. Social networking relies almost entirely on trust. Scientists have even discovered a trust hormone, oxytocin, which seems to make us more trusting!

Besides, why shouldn't we trust other people? Most of the time they are who they say they are, and you can take people's requests at face value. We rarely believe that anyone intends to deceive us. But every now and again we come up against someone who is trying to deceive us, whether that person is a fraudster, con man, prankster, or social engineer. We trust that social engineers are who they say they are. We trust them enough not to verify this or to check—*really* check—their ID cards or validate their requests. Some people are simply more trusting than others and will believe the caller when she claims to be the bank manager and requests that they hand over their credit card to that courier that she is sending around to their house.

In the workplace, we may be even quicker to trust other people for a number of reasons. Sometimes we assume that someone else has vetted them or authorized them to request certain information. It is also easier to trust people and comply with their requests—we are all busy after all and want to get our jobs done as quickly and as painlessly as possible. We may trust people in the workplace because they look like they belong or simply because we like them. It may also be a result of social compliance—everyone else seems to trust them so we do too.

A study at the University of Waterloo that observed children at home found that a four-year-old child tells a lie once every 2 hours, while a six-year-old lies every 90 minutes[1]! Children's early attempts to lie are usually glaringly obvious. A child covered in cookie crumbs might deny that he has stolen a cookie if he'll avoid punishment. This behavior is fairly typical. In fact, researchers have found that the complex brain processes involved in formulating a lie are an indicator of

---

[1]The Nature and Effects of Young Children's Lies, Anne E. Wilson, Melissa D. Smith, Hildy S. Ross

intelligence. And we get more skilled at lying as we become older. Studies show that up to 25 percent of our daily interactions involve a lie (and probably more on social networking), so why do we trust people so implicitly?

Detecting Deception

We are not very good at detecting deception. We want to believe we are hearing the truth. Psychologists Paul Ekman and Maureen O'Sullivan spent over 20 years studying people's ability to detect deception in a study they called the Wizards Project. Their research showed that most people can detect deceit only about 50 percent of the time, drawing parallels with the statistical equivalent of flipping a coin. Individuals trained as psychiatrists and law enforcement are no more successful at identifying lies than college freshmen. This study was the inspiration for the Fox crime drama television series, *Lie to Me*, where a team of deception experts assist law enforcement and government agencies to expose the truth.

Of more than 15,000 people tested, Ekman and O'Sullivan identified only 50 people with an exceptional ability to spot lies, who they called truth wizards. In their tests, they showed participants video footage and asked them to judge whether the person in the video was telling the truth or lying. A *truth wizard* was defined as someone who could identify deception with an accuracy of at least 80 percent. It seems that truth wizards were better at picking up micro-expressions. However, no truth wizard was found to be 100 percent accurate, so even they could potentially be fooled by social engineers along with the rest of us. Furthermore, they seem to rely on visual clues to spot deceit. Would they be able to identify a social engineering attack in which the social engineer is not present, that comes in via email or phone perhaps?

One of the certified truth wizards publishes a blog, under the pseudonym Eyes for Lies (blog.eyesforlies.com), in which she examines criminal cases and gives her opinion on whether the defendant is lying. She has kept a score on her blog for over seven years and has an accuracy rate of 95 percent after identifying truth and deception in 38 out of 40 people before the truth was known by watching media clips. The Eyes for Lies truth wizard has used her skills to give an opinion on many high-profile criminal cases, mostly involving murders, and sometimes on celebrities such as Michael Jackson (did he molest children?), Britney Spears (was her marriage breaking up?), or Tom Cruise and Katie Holmes (were they really in love or did they just want to promote their movies?).

How truth wizards have such high deception-detection rates is still being studied. O'Sullivan noted in the Wizards Project that

> Our wizards are extraordinarily attuned to detecting the nuances of facial expressions, body language and ways of talking and thinking. Some of them can observe a videotape for a few seconds and amazingly they can describe eight details about the person on the tape[2].

---

[2]www.eurekalert.org/pub_releases/2004-10/ama-lad100804.php

Truth wizards seem to have a natural instinct for whether people are telling the truth. The truth wizard in the Eyes for Lies blog believes that her biggest clues to deception are

- Inconsistencies in emotions
- Odd word choices
- Inconsistencies in fact
- Inconsistencies in personality/character
- Micro expressions—expressions that last a fraction of a second and mostly go unnoticed

But we are not all truth wizards. Most of us tend to rely on inaccurate methods such as eye contact and body language to detect a lie. We do not get to practice knowingly against good liars, so we do not get to keep score on detecting lies and deception. Effective attackers know this and act accordingly. They may maintain eye contact when telling lies or trying to deceive people, or avert eye contact to make their victims believe they are lying. Good acting skills are quite useful in physical social engineering scenarios. Consider the visual clues and body language that President Clinton used back in 1998 when he was suspected of having an affair with his intern, Monica Lewinsky. He looked directly into the camera and confidently declared, "I did not have sexual relations with that woman, Miss Lewinsky."

Why Do We Trust?

Think about who you trust and why. You probably trust your friends and your family, maybe your teammates at your sports club. You probably trust at least some of your colleagues and chances are you trust your boss to some extent. Some people trust politicians—that's open to debate, of course. But what about people we don't know or recognize? Why do we trust and get taken in by social engineers? What leads us to trust a complete stranger? Trust must be earned, and social engineers earn it quickly.

The propensity to trust may be a result of *in-group favoring*, where people intrinsically trust or favor other people within their group, whether it's their department at work, other people of the same nationality, or other members of their sports club. We are more positively inclined toward another individual if he or she appears to be part of our group, or "one of us." If a social engineer can somehow become part of his target's in-group, his target is far more likely to trust him. Becoming part of the in-group can be as basic as dressing like the people in the office. If the social engineer is wearing a suit, just like the rest of the staff, he is far less likely to be challenged than if he is wearing jeans and a t-shirt when everybody else is dressed more smartly. Social engineers find it advantageous to research their targets and establish the group membership of the target of their attack.

The SPICE Model

In his book, *Split Second Persuasion: The Ancient Art and New Science of Changing Minds* (Houghton Mifflin Harcourt, 2011), author and psychologist Kevin Dutton says we trust some people instantly because of five key triggers, which he calls the

The Trust Game Study

Psychologists Joyce Berg, John Dickhaut, and Kevin McCabe designed their "trust game" (also known as the "investment game") for their 1995 experiment on "Trust, Reciprocity, and Social History."[3] The game was designed to study people's propensity to be trusting and trustworthy. In the game, two players were given $10 as a show-up fee. One of the players was appointed decision maker and was permitted to send all, some, or none of their $10 to the other player. The rules were that every dollar sent would be tripled by the experimenter before it reached the second player, who must then decide how much money to keep and how much to send back to the first player.

The hypothesis of the study was that the first player wouldn't trust the second because she'd assume that the second player would keep the entire amount and, therefore, would send no money. But this is not what happened in the experiments. On average the first players sent more than $5 and around one-third of the second players reciprocated by sending back more than the original amount sent. This implies a certain amount of trust between the two strangers playing the game. To trust someone you need to accept a certain level of risk that they might betray you. So what is it, other than the obvious possibility of making a few bucks, that leads us to accept that risk and trust someone we don't know?

[3]Joyce Berg, John Dickhaut, and Kevin McCabe, "Trust, Reciprocity, and Social History," *Games and Economic Behavior* 10 (July 1995): 122–142.

SPICE model. Each of these triggers is part of the "DNA of persuasion" that makes a person sufficiently persuasive and compelling to be instantly trustworthy. This relates closely to social engineering: it is easier to persuade someone who trusts you. Social engineers excel in Dutton's five major axes of persuasion, the SPICE model:

- **Simplicity**   They use plain language and direct rhetoric.
- **Perceived self-interest**   They let the other person think he or she is getting what he or she wants.
- **Incongruity**   They use distraction or something unexpected to throw people off course.
- **Confidence**   They make their request with confidence to increase the likelihood of it being accepted.
- **Empathy**   They make it personal so people will want to act.

Simplicity   We tend to trust short, simple messages. These messages are quick to process, making people think they are true. Dutton found that the simpler, the shorter, and the sharper the message, the more likely it was to convince the listener. Politicians and journalists are experts at getting their messages across quickly. So are social engineers. One of the shortest, simplest email attacks that I have seen is simply an email with the subject "Crime" and the message "Happened near us. Read the story here."

Perceived Self-Interest   To motivate their targets to take action, social engineers may appeal to their target's self-interest. What's in it for them? If social engineers can convince their targets that complying with their requests would be good for them, their targets are more likely to go along with it. The social engineer may offer something of value, like an opportunity to win a trip to Paris, or even just a favor—knowing you can call in a favor with someone purporting to be from the IT department could be a very useful tool in most organizations. Salespeople are the experts in this area. They are trained to relate their products to their customers' needs. Salespeople who don't relate their products to their customers' needs are much less successful. Trust can be built quickly if there is some semblance of perceived self-interest, as in the trust game study.

Incongruity   Social engineers may try to break the monotony of everyday patterns by doing something out of the ordinary. Often people will not know how to react. In a distraction attack, the social engineer creates a distraction so her victim doesn't notice the real attack occurring. Many people are probably familiar with the "invisible gorilla test" by Simons and Chabris, where viewers are shown a short video of a group of people in black or white t-shirts passing a basketball around. The viewers are asked to count the number of passes made by the players wearing the white t-shirts. During the video, a person in a gorilla costume comes in and beats his chest. Barely half the people viewing the video for the first time notice the gorilla, as they are too busy focusing on where the ball is. The "invisible gorilla test" along with lots more selective attention tests are available to watch at www.theinvisiblegorilla.com/videos.html.

   Incongruity can be an effective technique when it comes to targets working in more monotonous job functions, such as call center staff. Call center staff often have a set script that they are required to follow. Having to break out of this script can make for a more interesting call, from the point of view of the call center agent. The social engineer's request is more likely to stand out if it is not part of the normal day-to-day operations. On the other hand, there is a lot to be said for blending in with the normal day-to-day functions so that your request doesn't stand out.

Confidence   A bit of confidence can go a long way. It's amazing how much people will trust you if you are confident enough. Actors, dancers, musicians, and other performers are often told if they make a mistake on stage just to continue on confidently and no one will notice. Act big and people will believe you are big. New York student Brett Cohen, pictured in Figure 3-1, did this with flair in August 2012 by hiring bodyguards on Craigslist, paparazzi, and an entourage, which convinced people he was a celebrity. He spent three hours in Times Square posing for photos with members of the public who assumed he was a famous actor or singer. When asked if he knew of Brett Cohen, one passerby replied that he thought his new single was quite good. Another praised his performance in a Spiderman movie. Two policemen even asked for a photo with him! Cohen put together a short video on YouTube called "Fake Celebrity Pranks New York City." His rouse was effective because passersby saw a confident "celebrity" who looked the part and was surrounded by his entourage, which lent credence to the deception.

FIGURE 3-1 Brett Cohen poses for a photo surrounded by members of the public.

Empathy Social engineers often appeal to people's sense of empathy, either by convincing targets that they are concerned about them or by evoking a sense of empathy in their targets so the targets end up concerned about the social engineer. In the first case, the social engineer tries to make her target feel that she cares about him and so builds up trust. I have done work with call centers that have been compromised by someone who rang up to thank the call center agent for his hard work (which is also incongruous). In Internet dating scams, victims are taken in by individuals who profess friendship or romantic interest.

In the second case, the social engineer tries to evoke feelings of empathy or concern for her target. This method is frequently used by 419 scammers who may incorporate some kind of sob story into their email request. In the example shown in Figure 3-2, Mr. Salam Ahmed tells his target that one of his bank clients died in a plane crash along with his entire family. He even provides a link to the BBC news article about the Paris Concorde plane crash in 2000 to verify his story, shown in Figure 3-3. What further proof would you need?!

Appearing Trustworthy

What would make you trust a stranger? Has he shown you the appropriate credentials? Does she look trustworthy? People seem to think I am trustworthy even though I am pretty open about working as a social engineer for a living. I suspect it may be because I am female, and I am not very physically imposing. I have big eyes, an Irish accent, and I smile a lot. I also suspect that this is why I always end up with the weirdo on the bus sitting next to me, but that is another story....

There are a surprisingly large number of studies on trust and on what features or characteristics can make a person appear more trustworthy. I have included some examples in Table 3-1. Some of the studies are quite entertaining, although they don't necessarily correlate with each other. Amusingly, the phrase "barefaced lie" dates back to Shakespeare's Britain, when men without facial hair were considered to be more shameless in their deceit than men with beards! More than anything, we tend to trust

> Greetings,
>
> This message might meet you in utmost surprise; however, it is just my urgent need for foreign partner that made me to contact you for this transaction. I am a banker by profession from Burkina Faso in West Africa and currently holding the post of Director Auditing and Accounting unit of the bank. I have the opportunity of transferring the left over funds ($12.5million) of one of my bank clients who died along with his entire family on 31 July 2000 in a plane crash. You can confirm the geniuses of the deceased death by clicking on this web site http://news.bbc.co.uk/1/hi/world/europe/859479.stm hence; I am inviting you for a business deal where this money can be shared between us in the ratio of 60/38 while 2% will be mapped out for expenses. If you agree to my business proposal. Further details of the transfer will be forwarded to you as soon as i receive your return mail.
>
> 1.Your name.................
> 2.Your phone.................
> 3.Age.......................
> 4.Sex.......................
> 5.Profession...............
> 6.Address.................
>
> Best regards.
>
> Mr. Salam Ahmed

FIGURE 3-2   A 419 scam email designed to make the recipient feel sorry for the sender

FIGURE 3-3   The news story that the 419 email refers to

TABLE 3-1   Features or Characteristics Can Make a Person Appear More Trustworthy

Characteristic	Effect on Trustworthiness	Source
Vocal pitch and volume	Lower voices are considered more trustworthy and more intelligent.	Benjamin Waber, Michele Williams, John S. Carroll, and Alex "Sandy" Pentland, "A Voice Is Worth a Thousand Words: The Implications of the Micro-coding of Social Signals in Speech for Trust Research," in *Handbook of Research Methods on Trust,* eds. Fergus Lyon, Guido Mollering, and Mark N. K. Saunders, Edward Elgar Publishing, 2011.
Gender	People trust others of the same gender.	Aurélie Bonein and Daniel Serra, "Gender Pairing Bias in Trustworthiness," *The Journal of Socio-Economics* (October 2009): 779–789.
Gender again	Females score slightly higher on scales of trust.[4]	A. Feingold, "Gender Differences in Personality: A Meta-analysis," *Psychological Bulletin* 116(3), (November 1994): 429–456.
Gender yet again	Men are more trusting than women, and women are more trustworthy than men.	Nancy R. Buchan, Rachel T. A. Croson, and Sara Solnick, "Trust and Gender: An Examination of Behavior, Biases, and Beliefs in the Investment Game," *Journal of Economic Behavior & Organization* 68(3–4) (December 2008):466–476.
Regional accents	Certain regional accents are perceived as more trustworthy. For example, in the UK, the Scottish accent has been voted as the most trustworthy (think Sean Connery) with the Liverpudlian accent rating lowest. This is why many call centers are based in Scotland.	Survey for the David Ormerod Hearing Centres (www.davidormerod.co.uk/)
Foreign accents	On the other hand, people with foreign accents are perceived as less trustworthy.	Shiri Lev-Ari and Boaz Keysar, Why Don't We Believe Non-native Speakers? The Influence of Accent on Credibility, *Journal of Experimental Social Psychology* 46 (2010): 1093–1096.

[4]Government officials in Mexico City created all-female teams of traffic wardens in the belief that female officers are less likely to take bribes (J. Treaster, 1999. "Equal Opportunity in Mexico City: Counting on Women to Be More Honest than Men," New York Times, August 15, Section 4, p. 3.

(Continued)

TABLE 3-1   Features or Characteristics Can Make a Person Appear More Trustworthy

Characteristic	Effect on Trustworthiness	Source
Eye color	People with brown eyes appear more trustworthy than people with blue eyes (unless it's a man with a broad face—see next point). The study concluded that it was not the brown eye color but rather the facial features associated with brown eyes that caused a stronger perception of trustworthiness.	K. Kleisner, L. Priplatova, P. Frost, J. Flegr, "Trustworthy-Looking Face Meets Brown Eye," *PLoS ONE 8(1) (2013): e53285.*
Face shape	Men with wider faces are trusted less.	M. Stirrat and D.I. Perrett, "Valid Facial Cues to Cooperation and Trust: Male Facial Width and Trustworthiness," *Psychological Science* 21(3) (March 2010): 349–354.
Facial expressions	We trust women more when they are smiling.	K. Schmidt, R. Levenstein, Z. Ambadar, "Intensity of Smiling and Attractiveness as Facial Signals of Trustworthiness in Women, *Perceptual and Motor Skills* 114(3) (June 2012): 964–978.
Fake facial expressions	But we don't trust people if the smile looks fake.	Eve Krumhuber, Antony S. R. Manstead, et al., "Facial Dynamics as Indicators of Trustworthiness and Cooperative Behavior," *Emotion* 7(4) (2007): 730–735.
Attractiveness	Attractive individuals are perceived as more trustworthy than unattractive individuals.	Erin Shinners, "Effects of the 'What is Beautiful is Good' Stereotype on Perceived Trustworthiness," *Journal of Undergraduate Research XII* (2009).
Profession	The most trustworthy professions are Nurses Doctors Teachers Lawyers Estate agents (really?) Bankers (seriously?) Journalists (now you are kidding me!) Politicians (hahaha) Law enforcement, military, and even firefighters do not make the list, not to mention taxi drivers, cleaners, and other people we innately trust in our day-to-day lives.	Which? Survey of 2,060 people, 2012, (www.which.co.uk/).

people we consider to be similar to ourselves, so if a social engineer can build rapport on this basis, he has a reasonable chance of achieving the desired outcome.

We are particularly likely to trust people who are in a position of authority and to comply with their requests, which brings me on to my next point: social engineering can be quite successful when the social engineer assumes a position of authority.

Respect for Authority

From the moment we are born, we are conditioned to respect and obey those in authority, starting with our parents and teachers and moving on to our bosses in the workplace, law enforcement, and generally anyone in a uniform. Most people obey authority unquestioningly. If a police officer approached you in the street and asked to see your ID, would you hand it over? Most people would. If a police officer came into your organization and told you she had to investigate some reported activities on the roof of your building, would you let her in? Verizon did: in the example described Chapter 2, security guards allowed people who appeared to be police officers into the data center, where they promptly stole thousands of dollars' worth of infrastructure.

People tend to comply with requests made by individuals whom they perceive to be in positions of authority. Therefore, social engineers can achieve the desired response from their targets by making an assertion of authority. Obedience involves a hierarchy of power or status, so when the social engineer making the request has a higher status than the person receiving the request, the target is more likely to comply with the request. The social engineer may play roles such as that of a law enforcement officer, senior staff member within an organization (any kind of senior executive), an important client, or the Prince of Nigeria. Not only do we feel compelled to obey authority, but also we do not even feel permitted to challenge it, which is what social engineers are counting on.

Sometimes social engineers leverage vested authority, pointing out that those in authority have given their authorization. The authority game can backfire, however, by provoking a reaction in the target in which he feels inclined to fight back and refuses to comply with the request. As I do not have the physical appearance of someone in authority (more on that shortly), in my own social engineering scenarios, I often play the role of the personal assistant (PA) of someone in power, for example, the PA to the CEO of a key customer of the organization I am targeting. This way, I use the vested authority of the CEO but can also try to build rapport with my target who is unlikely to be the CEO.

In March 2013, MI5, the British intelligence agency responsible for protecting the United Kingdom against threats to national security, issued a public warning that fraudsters had been attempting to obtain money from people by using the agency's name. Members of the public, both in the UK and abroad, received requests for money by email or phone from individuals claiming they worked for the agency. Some fraudsters even claimed to be Sir Jonathan Evans, MI5's Director General at the time. In terms of playing the role of someone in authority, this takes the cake. Like any intelligence agency, MI5 pulls rank on just about everyone! Most people will comply with its requests. The social engineers in this instance risked creating a far-fetched and, therefore, less believable scenario, but it clearly convinced some members of the public.

The Milgram Experiment

The Milgram Experiment is possibly the most famous psychological study on obedience. Conducted in 1961, when Adolf Eichmann, the Nazi war criminal, was brought to trial to face charges for atrocities committed in World War II, Stanley Milgram, a psychologist at Yale University, sought to understand the justifications of the accused. Eichmann used the defense that he was following the orders of his superiors. Milgram decided to test just how far people would go in following orders of their so-called superiors when it involved harming another person. He began his experiments to answer the question, "Could it be that Eichmann and his million accomplices in the Holocaust were just following orders? Could we call them all accomplices?"[5]

Milgram's experiment involved pairing each volunteer with another person; they then drew lots to assign one as the "learner" and one as the "teacher." However, the draw was fixed so the participant was always the teacher, and the learner was one of Milgram's associates. The third role of "experimenter" was played by an actor dressed in a white lab coat. The so-called learner, an associate called Mr. Wallace, was led into a room, strapped into a chair, and had electrodes attached to his arm in view of the teacher. The teacher and experimenter then went into an adjoining room that contained an electric shock generator and a row of 30 switches ranging from 15 volts

(which would supposedly deliver a slight electric shock) to 375 volts (which would deliver a severe shock) to 450 volts (which can cause dielectric breakdown—severe internal burning—of the skin). The switches were also labeled in groups with verbal designations such as "slight shock" (15 volts), "moderate shock," "danger," and "XXX" (450 volts). (Although voltage doesn't kill without amperage, most people are unaware of this, and besides, it can still hurt.) The illustration shows the set-up for the experiment.

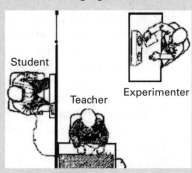

The learner was given a list of word pairs to learn. The teacher was required to test the learner by naming a word and asking the learner to recall its word pairing from a list of four choices. Every time the learner made a mistake, the teacher was required to administer an electric shock, increasing the shock level by 15 volt increments for each mistake. If the teacher refused to deliver an electric shock, the experimenter in the white lab coat would request that the teacher continue, using one of the following requests:

- Please continue, or please go on.
- The experiment requires that you continue.
- It is absolutely essential that you continue.
- You have no other choice, you must go on.

[5]Stanley Milgram, Obedience to Authority: An Experimental View, Harper and Row, 1974.

If, at any point, the teacher asked if the learner would suffer permanent physical harm, they were told, "Although the shocks may be painful, there is no permanent tissue damage, so please go on." If the teacher pointed out that it appeared the learner wanted to halt the experiment, they were told, "Whether the learner likes it or not, you must go on until he has learned all the word pairs correctly, so please go on."

The experiment finished when either the teacher wanted to stop after all four of the verbal requests were given or the maximum voltage of 450 volts was administered three times in succession.

The result was that all of the participants delivered electric shocks to 300 volts, with almost two-thirds administering the highest level of 450 volts. Milgram concluded that, "The extreme willingness of adults to go to almost any lengths on the command of an authority constitutes the chief finding of the study." This finding is certainly confirmed by the number of successful social engineering attacks in which the social engineer assumes the role of someone in a position of authority.

Factors that Increase Our Tendency to Obey

Certain factors can increase a person's tendency to obey an authority:

- **Legitimacy of the authority**   We are more likely to obey a credible authority figure. From a social engineer's point of view, this may involve wearing a certain costume (for example, that of a police officer, a telecom engineer, or even a cleaner) or presenting false credentials.
- **Social isolation**   We are more likely to obey an order when we are isolated and cannot appeal to others. This is one of the reasons why social engineers may try to put their victims under pressure to take an action quickly. Social support reduces obedience, so if the potential victims can ask others, they are less likely to comply with the order.
- **Gradual commitment**   Once the participants in the Milgram Experiment had already given lower-level shocks, it was harder for them to resist the request to give higher-level shocks. A social engineer might start with asking for smaller bits of information and then build up to bigger pieces of information.
- **Justifying obedience**   People are more likely to obey orders if they believe they are serving a justifiable cause. In the Second World War, Nazi propaganda made German people believe they were serving a justifiable cause. Social engineers may also use this kind of pressure to convince people to comply with their requests. This can result in a situation in which the victim may think, "I wouldn't do this usually but seeing as it's for a good reason..."

Indicators of Authority

There are various indicators that we associate with people in authority. Social engineers can use these to make their scenarios more believable. We will look at these indicators in more detail in Chapter 6, when we talk about how to create a believable social engineering scenario, but here is a brief summary:

- **Uniforms** Uniforms are very overt symbols of authority that we associate with the police and the military. Social engineers use uniforms to their advantage, sometimes playing the role of law enforcement, telecom engineer, pest control expert, business executive, and more.
- **Wealth** We associate wealth and symbols of wealth with authority. Fraudsters certainly play upon this. Look at Bernie Madoff, who, in 2009, admitted to operating the biggest Ponzi scheme (worth an estimated $50 billion) in history. Madoff had a following of loyal investors who unquestioningly believed his promises of 10–12 percent annual returns. Madoff was so wealthy and so highly regarded as a hedge fund manager that people automatically assigned him an authoritative role and didn't necessarily perform their due diligence.
- **Physical attributes** Certain physical attributes, for example, your age, height, or posture, or even being in physically good shape, can make you look authoritative.
- **Attitude** If you act like you are in charge, most people won't challenge you.
- **Voice/accent/vocabulary** How we use our voices and even our vocabulary can affect how authoritative we appear to other people. As children, we know when we are in trouble just by the way our parents or teachers say our name. Sometimes we may find certain accents or vocabulary intimidating or even threatening.

Often people are keen to help or assist even when the person who has made the request is not in a position of authority. As described next, sometimes social engineering often works because people are genuinely helpful.

Helpfulness

People like to help other people. We often feel compelled to help other people, even strangers, particularly if it is within the work environment. For many people, their job involves helping others. Customer relations is a key aspect of jobs for call center agents, receptionists, and help desk staff, for example—areas that are often our first line of defense when it comes to social engineering. Call center staff may be measured according to the number of calls they successfully complete. To get through calls as quickly as possible in this environment, you need to have a happy customer on the end of the phone.

We sometimes even help people without being asked. If we see someone carrying two cups of coffee, we hold the door open for them. Most people, when opening a door, will hold it open for the people behind them even if they don't have their hands full. If someone asks directly for help, most people are extremely reluctant to refuse.

Most of us have probably been in the situation where we step into an elevator and someone shouts out to hold the door. We may not want to wait around holding the door, but nearly everyone does.

Some social scientists believe that *altruism*, the practice of unselfish concern for the welfare of others, is programmed into the human genome, that we have a natural urge to be helpful. Author and development psychologist Michael Tomasello writes in his book *Why We Cooperate* (The MIT Press, 2009) that when an 18-month-old infant sees an adult, even an unrelated one, whose hands are full and who needs assistance with opening a door or picking up a dropped clothes peg, that infant immediately helps. The same goes for a social engineering scenario in which the social engineer is carrying two or three cups of coffee and reaches a door she cannot open; someone will inevitably open the door. Biologists and social scientists in this camp claim that the urge to help appears to be innate because it appears so early in a child's development—before many parents start teaching their children the rules of polite behavior.

Tomasello also writes that infants will help by providing information. From the age of 12 months, a child will point at objects that an adult pretends to have lost. It seems that we are innately programed to help social engineers with their information-gathering processes! We just love providing information. Have you ever phoned a contact to be told they were away on holiday or at a training course, when a simple out of office message would suffice? Such information seems harmless but is golden to a social engineer.

Of course, people do not always help others out of the goodness of their hearts. Sometimes people will help because they have other motivations for doing so.

Motivators to Aid the Social Engineer

Social engineers often try to motivate their targets, in either a positive or a negative fashion, to help them. On the positive side, the social engineer may offer some kind of financial incentive or other bribe or even just owing a favor. On the negative side, the social engineer may threaten his victims, scare them, or make them think they will get into trouble for not complying with his requests.

Positive Motivations: Reciprocity

Reciprocity is an extremely effective principle when it comes to influencing people. Social engineers often give or offer something to their targets so the targets feel obliged to reciprocate. We tend to comply with requests when the person who has made the request has given or promised us something of value. Even giving victims a chance to do their good deed for the day can be effective (this may be why charity scams are so widespread). It could even be something as simple as a bar of chocolate.

Carlos Hector Flomenbaum, the Antwerp diamond thief, built a rapport with staff at the bank he robbed by bringing them chocolates. Most security professionals will be familiar with the oft-repeated experiment where passersby are asked to give up their passwords in exchange for a chocolate bar. Typically, this experiment is performed in the run up to the Infosecurity trade show in London. The number of people willing to disclose their passwords in recent years has dropped, but it is still surprisingly high. In 2004, the number was at 70 percent but, by 2008, it had dropped to 21 percent. That's still one in five people! No one seemed to verify whether the passwords were real, but when you ask people for information on the spot they mostly tell the truth, so I'm sure at least some of the passwords were valid.

The 2008 survey also showed that 45 percent of women were happy to disclose their passwords in return for a bar of chocolate, compared to only 10 percent of men, leading to headlines around the world saying that women give out passwords for chocolate. (If you ever try to bribe me with chocolate, please note that I only eat high-quality dark chocolate.)

The potential to make a quick buck is also why Nigerian 419 scams are still successful, despite having been around in one form or another for at least 300 years. Victims of these scams believe they stand to make a significant amount of money. Some social engineering scams and other cons involve informing clients that they could *save* money. For example, toward the end of the tax year in the UK, there is usually a round of phishing emails purporting to be from HM Revenue & Customs, which inform recipients that they are entitled to a tax refund. An example is shown in Figure 3-4.

Selecting this link takes you to a fraudulent web
page that looks similar to a genuine HMRC page.

To:
From: info171581@inbox.net
Subject: Tax Refund Notice !

 **HM Revenue & Customs**

Tax Refund Confirmation

After the last annual calculations of your fiscal activity, we have determined that you are eligible to receive a tax refund of 468.50 GBP. Please submit the tax refund request and click here by having your tax refund sent to your bank account in due time

Please Click "Get Started" to have your tax refund sent to your bank account, your tax refund will be sent to your bank account in due time take your time to go through the bank we have on our list

Get Started

Note : A refund can be delayed a variety of reasons, for example submitting invalid records or applying after deadline.

Best Regards

HM Revenue & Customs

Source: www.hmrc.gov.uk/security/example1.pdf

FIGURE 3-4 Fraudulent tax rebate email.

So people will often return the favor if you offer them something—*quid pro quo*. But even more than that, people like to get something for nothing. Few people will refuse a free USB key. That's why so many social engineering tests involve scattering USB keys in an area where they are likely to be picked up by staff working at the target organization.

Negative Motivations: Pressuring the Victim

A number of social engineering techniques rely on threats or scaremongering to apply pressure to the target. A typical phishing attack that looks like it comes from your bank will threaten to cut off your credit card if you don't click the link and update your details. Some social engineering attacks may rely on the victim thinking he is not doing his job properly if he doesn't comply with the social engineer's request. Targeted individuals may be concerned that if they don't give information to the very important-looking person claiming to be the CEO of one of their organization's most profitable clients, they may get into trouble or even lose their job. In other attacks, social engineers may use time pressure to trick their victims into complying with their request—I need access to this document *now*!

One of the best email attacks I have seen involves sending the recipient an e-ticket receipt for a plane journey with British Airways. Naturally, the ticket is attached to the email. The recipient is supposed to open the attachment in order to rectify the apparent mistake but, instead, unwittingly installs malware on the computer.

Many scams play on victims wanting to maintain their online reputation. A popular phishing scam involves sending an email to the recipient that says, "I saw you in this video on Facebook? Who posted this of you? Hah! Skip video to 1:45 ! Type in with no spaces and search your name on www.*****.com." Another scam plays on victims' fear of having their eBay score affected negatively, telling them they haven't paid for a recently won item—Please Click Here to Pay. All of these scam emails either redirect the user to a malicious website or use attachments that install malicious software such as a virus, Trojan, keylogger, or other malware.

Social engineers and fraudsters have always played on people's fears. In today's world, guessing what people worry about—whether it's their financial position, their reputation, or their job situation—is not hard. Many surveys on social networks ask people what their deepest fear is. People write all kinds of things, from their football team losing to a fear of spiders. This information is always useful to a social engineer, who could potentially threaten her target with a tarantula until he hands over the requested information...

Lack of Personal Responsibility

Few people want to take responsibility for an action, particularly in the case of physical social engineering. I have done so many social engineering tests where I have obtained unauthorized physical access to a building and wandered around, rarely to be challenged. Why do people fail to act in these situations? I've asked myself over and over why so few people challenge me and have come to the conclusion that it is usually for one of the following reasons:

- People do not think it is their job to challenge me, unless it is very obviously part of their job role, for instance, a security guard.
- People assume that somebody else is dealing with me or has authorized me to be in the building.
- People don't want the hassle of a confrontation.

Bystander Effect

In 1964, a 28-year-old woman named Kitty Genovese was stabbed to death outside her apartment block in Queens, New York. The story goes that although several of her neighbors heard her scream, none of them came to her aid and not one of them called the police until it was too late. This event became the impetus for research on the psychological phenomenon that became dubbed the *bystander effect* by psychologists John Darley and Bibb Latane. The bystander effect is the social phenomenon in which the presence of other people reduces helping behavior. In a series of experiments, Latane and Darley found that the amount of time it takes a person to take action and seek help varies depending on how many other people are in the room. The greater the number of people present, the less likely people are to help a person in distress.

In one of their experiments, the room in which participants were filling out questionnaires began to fill with smoke. When participants were alone, 75 percent reported the smoke to the experimenters. When they were in the room with two other people, 38 percent of participants reported the smoke. In the final group, the two confederates in the experiment noted the smoke and ignored it, leading to a drop to 10 percent of the number of participants who reported the smoke; some participants even stayed in the room until it became hazy!

In another experiment, Latane and Darley faked epileptic seizures on the streets of New York City. When there was only one bystander, they were helped 85 percent of the time. But when there were five bystanders, they were helped only 30 percent of the time.

Psychologists claim that two major factors contribute to the bystander effect. The first factor is the presence of other people creates a *diffusion of responsibility*; people are less likely to take action in the presence of others because they feel less responsible for helping someone in need if more people are present. People familiar with this concept know that if there is ever an emergency situation, for example, someone at your train station collapses, you are supposed to pick one individual and ask them to take a particular action.

The presence of other people lowers the chances of anyone intervening because everyone assumes that someone else will provide the necessary help. Being in a crowd, or on an office floor, can make it easy to avoid personal responsibility for taking action. Consider again the scenario where a stranger is walking confidently around an office building. The stranger blends in with other office workers in terms of appearance and seems to know where she or he is going. Who is going to challenge this individual or ask to see some ID? In my experience, very few.

The second factor in the bystander effect is we look to others for guidance in ambiguous situations. If no one else is doing anything, then we assume that there is nothing that needs to be done, an effect referred to as *pluralistic ignorance.* If other people present fail to act, individuals often assume that a response is either not needed or inappropriate. In the aforementioned scenario, where a stranger is walking around an office area, staff may assume that because no one else has challenged the stranger, then nothing needs to be done.

With the bystander effect, researchers have found that bystanders go through the following five stages and, at any of these stages, can choose to take an action or do nothing:

1. Notice the event.
2. Realize there is an emergency.
3. Assume responsibility.
4. Know what to do.
5. Take action.

Let's consider each of these stages from an emergency point of view—the smoke in the room experiment used by Darley and Latane—and from a social engineering attack point of view—a physical social engineering scenario in which an unidentified person is roaming unescorted around an office.

Bystander Phase	Smoke Emergency	Physical Social Engineering Attack
Phase 1: Notice the event.	The bystander observes smoke in the room.	The bystander observes an unidentified individual in the office.
Phase 2: Realize there is an emergency.	Smoke means fire. The bystander realizes that people could be in danger.	The bystander realizes that the unidentified person may be an impostor.
Phase 3: Assume responsibility.	The bystander realizes that help is needed and that she has the capacity to assist.	The bystander understands that something needs to be done about this individual and that she can potentially do something.
Phase 4: Know what to do.	The bystander decides on the most appropriate course of action, for instance, to ring the fire alarm.	The bystander decides that the unidentified person needs to be challenged.
Phase 5: Take action.	The bystander actually rings the fire alarm.	The bystander actually challenges the unidentified person or asks a security guard or other "authority figure" to do so, thus acting by proxy.

In these situations, people sometimes realize there is a problem but fail to take action. They can choose to act or not at any point during the five stages. But how can people take action if they don't even realize that there is a problem and they haven't even noticed the event?

Lack of Awareness

Often social engineering works because people don't realize it's a problem. Even when they do realize that it is a threat, they may think they would not fall for such scams or they are not aware of what the right course of action is.

Social engineering has become easier over the past few years as people publish so much information about themselves on social networks. Creating a sophisticated, targeted, and above all realistic attack is much more effective when the attacker has so much personal information to choose from. This being the case, why do people publish so much information online and why don't they take precautions to ensure that this information is not available to absolutely everyone on the Internet? It's because people are not truly aware of how this information can be used against them. Often, people don't believe they will be targeted or don't recognize the real risk that comes with being targeted. The "what have I got to lose" mentality is rather widespread.

People Don't Realize Social Engineering Is a Threat

Many people just aren't aware that social engineering exists at all. When they find out that they have been targeted, they don't even realize that it was a scam. They don't know what social engineering is. How can they be expected to defend against it? When the first phishing attacks started appearing in the mid-1990s, they were very successful as no one had ever come across them before. Around this time, AOL was the top Internet access provider and so a natural target for attackers. Initially attackers used algorithms in programs such as AOHell to create fake credit card numbers that they used to open AOL accounts, which, in turn, were used to send spam or other fraudulent messages. When AOL enforced security controls to prevent the use of randomly generated credit card numbers, phishing as we know it today was born. Phishers posed as AOL staff and used instant messaging and emails to trick users into verifying their accounts or confirming their billing information. Users had no reason not to believe these emails, so the success rate was high.

As our awareness of these scams has increased, phishers started sending these emails or messages from what appeared to be our friends' accounts. Up until that point, we had no reason not to trust our friends and so we clicked the links or opened attachments that they sent us. We have to be aware of the risk to defend against it.

People Don't Think They Will Be Targeted by Social Engineers

As security professionals, how often do we hear people ask, "Why would they come after me? What do I have that's of value?" This dangerous mentality is all too commonplace nowadays. If people don't believe they will be targeted (because they don't fully understand the risk), then they will not take adequate precautions to prevent against social engineering.

Some people claim they don't care if they fall for a social engineering scam, that is, until they fall for one! This idea may also be driven by the "what have I got to lose" mentality.

People Think They Would Never Fall for a Social Engineering Scam

Some people have a misplaced confidence that they will never fall for a social engineering scam: "It would never happen to me." They think they know how to avoid scams—and they do know how to avoid an awful lot of scams. But no one knows how to avoid every scam. Every one of us is liable to be stung by a social engineer. In fact, the more you study social engineering or execute social engineering tests, the more you realize how much of a potential target you yourself are.

Sometimes people who believe they can't be scammed become attractive targets for social engineers. Bertha Heyman, a successful con artist in America in the late 1800s, was quoted as saying, "The moment I discover a man's a fool I let him drop, but I delight in getting into the confidence and pockets of men who think they can't be 'skinned.' It ministers to my intellectual pride."

People Don't Know What to Do When They Face a Social Engineering Attack

Sometimes people may recognize that they are in a social engineering situation, but they don't know what the correct course of action is, so they take the wrong action or even no action at all. Most people want to take the right course of action in any scenario, but unless they know what this is, how can they take it? They want to do the right thing, but they don't know what it is. This is one of the reasons why good security policies and training and awareness are so important. If your staff knows what to do in a social engineering situation, they are more likely to deal with it in the most effective manner.

Final Thoughts

Social engineering attacks are limited only by the attacker's imagination. There are hundreds of examples of social engineering attacks and many reasons why social engineering techniques work. In this chapter, we have looked at some of the key reasons why social engineering works and the aspects of human nature that social engineers and other fraudsters attempt to exploit.

Many psychological studies have investigated different aspects of the human condition. Some of these studies can help us understand why we fall repeatedly for social engineers and con artists. We are only human, after all, and therefore mostly but not entirely predictable. Everyone is different. Running a social engineering test is not like testing a machine or a network; there are no absolutes when it comes to human beings, bar death and taxes—and social engineers try to get around even the latter!

As security professionals, to prevent social engineering attacks from being successful, we must try to understand why they work. And in the immortal words of former President of the United States, Ronald Reagan, "Trust but verify."

4 Planning Your Social Engineering Test

There was no such thing as luck. Luck was a word idiots used to explain the consequences of their own rashness, and selfishness, and stupidity. More often than not bad luck meant bad plans.
—Joe Abercrombie, *Before They Are Hanged*

Over the next few chapters we will look at how to plan, execute, and report on a social engineering test. The social engineering testing methodology presented here can be tailored for each test as no two social engineering assignments are the same. As with any project, the first step is the planning phase.

The key to running a successful social engineering assignment is in the planning. Although social engineering has been around for a long time, the concept of performing social engineering tests is relatively new. Often clients don't know what they want or don't know what to expect from the test. During the planning phase, you will work with the client to figure out what you will test, when you will test, and how you will go about it. The objective of the planning phase is to develop a project plan with the relevant authorized people to achieve specific, agreed-upon goals.

The planning phase of the social engineering assignment, which I cover in this chapter, includes the following activities:

- Assessing the threat
- Scoping the test and setting goals
- Planning the project
- Defining the rules of engagement

Considerations Before You Meet the Client

If you are meeting your client face-to-face at any point throughout the planning phase, consider how this might impact any physical security scenarios you are going to use. For example, if you go into your client's office and sign in as a security consultant one week, will anyone recognize you if you return using an alias the next week? Visiting in advance is useful in terms of learning how the visitor process works, but it skews your knowledge if your client is looking for a black box assessment. You could get around this by meeting in a different location. However, if you choose to do this, you must be sure that the person you are meeting really does work for your target organization and is authorized to engage you as a social engineer!

Remember, you must always seek authorization from your client before performing a social engineering test. If you are going to use social engineering techniques as part of a penetration test, you should obtain explicit permission to do so. For your own protection as a security professional, a contract granting explicit permission for social engineering activities ensures that you are covered in case of unintended or difficult scenarios.

Assessing the Threat

The first activity you will perform as part of the planning phase is a high-level threat assessment. The purpose of the threat assessment is to establish what your client is seeking to protect and who they are seeking to protect it from. You'll use this information as the basis of the social engineering test, so your test is reflective of the actual threat that your client is facing from social engineers.

Start with finding out what your clients are concerned about and what they are trying to protect. They may have a call center that handles a lot of personal information. They may be developing a new product and are concerned about intellectual property relating to the project being leaked to the press or falling into the hands of competitors. What would be the impact of a successful social engineering attack? It may be the financial impact of losing data, the reputational damage that results from a social engineering attack or corporate espionage, or even a drop in share prices. This background information will influence the type of social engineering test you perform. For example, if your client is a financial organization that deals in mergers and acquisitions (M&A) and is concerned about losing or leaking M&A information, the objective of your social engineering test will likely be to access information relating to M&As (or test information to this effect).

Find out from your clients what is driving the need for a social engineering test. Has there been a security breach in which your clients know or suspect social engineering was used? Do they know about any attacks that have targeted their competitors? Has a social engineering incident been in the news lately? Maybe they are looking to increase awareness and use the social engineering test purely as an educational exercise for employees, or maybe they are looking to identify vulnerabilities in their security posture.

Types of Attackers

Consider the types of attackers that may target your clients. They generally fall into the following categories, described in Chapter 1, or into a combination of them, any of whom may use hacking techniques as part of their attack:

- Opportunists with little preparation and little to no budget
- Well-funded and prepared attackers
- Trusted insiders

Opportunists with Little Preparation

If the social engineering test is driven by a client who is concerned about opportunists with little preparation and little to no budget (petty criminals, pranksters, and so on), the test will be relatively short and require little preparation or scenario creation. It may involve attempting to gain access to the building through open doors or via tailgating somebody into the building, or it may involve sending a blanket phishing attack that has not been customized for your target organization.

Well-Funded and Prepared Attackers

Your client may be concerned about well-funded attackers who are well prepared. These adversaries can afford to undertake more sophisticated attacks that occur over a longer period of time. The social engineering test that you devise to reflect the types of attacks an organized external attacker would perform will, therefore, involve creating a sophisticated scenario that takes place over an extended period of time. In my experience, this type of social engineering test is the most common.

Trusted Insiders

As described in Chapter 1, an insider attack can be done from a number of perspectives, therefore, so can your social engineering test. From a testing point of view, trusted insider tests involve your clients giving you some level of access to their building or systems, and/or appointing you as a member of staff or approved third party with access to the organization. Such tests use quite detailed scenarios that can require a lot of planning and preparation and may require a longer execution time if you are playing the role of a known staff member or third party.

Current Awareness Levels

What have your clients done to date to minimize their exposure to social engineering attacks? Is the staff aware of the social engineering threat? They may have had specific social engineering training, or there may have been a poster or email campaign to make staff aware of the problem. Asking the following questions is useful:

- Does the staff know what social engineering is?
- Have they had any training or awareness campaigns for social engineering?

- Have staff been told what to do if they suspect they are being social engineered? Is this documented anywhere, for example, in the security policy?
- Is there a formal process for flagging social engineering attempts?

If the staff has had no training whatsoever and has not been made aware of what social engineering is, is it fair to test them? Ensure you talk this through with your clients so they make the decision to perform a security test from an informed perspective.

Once you have completed the threat assessment and understand the types of social engineering threats faced by your client, the next step is to scope the social engineering test.

Scoping the Social Engineering Test

Scoping the social engineering test involves gathering the information you require to start a project and assessing how long it will take to complete the test. Social engineering tests can be difficult to scope. How do you predict how long it will take to run through a scenario successfully? The more time you have the more sophisticated scenarios you can devise. You could spend months doing the research and reconnaissance phase and building a highly sophisticated attack, but unfortunately most budgets won't allow for this.

In the scoping phase, you

- Decide what type of test to perform
- Figure out how much time to allocate to the test
- Agree on goals and deliverables

 Going over budget is common, as social engineering is so interesting and so much fun that testers can get carried away. Once you start your social engineering assignment, thinking of anything else is difficult. It will be on your mind 24/7.

Type of Test

Your social engineering test may be an onsite or a remote test (via telephone, email, or even fax), or a combination of the two. It may involve some technical aspects or even be combined with a penetration test. At the planning stage, you decide what type of test is appropriate, although the detailed scenarios come later after you have done your research and reconnaissance phase. The test could involve

- Attempting to gain physical access to a specific location
- A phishing test to trick staff into opening attachments or clicking links
- Attempting to elicit sensitive information over the telephone
- A bait-and-hook test, such as scattering USB keys around an office

Or your test could also be any combination of these. The type of test you choose will be largely driven by the threat assessment that you have performed. It should accurately reflect the types of social engineering threats faced by your client.

Obtaining Information in Advance

You need to decide what level of information is appropriate to obtain from your client in advance of the test. Similar to penetration testing, social engineering can be done from a black box or white box perspective, or somewhere in between, in which case you have a limited amount of knowledge. The more information you receive in advance, the less time you will have to spend obtaining it yourself, so there are financial benefits for your client to provide certain information ahead of time. For a physical test, this material may include

- Floor plans
- Locations of key areas, such as the server room and the CEO's office
- ID cards
- Details on security controls such as locations of CCTV video cameras

For an onsite test, find out if the security guards are armed or if there are any guard dogs. The physical safety of both you and your team comes first. If you have any concerns about being physically hurt during the course of your test, call it off or do a remote test instead.

For a remote test, you may wish to obtain the following information in advance of the test:

- Call center scripts, otherwise, the first part of your test will involve making repeated calls to your target to map out the various calling options and scripts
- Telephone numbers or email addresses to target
- Types of systems in use so you can use technical attacks that are more likely to succeed

A full information questionnaire is provided in the sidebar at the end of this chapter. I've included a combination of scoping and reconnaissance questions.

Time to Allocate to Test

How long your social engineering test takes will be determined by a number of factors, of which the chief one is budgetary. In an ideal world, you could perform the test over a series of months or even years, but few social engineering tests get this kind of sign off.

The following questions address other factors that influence how long the test will take:

- For an onsite test, how many locations do you need to test?
- For a remote test, how many individuals are you targeting? Remember, if it's a phone test, you will need to include a delay between calls so your voice isn't recognized.
- How many scenarios are you going to attempt?

- How sophisticated are the scenarios you are going to use? Tailgating may only take a day, but setting up a more involved scenario, or long con, such as ingratiating yourself as an employee or service provider, or attempting to execute a complex physical breach can take months.
- When does the test need to be completed? Your client may have certain deadlines, for example, audit committee meetings, that require the test be completed by a certain date.

A good social engineering test is never rushed. If you are contracted to call 30 people as part of a remote telephone social engineering test, there is no point in calling them all on the same day. The receptionist may recognize your voice, or your number may be flagged. What if the people you are calling sit next to each other and find it suspicious that you are calling each of them? Similarly, if you are doing an onsite test, if you turn up pretending to be a cleaner one day, you need to leave a bit of time before you turn up as the telecom engineer. The best way to avoid this situation is to agree to a certain number of testing days that can be delivered over a longer period of time, so you may agree to perform five onsite testing days over a one-month period, or make 30 phone calls over the period of three weeks, for example.

In some instances, you may also need to set cutoff times. A cutoff primarily applies to bait-and-hook tests, where you set the bait and wait for a target to "get hooked," but also to anything requiring a call back. For example, if you drop a USB key as your bait, how long do you wait before someone plugs it in or the social engineering test is considered a failure? Similarly, if you send a phishing email, how long should you wait for a response? These situations should be discussed with your client. How long you wait usually depends on how soon the test needs to be done and the budget.

Goals and Deliverables

The purpose of the social engineering test is to achieve specific goals that have been agreed on with your client. What you did to achieve these goals and whether you achieved them is described in the deliverables for the project, usually in the form of a report.

Goals

Your social engineering test should have a clear goal. In my experience, goals can be as varied as trying to attend a premier league football match without a ticket, obtaining information about internal projects at the local pub, or even eating lunch in the canteen. A typical goal might be

- Gaining access to the client's network either onsite or remotely
- Sniffing network traffic
- Obtaining an internal IP address

- Accessing a certain location, such as a server room or CEO's office
- Removing target assets (laptops/project plans/other sensitive data) from a physical location
- Obtaining remote access to sensitive data, such as client information

If you are going to take sensitive data offsite, or download a local copy in the case of a remote test, remember you are responsible for keeping it secure and may even have data protection or privacy requirements to fulfill. Because of this, clients often request in a physical social engineering test that you leave evidence onsite as proof you have gained access, rather than taking data offsite. I use stickers or business cards as my calling card to say I've been there. My calling cards note the name of the tester who has gained access and the time and date of the test. I don't want a client calling me in a year's time because she thinks I have just penetrated the building! I keep notes and usually take a photo of the calling cards I leave and where I leave them as I go along, as recalling where I've left them after the test can be difficult. One of my former colleagues likes to leave a comic book as her calling card. The advantage of this is it provides good reading material for any lulls during the test, for example, when you are hiding in the bathroom and waiting for all the staff to go home!

For me, a typical physical social engineering assignment involves gaining access to a certain location, leaving a calling card, and making a note or taking a photo of the types of sensitive information I can access (although not necessarily of the information itself). In terms of remote testing, phishing programs are very popular, in which case the assignment involves crafting a phishing attack that is designed especially for my target organization, sending the phishing email, and tracking how many people click through on it.

Deliverables

The deliverables for a social engineering test usually include a report with photographs, screenshots, and possibly audio or video recordings of the social engineering fieldwork, depending on whether you were authorized to make recordings (and taking into account the local laws on data protection and privacy). The report typically contains a description of what you did, the outcome of the test, and any recommendations on how to improve physical or logical security and security awareness. Sometimes the report contains statistics on the numbers of people who fell for the social engineering attempt. Social engineering reports can be difficult to write after all the fun of the social engineering test and may take longer to write than you might expect. Chapter 8 provides more information on how to write a social engineering report.

Some clients may not require a report and prefer simply to have a meeting to discuss what you did and how you did it. Unfortunately, this kind of client is rare! Other deliverables may include plans for a social engineering awareness program based around your social engineering test.

Planning the Project

Once your client has agreed to do a social engineering test and allocated a budget, you can put together a project plan. The project plan shows how the goals of the test will be achieved within the agreed timeline and budget. Your overall project plan consists of the following elements:

- **Test plan**   Developing the scenario and deciding on targets
- **Team plan**   Establishing roles and responsibilities and assigning these to individuals
- **Communications plan**   Defining the lines and frequency of communication
- **Risk management plan**   Identifying any potential risks or pitfalls that may occur during the test

Test Plan

You have already decided what type of test you are going to do. Now you have to decide who you are going to target and start thinking about the type of scenario you are going to use. Once you have done this, you can put together your testing team and start assigning roles.

Deciding Who to Target

The client who has contracted you to perform a social engineering test may have a certain individual or, more frequently, group(s) of people who they would like you to target during the test. If the client has not selected anyone, then you need to decide who to target as part of your test. In my experience, my clients and I usually chose to target staff within the following categories:

- Frontline staff, such as receptionists, help desk staff, call center agents, and any other people who deal with the public or enquiries from third parties
- People with direct access to the information that you want, such as IT departments, financial departments, or human resources, and especially personal assistants to senior individuals within the organization—although PAs are notoriously hard to get past!
- Senior staff, such as C-suite executives, usually as part of an awareness-raising initiative and especially if they have public profiles available online
- Random sample of employees, often for group attacks, such as phishing

In terms of softer targets, temporary staff and new joiners may be easier targets for social engineers, as they may be unfamiliar with the correct processes and procedures within your target organization; however, it may (or may not) be a little unfair to target such people from an ethical point of view. Also, building targeted attacks against employees who have a lot of personal information publicly available, particularly on social media websites, is easier. However, if you are going to use information from personal profiles in your social engineering test—even if it is publicly available—get permission from your client first.

Selecting a Scenario

Some clients will have a specific scenario that they may want you to try. Scenarios that clients have asked me to test in the past have been pretty random and include

- Pretending to be the new CEO at a company conference. This scenario was geared more toward awareness raising rather than testing a potential vulnerability. It would take a lot of guts and be rather unrealistic for a malicious social engineer to open a conference in person as the new CEO!
- Pretending to be an employee from another office. In one particular case, many employees wore a T-shirt with a company logo on it, so I was given one of these shirts to wear for the test.
- Going to the local pub to listen to what employees were saying about work projects.

Otherwise, you will need to brainstorm potential scenarios. In my experience, 90 percent of your potential scenarios can be discounted because they are illegal, unethical, unrealistic, or cannot be performed within the budget or timeframe. Of the remaining 10 percent, you will have to decide which scenario is most likely to succeed and is best suited to achieve your goal. Your clients may or may not wish to be involved in the scenario selection. If they do wish to be involved, you can prepare a menu of potential scenarios and costs for each one. Of course, whichever scenario you choose will influence the costumes, props, and equipment you will need for your test. Chapter 6 describes how to create a scenario for your social engineering test. Once you have developed your scenario, you can gather your team.

Team Plan

Identify the roles first within the social engineering project, then within your chosen scenario. You may want someone to manage the project who won't be involved with the test, so she can communicate with your client without worrying if she'll be recognized—whether in person or over the phone—while the test is taking place. Describe the roles and responsibilities for each person working on the project. Typical roles for a social engineering test include

- Project manager
- Researchers
- Scenario developers
- Testers who will use the developed scenarios to attempt to gain access
- Report writer

Your chosen scenario may involve bringing further people onto the team. If you are an English speaker and you are targeting a French company, your scenario may require using a native French speaker. You may even wish to involve actors. If your scenario involves pretending to be an elderly Italian lady, you may want to recruit someone who can play that role. Scenario development can include a lot of rehearsing and role playing, so, in some ways, it is similar to being an actor. Your typical penetration tester does not necessarily have these skills, so he's not always the best person to execute the test.

Communications Plan

Communication with the client is one of the most important aspects of a social engineering test, particularly as the client often hasn't had any experience in running social engineering tests and may not know what to expect. It can be a strange relationship—you are trying to dupe employees at your target organization while maintaining an honest relationship with the person who has contracted you to do the test. The frequency with which you interact with the client and how up to date you keep them about how the test is progressing can help the client feel more at ease with the execution of the social engineering test.

Establish lines of communication in advance of your test, with contact points from both your own project team and your client organization. You need to be able to contact someone from your target organization in case of an emergency and vice versa. Perhaps the security guard has apprehended you; someone has called the police; or you've come across potentially incriminating material such as pornography.

Your emergency list should include contact details (including cell phone numbers) for at least two individuals at your target organization. The second contact is handy as a backup, in case you can't get through to your first contact. Likewise, your client needs at least two points of contact from your social engineering team.

You should establish a communications plan with your client that includes an appropriate schedule for updating them on your progress. Some clients like to be very involved, especially those who have never had a social engineering test before; others prefer less involvement so they are not aware of how or when you are doing the test and therefore can also be tested to an extent.

You should also establish a communications plan with your own team, with regular meetings throughout the whole project. In my team, we always go out in pairs for onsite social engineering tests, in case something goes wrong. Both team members are not always involved in the scenario, but the second individual will always be nearby—even if it's in a coffee shop near the building you are attempting to access. There are a number of advantages to doubling up in this way:

- It's safer if something goes wrong.
- The second person can cause a diversion while the first person attempts to gain access.
- The second person can alert the person doing the test if there are any security guards or other unexpected individuals around.
- Two people might look less suspicious than one person (especially if it's a male and a female).

Tip   Always ensure someone knows where you are going and when, so he or she can raise the alarm if you don't check back in.

Risk Management Plan

Risk management is an important part of the social engineering test. You can never fully predict what will happen during a test and how people will react to your test scenarios, so you have to be as prepared as possible. Identify potential risks to your project and take measures so you can be prepared if something goes wrong. Common project risks when it comes to social engineering are

- You don't have enough time to complete the test or perform enough research and reconnaissance. You need to give yourself adequate time to do this and use your time wisely.
- You can't think of a realistic scenario that is likely to work. It may be that you need to do some more research until you can come up with a more realistic scenario.
- You don't have the budget to execute your ideal scenario (props and setup are too expensive, or you don't have enough time). This very much depends on what budget you have agreed on with your client. You have to work with what you've got.
- Client requirements are not properly understood, either by you or by the clients themselves. Talk your client through what social engineering testing involves and listen to their concerns.
- Your test doesn't accurately reflect the risk that your target faces. A threat assessment should be performed before designing your test so that your scenario reflects the risk your target faces.
- Poor communication results in misunderstandings. Regular communication with your client can help to avoid this.
- You are discovered early in the test. Do you send in a different team member or try another scenario?
- Your scenario is unsuccessful. Do you try another scenario?
- Someone at your target organization calls the police. Do you explain what you have been doing, present your contract and get out of jail free card - or make a run for it?!

Consider how you will deal with each of these potential pitfalls. If you are discovered early into the test, should you inform the discoverer and progress with your chosen scenario or switch to a different scenario? If you are not getting anywhere with your scenario at all, for example, no one is responding to your requests for information over the phone, do you continue or try a different scenario? These examples very much depend on the budget for your test.

Remember what the goal of your test is throughout the social engineering project. If there are going to be any adverse effects as a result, notify your client and get permission for this. For example, in many buildings, the doors automatically open if a fire alarm rings to help staff exit the building quickly. Of course, this means it may be easier to get into the building then as well. But if you select a scenario that involves setting off a fire alarm and the entire staff exit the building, this can impact business operations. Similarly, if you remove a laptop as part of your test, the person who owns the laptop may have his work disrupted. Always seek explicit permission for scenarios that involve any kind of downtime and think through each scenario to see what these pitfalls may be.

Defining the Rules of Engagement

The rules of engagement are the specific rules that determine when, where, and how the social engineering test will run. Your entire social engineering team should be aware of the rules of engagement prior to embarking on any testing activities. The rules of engagement for a social engineering test can include

- Restrictions on testing, such as times of the day you can or cannot test, the time window during which you can perform the test, locations you may not attempt to access, information that is out of bounds
- Under what circumstances the test is to be called off
- What permission and contracts you need to do the test
- Who should be informed about the test

Restrictions on Testing

Are there any restrictions on when you perform the test? For example, if it is an onsite test, does it need to be done during work hours or can you attempt to access the location after hours? If there is a system going live or some other important event happening (I've had everything from company conferences to sports events), can you test while this is happening?

There may be restrictions on locations that you can attempt to access. If it's a production plant, you may not be allowed to access the production floor, for example. If there are any areas where hazardous materials are used, you are unlikely to be allowed to access them, even for social engineering purposes. Some organizations do not permit you to go into the HR area because of all the personal information stored there.

Calling Off the Test

Decide with your client the circumstances under which the test should be called off. For example, if you are caught by one employee, should you continue with the test or finish it? Obviously, you create your scenario or cover story so you don't get caught, so if your cover story is blown, do you continue?

In one test in which I was involved, the client had some equipment stolen during the test window. The client called the social engineering team and asked them to return it, only to find that it wasn't part of the test and the organization had actually been burgled! This kind of incident needs to be flagged as soon as possible. In this case, the social engineering test was called off.

Permission to Test

You need to seek permission to perform the social engineering test. As described in Chapter 2, you need the following documents before embarking on any social engineering activities:

- A signed contract
- A Get Out of Jail Free (indemnity) card with an explanation of what you are doing, identification details for the person(s) performing the test, and contact details for whoever has authorized the test within the organization
- Written approval for the scenario you are going to use
- If your test involves any technical aspects, permission to attempt to access the organization's network

As with a penetration test, third parties may be involved, and if they are, you may need to get their approval before doing the test. The types of third parties that may be involved are

- Outsourced facilities management or security
- Landlords of buildings that are not directly owned by your client
- Other organizations within the same building
- Third-party call centers

Tip Perform a third-party analysis as part of your scenario creation (see Chapter 6). However, should you choose to impersonate any of these third parties, you will need to seek their permission and stay strictly within the bounds of the law.

Who Should Be Informed About the Test

Establish who needs to be aware of the test in your target organization: this is usually the person who has authorized the test and a backup contact, should the authorizer be unavailable. Apart from that, it is better to limit the number of people who know about the test so it gives a better indication of whether a malicious social engineering attack would be successful. The fewer people the better, although one or two people need to know. I have found that when employees know that a social engineering test is occurring, they put extra controls in place that are removed after the course of the test, from blocking doorways that are usually left open, to putting extra security guards on duty, and even being more suspicious on the telephone.

In one of my favorite social engineering tests, I had to gain physical access to a server room in a particular building. The security staff and receptionists were informed that there would be a social engineering test during that particular week. When I arrived at reception with my scenario, the receptionist called the head of security, who took me aside to be questioned. He apologized and said that was not the usual procedure, but he had to do it that week as they were having social engineering tests. I asked what social engineering tests were. When he explained, I exclaimed my amazement that people do that kind of thing for a living. He laughed and waved me through!

Case Study: Social Engineering a Banking Call Center

The following table provides a high-level overview of the plan for a social engineering test I performed with my team. The test was for a bank that wanted us to attempt to access particular test accounts specifically set up for the test (but which appeared real to the call center agents), so the bank could assess how vulnerable the call center was to social engineering.

Threat Assessment	**Type of attacker**	Opportunists looking to steal identities or make transactions on their victims' accounts.
	Current level of awareness	An awareness program via posters and email had taken place, but there was no direct training.
Scoping the Test	**Type of test**	Telephone social engineering.
	Information required in advance	—Call center telephone numbers.
		—Call center scripts, including automated call options (for example, dial 1 for bank balance, 2 to speak to an operator, and so on).
		—Details for the test accounts set up for the purpose of the test. We tested these rather than real accounts so we wouldn't breach any data protection or privacy laws.
	How many days required	This particular test was limited to 15 days effort, of which 3 were set aside for reporting and analysis.
	Goals	To access account information for the accounts set up for the test without going through the full authorization process with the call center agent.
	Deliverables	A report containing details of the scenarios used and statistics on how successful they were. The report was to be accompanied by a spreadsheet that listed for each call:
		—The exact time it took place (so they could revert to their own recordings of the call)
		—The particular scenario used
		—Whether it was successful
		—If it was successful, what kind of information we were able to obtain about the account
		As well as giving an indication of the level of security awareness in the bank's call center, the test results were intended to help the bank decide what kind of awareness-training program, if any, to provide to the call center staff.

Project Plan	**Who to target**	We were to target as many call center agents as possible during the course of the 15 days.
	Scenario selection	We agreed on a selection of half a dozen or so scenarios, for example:

—Pretending to have lost certain information required to authenticate the caller to the call center agent

—Mumbling some of the authentication data so it wouldn't be understood by the call center agent (rather like a fuzzing attack in penetration testing)

—Claiming to be calling on behalf of the account holder

—Using a sob story to bypass authentication

—Acting overly friendly toward the call center agent in an attempt to elicit information

	Team	Our team consisted of a project manager and five callers, a mixture of males and females of various ages and with a selection of mostly British accents.

Each caller was to make five calls a day throughout the course of the test from a different telephone number or a hidden number each time.

	Communications plan	This test was not particularly high risk and didn't have many pitfalls that we were able to identify in advance. Therefore the client was relatively comfortable letting us work through the test without being involved. We agreed to give weekly updates and to notify the client if any particular scenario was repeatedly successful.
	Risk management plan	Potential pitfalls identified were

—None of our chosen scenarios were successful. This was not the case, however. We tried a selection of approximately half a dozen scenarios.

—Our voices would be recognized by the call center agents. To avoid this, we used a team of five individuals and restricted our calls to five a day.

(Continued)

Rules of Engagement	Restrictions	We were only permitted to attempt to access test accounts that we were notified of in advance.
		We were not allowed to make any transactions on the account, such as transferring funds or ordering a new debit card. We were allowed to change account details such as the postal address or email address associated with the account.
	Calling off the test	We had no particular reason to call off the test. If our social engineering attempts were flagged, we were to continue with our calls until the 15 days were up, so we could get an idea of what proportion of the calls leaked information.
	Permission to test	We had an appropriate contract in place that described the test and the chosen scenarios.
		We also got a Get Out of Jail Free card for each member of the team to cover them personally.
	Who should be informed	The Internal Audit Team was aware of the test as they commissioned it. They also informed the most senior call center manager so the manager could report back on whether any of our social engineering attempts had been escalated.

Pre-engagement Questionnaire

These are some of the questions I ask clients prior to performing a social engineering assignment. I ask a mix of scoping and reconnaissance questions. They do not have to answer every question, but the more information they can provide the better.

- What is the budget for your test?
- What is the goal of the test? For example, should we try to get network access or target specific information?
- Are you aware of any malicious social engineering attempts against your organization?
- Have you had social engineering testing done before?
- Are staff aware that a social engineering test will be taking place?
- Have staff been trained in social engineering awareness and defense?
- When does the test need to be completed?

For an Onsite Social Engineering Test
- How many locations are you planning to test and where are they?

For each location, please consider the following questions:

- Is the building a managed office?
- Is it a shared facility?
- How many floors are there? Which floor are we attempting to access? What's on each floor?
- How many entrances are there? Please include fire escapes and garages/car parks.
- Is there a server room? Is it in scope to access it?
- Do staff wear suits?
- Are security guards armed?
- Do the security guards have dogs?
- Are security/facilities management aware we are performing the test?
- Do staff wear badges?
- Are there any meeting rooms or places to hide in?
- Are there any hot desk or shared working areas?
- Do bathrooms require swipe-card access on all floors?
- Do visitors get swipe cards?
- What time does the building open and close?
- Can we attempt to gain access to the building outside of normal working hours?
- What time do the cleaners come in?
- Are there any other third parties who regularly access the building?
- Are there any areas we are not permitted to access over the course of the test?
- What physical security measures are in place, such as CCTV, security guards, turnstiles?
- Can we remove sensitive documents/media? If not, can we photograph them?
- If we find an access pass, can we take it?
- Do we need to leave a token as evidence?
- Can we plug our own devices into the network if we get inside the building?

For a Remote Social Engineering Test

- How many employees do you want to test?
- Who are they? Is there any particular group we should focus on, for example, receptionists, help desk staff?
- Will contact details for these individuals (phone numbers for telephone attacks or email addresses for phishing attacks) be provided?
- If you are targeting a call center, is there a standard script?
- If it's a telephone attack, how many call attempts should we try for each number?
- Can we use information from employees' social media accounts, assuming it is publicly available?
- How sophisticated should the scenario be, for example, for a phishing attack, will it be a general phishing attack aimed at a number of staff members or a more focused spear-phishing attack that is targeted at a particular individual?

Final Thoughts

At the end of the planning phase, both your testing team and your client should be confident that you are proceeding with a social engineering test that is both fair and worthwhile. You will have designed a project plan with clear goals and done as much preparation as possible to ensure that the social engineering test will proceed smoothly and within an agreed-upon scope and budget. As you go through the next phases of the social engineering test, performing your research and reconnaissance, creating an in-depth scenario, and executing the test, you can refer back to your project plan, constantly adjusting it for optimal performance and effectiveness.

5 Research and Reconnaissance

Ask and it will be given to you; seek and you will find.
—Matthew 7:7, *The Bible*

Once you have put together your project plan, scoped the social engineering test, and obtained all relevant authorizations, you can move on to the research and reconnaissance phase. This phase involves collecting as much information as possible about your target within the timeframe and budget you have allocated (which is never enough—you can always do more!). The success of your social engineering test relies heavily on the research and reconnaissance phase as you will use the information collected during this phase to build a targeted and convincing attack scenario for your test.

Sometimes this activity is all that clients require—rather than a full social engineering test, they may just want you to do some basic information gathering and present a couple of scenarios to them. My favorite social engineering test ever was a simple information gathering exercise. A client was concerned that their staff talked about work projects during their regular Friday night pub gathering. They asked me to go to the pub one Friday to see how much information I could glean. I got loads—just through listening to people and by chatting to one or two staff members a myriad of information was revealed, such as employee names, project details, and general office gossip. Not only that, staff members were wearing ID badges (which I could have copied) and had left a few laptops under their table along with coats, wallets, and so on. It was a very successful exercise from my point of view, but the expenses were high!

In this chapter, we look at a number of sources that you can use during the reconnaissance and research phase. This chapter is by no means exhaustive; rather it is a compilation of the most popular sources (and sometimes the most unusual) that I have used for reconnaissance throughout the years. The more information you have about your target, the more successful your test is likely to be.

Intelligence Collection Disciplines (INTs)

The FBI defines five ways to collect intelligence, collectively referred to as intelligence collection disciplines, or INTs. They are

- **HUMINT or human intelligence** This intelligence is collected from human sources, either overtly (through interviewing a person) or covertly (through social engineering or espionage). On social engineering tests, you may come across situations where you overhear useful information being discussed, maybe in a coffee shop near your target location or in a nearby pub, as I did in the example just described. Perhaps you overhear someone discussing sensitive information on their cell phone. Alternatively, you may use social engineering techniques to mislead your target into revealing information, possibly as part of the active reconnaissance phase. This all counts as HUMINT.
- **SIGINT or signals intelligence** This is intelligence collected from the interception of electronic transmissions usually by ships, planes, ground sites, or satellites, including wiretapping.
- **IMINT or imagery intelligence** This information is collected largely from imagery satellites, aerial photography, and mapping data. You may use some IMINT for onsite social engineering tests if you look up your target location on Google Maps.
- **MASINT or measurement and signatures intelligence** This category concerns weapons capabilities and industrial activities.
- **OSINT or open source intelligence** This intelligence is collected from open sources, such as the media and public data.

In the research and reconnaissance phase of a social engineering test, you will primarily be concerned with collecting OSINT. The main difference between OSINT and the other types of intelligence is that OSINT is publicly available and, therefore, can be shared with anybody.

What Types of Information to Look for in the Reconnaissance Phase

During the reconnaissance phase, you'll want to gather three types of information. First, you need information that you can use to create your scenario, for example, if an employee has posted online that she is interested in learning about her ancestry, you could potentially use this nugget to create a test scenario. I did exactly this when an employee of my target organization posted online that she was looking to contact anyone from her Irish family tree. I contacted her on the pretense that I was part of her family tree and was also looking to connect. She trusted me straightaway—after all, I was family!

Second, you need information that will make your scenario seem more realistic and, therefore, be more likely to succeed, such as project names or staff names so you can name drop. Using this kind of information as part of your attack scenario can make it appear more legitimate and believable.

Finally, you need practical information that will be useful during your attack phase, such as office opening times, types of systems in use, and so on. This latter type of information is the most likely to be provided to you in advance by the organization that has commissioned the test, as part of the planning phase.

> **Tip** During the reconnaissance phase, familiarize yourself with any particular jargon used within your target organization. Make a note of any "lingo" used by staff or third parties who deal with your target organization. This includes things like project names, department names, staff names, or nicknames, and any other jargon that could make you sound like you know what you are talking about—even the name of the local pub!

An effective social engineer will piece together all the information gathered like the pieces of a jigsaw puzzle, to provide a bigger picture of how the target organization operates. Seemingly innocuous bits of information can be used and manipulated by social engineers to achieve their goals. In one social engineering test, the head of security had recently attended a Certified Ethical Hacker (CEH) training course and had completed a feedback form at the end of the course. The feedback form asked for a testimonial that could be used for marketing purposes. The training company posted the testimonial on its website, along with the head of security's name, title, and organization. It took us about five minutes of reconnaissance to discover this. Imagine our joy when we went to call the guy to update him on our social engineering plans and the receptionist kindly told us "he's away on holiday in Spain and won't be back for two weeks." Our plan was hatched. We phoned a colleague of his pretending to be someone who had attended the CEH course (naturally we had a lot of experience to back this up!) and explained that the individual in question had promised to send us a certain document before he went to Spain. All the apparently inconsequential pieces of information fell into place to create a believable and quite successful attack scenario.

Table 5-1 gives some examples of the types of information that it is useful to collect when searching through all the resources outlined later in the chapter.

TABLE 5-1   Types of Information to Collect in the Research and Reconnaissance Phase

Any personal information about employees	Employee names	Names of former employees
Business cards	Employee telephone numbers	Organizational charts
Company news	Employee whereabouts	Project names
Corporate jargon	Event information, for example, conferences or tradeshows	Roles and responsibilities
Customer details	Fax numbers	Security controls in place
Details about any third parties used	Financial information	Signatures
Employee email addresses	Logos	Technologies in use

Why Knowing When Someone Is Out of the Office Is Useful

I've often called an organization to ask for someone I already know is out of the office, telling whoever answers that she or he promised to send me a particular document before leaving town. One organization I worked with had previously experienced an attempted social engineering attack when the attackers found out the CEO was going to be out of the office. They called the CEO's PA claiming to be the CEO's brother and said they needed money to be wired to them urgently. The CEO was on a plane at the time. Luckily, the PA was suspicious as she had never heard the CEO talk about a brother before and insisted on speaking to the CEO before wiring the money to the caller. When he landed, the CEO confirmed that he didn't have a brother and that it was a scam.

You can find out if someone is out of the office in a number of ways:

- Check social media sites for travel plans or status updates.
- Send the person an email to see if you get an out-of-office response.
- Call reception and ask to speak to the person. If the individual answers, hang up or ask to speak to someone else who may or may not exist within the company ("I'm sorry, wrong number!"). Don't try this too often on a test or your target organization might get suspicious, however.
- Call your target's PA or secretary and ask to set up a meeting with the target. By finding out when he's in the office, you can deduce when he's not in the office.

Where to Look for Information

The reconnaissance phase will almost certainly involve passive reconnaissance, where you have no interaction with the client, but it may also involve some element of active reconnaissance as well, where you may interact a little with the client, for example, phoning to see when a certain individual is in the office or attending the same conference as your target organization so you can interact with its staff to glean information from them. Active reconnaissance via social media is rarely permitted because of the legal and ethical issues involved. Using social media for passive reconnaissance is fine, however, as long as you restrict it to what is publicly available and it has been approved by your client.

If you are doing an onsite test, you need to visit the physical location you are targeting to "case the joint" (more on this later in the chapter in "Physical Reconnaissance"). For all other tests, you need to procure as much information as possible from publicly available sources—*Open Source Intelligence (OSINT)*—such as company websites, social networks, newspapers, and other sources. You can use various methods for collecting such OSINT. Some potential sources for passive reconnaissance, or OSINT, are presented in Table 5-2. You can obtain, of course, a lot of information from search engines, especially with a bit of Google hacking. Johnny

TABLE 5-2   Potential Sources for Passive Reconnaissance

Annual reports	Discussion boards, online group forums, Usenet, and newsgroups	Official filings
Blogs and tweets about or posted by your target organization or its staff	Event calendars	Online developer forums
Commercial sources such as Factiva	Gray literature	Recruitment websites
Company websites	Job ads and employee resumes	Search engines
Corporate blogs, employee blogs (personal or corporate)	Metadata	Social networking sites
Court/council records	Newspapers and the press	Whois records and DNS data

Long's book, *Google Hacking for Penetration Testers* (Syngress Media, 2007), is a great reference on this subject. A search on newsgroups, for example, can reveal all kinds of information, from technical queries published by developers to project names, contact details, and more. Not everything can be gleaned through search engines, however, and sometimes sorting through the hundreds of pages returned can be time consuming and monotonous. A number of tools, such as Maltego and FOCA, are available for quickly gathering OSINT and presenting it in a meaningful way.

Maltego, available from www.paterva.com, is the main player in this area. It determines relationships and links between entities and shows these in a visual representation that allows users to see relationships instantly, much like the whiteboard that police use on television to map out the relationships between criminals. An entity can be a person, organization, website, group of people, or more. Links are determined via open source intelligence. In Chapter 9, we'll look at some of the tools that social engineers can use, including Maltego, FOCA, and Metagoofil.

Company Websites

When you look at a company website (or its social media pages, if it has any), make a note of every name and corresponding role that you come across. Look for personal email addresses and phone numbers. Watch out for logos and signatures that are often found on annual reports. You can use these to spoof official-looking documents later in the test. Look for a section on company news and sign up for any newsletters being offered.

Throughout your reconnaissance of the company website and other sources identify third parties that your target organization deals with. Third parties can be business partners, website developers, cleaners, or even the person who sells sandwiches at lunchtime. You could potentially pretend to be from a similar company in your attack scenarios. If you know that your target company outsources its cleaning to a third party, you could pretend to be a cleaner to gain physical access, call the target on behalf of another cleaning agency, or if you know that the cleaners come in at 8 P.M. every evening, you could try to visit the office then. I have found that third parties who have physical access to other organizations don't necessarily receive the same training as, nor are they educated to abide by the same policies as, direct employees.

Many companies love to share what they are doing with the public, especially when it comes to charity work or staff parties, if not on their websites then potentially on their social networking sites. "Company News" pages can be a treasure trove of information for potential social engineers. I have used scenarios based on company news so many times during the course of my social engineering career, all as part of authorized tests:

- One organization published a company newsletter. The latest newsletter said that an employee had recently given birth to a baby daughter. It gave the usual information that you might expect with this news: date of birth, weight of the baby, the baby's name, and the name of both of the parents. We spoofed an email from the baby's father (the husband of the employee at the target organization), which included an attached photo of the newborn. We got a very high click-through rate on that particular test.
- Another organization listed new joiners on its company news website with a brief background of where they had come from. It gave us great fodder for our social engineering scenarios. In one case, we emailed some "new joiner material" to one of the people listed, who obligingly opened the email attachment. Remember that targeting new joiners may be considered unfair so it might be something to run past your client before trying out.
- Yet another organization posted a photo of its team that had just completed a charity fun run the previous weekend, with each individual identified in the text below the picture. We sent an email congratulating all the runners with the "results" of the fun run in an accompanying spreadsheet.

Another useful area to look for on the company website is the Recruitment section. In one of my earlier social engineering tests, I had to gain access to a financial organization based in London. I did some physical reconnaissance and found that their building was reasonably well secured. There were lots of security guards and receptionists, plenty of CCTV cameras, turnstile access, a bag scanner on the way in, and the building was even surrounded by water on three sides! Tailgating or any kind of casual physical access was certainly off the cards. During the reconnaissance phase, I found the Graduate Recruitment section on the target organization's website and decided to play the role of a graduate looking to join the company's graduate program. On the Graduate Recruitment section, the company had posted an article about two recent graduates who had joined. I emailed them (guessing the email address syntax is usually quite straightforward) and exchanged a number of emails with one of them until, finally, he invited me to his office to meet with him.

Here's the first email that I sent. I explained how I got his email address (obviously not true) and appealed to him for help, which can be very flattering.

Luckily the closing date for applications was coming up, so I was able to move this social engineering scenario along quickly.

Hello,

I hope you don't mind me emailing you. I found your graduate profile on your company website and got your email address from reception.

I am a final-year student studying Computer Science, Linguistics & French at university. I am currently looking for a job for when I finish university. I am very interested in your company's Graduate Development Programme. It looks like it has lots of variety and would be good experience for someone coming from an IT background who is looking to get into the financial side of things. Although I aim to have a career in finance, I am concerned about starting this with a degree in computer science. I was wondering what your opinion on this move may be, or if you know of any other graduates who may have done something similar who I could talk to.

The closing date for graduate applications is next Wednesday 23rd December, so I am trying to do all my research and get the application in as soon as possible. I would appreciate any views you have on this matter.

Thanking you in advance,

Sharon

One response came back with an out-of-office message saying that the recipient was away on assignment. The second guy replied as follows and was very helpful. He seemed like the easier target, so I chose him to move the test along.

Hi Sharon,

I am very impressed with your guile in getting my email address. I am more than happy to receive your mail.

You should not be at all concerned with whether your degree course is not relevant for the job. We pride ourselves on not being a Degree Snob organization. A lot of my fellow grads have come from backgrounds such as Physics, Classics, History, etc. so we aren't concerned with that. I think the fact you do computer science is a benefit, because you will have developed analytical and logic skills which are very important. Also your linguistics background demonstrates communicative skills. You will need to try and get this across in the application form.

If you need any other help on the application form feel free to ask—you can call me or you can email me. There will be an area on the form asking where you heard about the job—if you put my name down it will show that you've taken time and initiative to talk to me, and it's something I would certainly mention to the Grad HR Team.

As I said if you have any other questions feel free to ask.

When I read the part about putting his name down on the form, I was confident I would be able to get in. He would probably get some kind of financial incentive if I were successful in my application and took a job with the firm. I responded, trying to set up a meeting in his office either with him or someone from Graduate Recruitment.

Hi,

Thanks for replying. It is good to hear that your company does not insist on having finance or a business degree. I know some companies do, and that has put me off.

I am actually in London tomorrow and Wednesday for a last minute interview, so I was wondering if it might be possible to come in for a quick 15 minute visit and see the kind of thing you do in your company and maybe go through some of my answers on the application form.

Do you think I could meet you or someone from Graduate Recruitment to do this? Thanks again for all your help—it is very much appreciated.
Sharon

I only asked for 15 minutes. How could he refuse? He didn't.

Yeah—if you need directions just let me know. I will let Reception know you are coming so just report to reception and they will give you a pass.

I met the graduate who brought me to the office canteen and spent 15 minutes or so going through the graduate application form. When I was finished, I asked if I could wait in the canteen as I had a bit of time to kill before my flight home and would like to type up my notes on the form. Unfortunately for him, he told me that was fine, as long as I hid my visitors pass, as technically visitors had to be escorted at all times! So, in spite of all its impressive physical security controls, I compromised the organization based on the information posted in the Graduate Recruitment section of its website.

Analyzing Metadata on the Corporate Website

Metadata is data about data. In this context, metadata is data that describes the environment in which documents were created or that describes properties of the document itself. For example, whenever you create, open, or edit Word documents, information about you and the edits you make is automatically created and hidden within the document file. This can include your name and initials, the name of your organization, the local hard drive or server where you saved the document, and more.

Metadata left in documents published on the Internet or sent to others can be a good source of information for the social engineer who can use it to perform a more targeted attack. Metadata useful to social engineers includes usernames, email addresses, system information, and, indeed, any kind of corporate jargon or project names that you could use to make your attack scenario appear more realistic. If it's in scope (in theory, metadata is public information but it's always best to check), you can run a tool to extract and analyze metadata on the corporate website, such as FOCA by Informática64 or Metagoofil from Edge-Security. Both tools make great additions to your social engineering toolkit.

Tip Even photos can leak information in their metadata, including EXIF data such as the date and time the photo was taken, the model of camera used, and sometimes geolocation data. Tools such as TinEye (www.tineye.com) allow users to perform a reverse image search and find out where an image came from and where else it is being used online. You never know what kind of information the photos on your target organization's website might reveal and how this information could be used as part of your scenario.

Recruitment Websites

Job advertisements can give away a lot of information about an organization. A job advertisement for a position in IT can give away details relating to the types of systems in use, as well as the size and structure of the IT department. In one test, I applied for a job that was being advertised and actually was called in for an interview. Connecting to the organization's internal network was trivial once I was in the door.

Similarly, CVs and resumes contain a wealth of information about their author's current and even previous places of work. I know of several social engineers who have played the role of a recruitment agent so they could get their hands on this kind of information. The promise of a big enough salary increase can loosen lips!

Newspapers and the Press

Newspapers and the press can publish interesting information, particularly when it comes to trade journals. They may print stories about successful projects and staff movements within the industry, but they are also generally good for helping you pick up jargon related to your target's industry.

Local newspapers from the area in which your target organization is based can be great sources too. Local publications often print details about community involvement, along with news about developments at the organization. People sometimes drop their guard when it comes to speaking to reporters from local papers, as they don't see it as official as dealing with larger newspapers and don't necessarily expect anyone "important" to read it.

A number of services provide news alerts, such as the Google or BBC Alerts Services. Set up an alert for your target company for the period when your test is running, so you can keep abreast of any developments that might be handy during the social engineering test.

WHOIS

Do a WHOIS lookup for your target organization. You can do this via a command line utility for Unix or Linux, or use one of the WHOIS lookup facilities offered by the Regional Internet Registries, ARIN, RIPE and APNIC and a myriad of other websites such as www.whois.net.

The WHOIS database stores information about a specific domain name, some of which can be put to use by social engineers. A WHOIS lookup can reveal contact names and telephone numbers (probably for a more technical staff member) that may be useful in your scenario. I gained access to an office in Italy by saying I was there to meet with the technical contact listed on the company's WHOIS record, someone who was clearly based in the US. Because it was 8.30 A.M. local time, and there was an eight-hour time difference (so it was about midnight in the US office), no one was there to answer the phone and verify my meeting request. In the midst of all the confusion, they let me in.

Conferences and Public Events

If at all possible, I try to attend conferences or other public events (such as seminars or tradeshows) that my target organization will be attending. Tradeshows are great for collecting props for your social engineering scenarios, such as T-shirts and lanyards. You can even collect a few business cards that you can use (or copy) during your social engineering attack scenario. I have had great success, with tech companies in particular, obtaining T-shirts and lanyards at conferences that I then wear to their office so I look like an employee. Note that this type of reconnaissance can be either active or passive, depending on the degree of interaction you have with the staff from your target organization. A more active reconnaissance exercise might be to gather HUMINT from some of your target organization's staff. For example, you might start by asking them about their latest projects or how they implemented something. Alternatively, you could ask them who would be the best person to speak with about working for the company. You can then create a scenario where you social engineer a physical entry into the office by going for a job interview. Conferences and public events are also good places to organize follow-up meetings.

Official Filings

Official filings such as company reports, tax filings, environmental regulation–related filings can potentially contain anything from company directors' dates of birth and home addresses to office floor plans.

All companies in the UK must register with Companies House and are required to file annual financial statements and returns, which are considered public records. For a nominal cost (although basic information is free), you can request any of the filing history documents using the online WebCheck service at wck2.companieshouse.gov.uk. The types of information available include company incorporation documents, details about directors, and financial accounts. Ireland has a similar set up with the Companies Registration Office. US-based companies are required to register at the state level, and you can research them on the Secretary of State's website. Furthermore, you can reach publicly traded companies on the EDGAR database at www.sec.gov/edgar/searchedgar/companysearch.html, which currently has access to more than 20 million filings.

Commercial Sources

A number of commercial information sources either charge a subscription fee or a usage fee for access to their information. Sometimes you can access them at public libraries, however. The "big three" when it comes to commercial sources are

- **Factiva** http://global.factiva.com
- **LexisNexis** www.nexis.com
- **Dialog** www.dialog.com

These commercial information sources offer lots of information that is not necessarily publicly available on the Web, such as articles from industry newsletters, financial information, market research reports, and so on, and can search through these very quickly. Information is vetted for accuracy and completeness. Access to these services can be costly. The subscription models can be pricey, but all three services offer a pay-as-you-go option and, in some cases, offer a day pass that lets you have unlimited access for 24 hours for a flat fee. I used these sources regularly when I worked for a large organization that already had access to them.

Gray Literature

Gray literature is information that is not readily available but that can be obtained ethically and legally. Examples of gray literature include working papers, technical reports, technical standards documents, dissertations, data sets, case studies, conference papers, company journals, flyers, patents, and whitepapers. Gray literature is a great way to find out about projects and research that your target organization is performing. Such literature is full of jargon that can make your attack scenario appear authentic. It can also include potential targets (for instance, the authors of the papers in question) and give you a good reason to contact them. If they have published a conference paper on their latest scientific research, you could contact the authors to discuss their work. Maybe you could email them to say you found their paper interesting and have been doing some research of your own that may be of interest, which you have very kindly included in an attachment to the email....

Information Gathering on Social Networks

Social networks are a treasure trove of information for social engineers. Although I will rarely use social media as part of an attack scenario (for the ethical and legal reasons described in Chapter 2), I almost always use it for information-gathering purposes. Information to look for on social networks includes the following:

- Any kind of personal information (phone numbers, dates of birth, home addresses, work details, and so on). This information may be directly or indirectly available, for example, if an employee's friend posts a message wishing her a happy 30th birthday, it is a no-brainer to deduce the employee's date of birth.
- Company profiles and organizational charts.
- Event information (any tradeshows, conferences, or open days coming up).
- Answers to secret questions that can be used for authentication or to reset passwords. Such information is often publicly available too. Consider the case of US vice-presidential nominee Sarah Palin, who had her Yahoo! email account compromised during the 2008 election when the attackers found the answers to her secret questions in her biography! Social media users often post details that can be used to guess the answers to their secret questions—a pet's name, first car, school name, favorite sports team. People love to fill in surveys that contain these details, such as the example shown in Figure 5-1.
- Any kind of information that will help you to hone your attack scenario. For example, in one test, my team found that a guy working for our target organization was really into surfing and had a surfboard for sale. The ad was posted on a surfing website. He probably shouldn't have used his work email address for this. We exchanged a number of emails, of which the final one had a malicious attachment in the guise of a surfing photo. All this because of a simple ad for a surfboard.

TELL ME ABOUT YOURSELF- THE SURVEY by ▒▒▒▒	
Name	
Age	
Sex	
Birthday	
Birthplace	
Current Location	
School	
Height	
Shoe Size	
Eye Color	
Hair Color	
Skin Type	
Single?	
Do you Smoke?	
Do you do Drugs?	
Do you Drink?	
How many pairs of shoes do you own?	
MCDonalds or Burger King?	
Pepsi or Coke?	
Favorite Sport?	
Do you Sing?	
Chocolate or Vanilla?	
Do you shower daily?	
Do you want to get married?	

FIGURE 5-1   An excerpt from a survey on www.pimp-my-profile.com

Social networks can also help you understand your target's trust network:

- Who does your target work with?
- What is the name of your target's boss?
- Who are your target's family members?
- Who are your target's friends?

We see lots of "friend attacks" these days, where the attack looks like it's coming in from a friend or acquaintance. These attacks can be quite successful. USA Today reported on financial firm Terremark's network compromise in 2010[1]. Attackers gained access to a Terremark employee's (let's call him Bob) Facebook account. They accessed his contact list of friends and manually reviewed messages and postings on his profile. They noticed a message saying that Bob had been at a picnic with some of his friends over the weekend. When they saw this news, they sent individual

---

[1]http://usatoday30.usatoday.com/tech/news/computersecurity/2010-03-04-1anetsecurity04_cv_n.htm

messages to a dozen of Bob's closest Facebook friends, including Alice—a fellow employee at Terremark. The message read, "Hey Alice, look at the pics I took of us last weekend at the picnic. Bob."

The link in the message led to a malicious executable file, which, when Alice clicked it expecting to see the photos, installed a keystroke logger on her machine. Once an hour, the program sent a text file of Alice's keystrokes to a Gmail account controlled by the attackers. When Alice logged into Terremark's virtual private network, the attackers noted her username and password. They used Alice's login credentials to access Terremark's network, which they had access to for a matter of weeks.

The attackers gained control of two servers before they were detected. A friend of Bob's who had also received the original message mentioned to him that the picnic photos he had sent had failed to render. Bob got suspicious, and a technician uncovered the network compromise.

Specific Social Networking Sites

Occasionally, certain social networking sites have very specific information that can be worthwhile. I always check www.ratemynetworkdiagram.com, where members post pictures of their network diagrams and visitors to the site rate them according to "their own personal opinion of the flow, functionality, implementation, etc. of your network" (an example is shown in Figure 5-2). As yet, I've never had a client post a network diagram on this site (that I am aware of), but I live in hope.

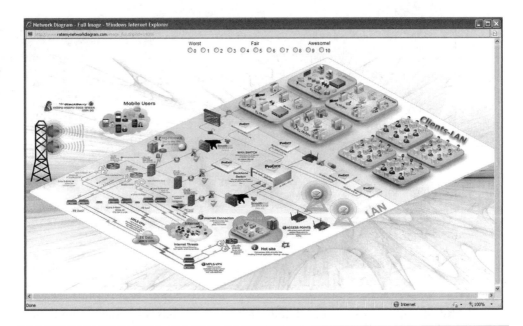

FIGURE 5-2   A network diagram submitted to www.ratemynetworkdiagram.com. This one rates quite highly!

One social media site I did actually get to use before it shut down in May 2011 was Blippy, where users could post details about their purchases. Users registered their debit cards and credit cards with the website and it automatically published whenever they made a purchase, what they had bought, and how much it cost. An employee at a company I was testing had posted about renting a movie on Netflix, similar to the posting in Figure 5-3. We spoofed an email with an attachment that looked like a voucher for free rental of the next movie in the series.

Geotagging sites such as Foursquare can be useful for tracking people. If people are checking into a local restaurant or coffee shop, then they are clearly *not* in the office—which is useful information for a social engineer, who can either target the individual wherever he has checked in, or target his office while he is away. Location sharing can have implications for your personal safety as well as your company's security. A really good website for awareness raising in this area was www.pleaserobme.com, which highlighted the dangers of location sharing by posting publicly shared check-ins. It showed a live stream of check-ins, which it referred to as "recent empty homes" or "new opportunities" aggregated from Foursquare and Twitter (see Figure 5-4). Another website followed this, www.weknowyourhouse.com, which showed tweets from people posting when they were at home along with a photo of their house based on the geolocation data associated with their tweets. You never know what social media website is going to pop up next!

FIGURE 5-3   Users posted details on recent purchases by registering their debit or credit card to Blippy.

FIGURE 5-4   Typical updates on www.pleaserobme.com

Using LinkedIn for Research

I start most corporate social engineering tests by using LinkedIn for some tactical research. It is useful for a number of things:

- Building an organizational chart for your target organization
- Identifying staff names and roles; you could potentially use these individuals as targets or even impersonate them (assuming you have the appropriate authorization). You can also drop their name in conversation: *<LinkedIn individual>* said....or *<LinkedIn individual>* needs this document...
- Identifying staff who previously worked at your target organization. A useful attack scenario is to call up as an account manager and say I used to work with *<insert name of previous employee here>*, who can help me now?
- Checking who is out of the office. The TripIt application on LinkedIn allows users to share their travel plans with their connections, so connections can potentially meet up or share tips on the destination. How often have you seen an update from one of your contacts along the lines of "John Smith is planning a trip to Barcelona in 5 days"?

(continued)

- Setting up fake profiles and linking to your target. For example, in the situation where it's highly likely that John from Company A knows Jane from Company B and they are not already linked, set up a profile that looks like Jane and send John a LinkedIn invitation. You could always make up an individual if there are any ethical or legal concerns about impersonating Jane. In fact, lots of people will connect with people they don't even know (demonstrated beautifully in the Robin Sage experiment described in Chapter 2), so you don't necessarily need Jane's profile. You don't even need to use LinkedIn. Most professionals know what a LinkedIn invitation looks like. You could spoof one with malicious links or malware. Even if your target doesn't use LinkedIn, we all get invitations.

Once I have the names of employees from LinkedIn (or other sources), I do more tactical research on them. I look them up on other social media websites and try to build profiles. I may target them or may use their names as part of my attack. I usually try to find individuals who have the most information published about them online and then use this to build a scenario.

In one example, we found a social networking profile for a guy who we had identified as an employee. Along with his salary details, where he had gone to school, and other really juicy information, he had posted his date of birth. We noticed that his birthday was coming up. So we had his birthday and a list of friends from the profile. We sent him a birthday card to his office, purporting to be from one of his friends. It was one of those cards that comes with a CD of the top music tracks from the year of your birth, like the one pictured here, along with a call home program that once inserted into his computer, connected back to one of our testing servers. He played it on his office PC straightaway, giving us remote access to his company network.

Physical Reconnaissance

If your social engineering test involves trying to gain physical access to a location, you will need to do some extra reconnaissance to, as mentioned earlier, "case the joint." You can do some of your physical reconnaissance remotely. For example, use Google Maps and Street View to see what the location looks like. Identify entrances and exits and notice what's around the building. Some local councils or governments may have building plans that you can access (although explaining why you need to see them may be a little tricky!).

At some stage, you will need to visit the location you are going to attempt to access. In this case, spend some time near the building, gathering as much information about it as you can to plan your attack scenario. Try to be inconspicuous; after all, you will be coming back at a later date under a different pretext, so don't let the target mark you as suspicious already. If there is a coffee shop nearby, where you can see the building, you could set up there for a few hours. Maybe you could park opposite the building and do your physical reconnaissance from your car. Walk around the building, if at all possible. Look for information like this:

- Where are the security guards located?
- Do smokers congregate in a certain area outside?
- Where are the CCTV cameras?
- Do staff wear and/or show ID cards? Can you copy them?
- What other kinds of controls are in place to prevent unauthorized access to the building (turnstiles, access cards, pin code entry, even defensive landscaping design)?
- Watch staff movements. What time do employees arrive or leave the office? What time do they have lunch? Is there a preferred café or coffee shop nearby?
- What else is going on in the building? (See Figure 5-5.) I had to get access to a data center in a basement that, quite randomly, had a training company in the same building. Signing up for a training class got me through the first line of defense in the building. Then I spent my lunch break roaming the building looking for ways into the data center.
- Are there any nonstandard ways into the building, for example, fire escapes, garages, loading docks? I've entered organizations through car parks and garages on countless occasions. Occupants of older buildings with no air conditioning sometimes prop doors and windows open in the summer time, which can potentially be used to gain access, such as the example in Figure 5-6. In Figure 5-7, staff have actually tied back the door so it does not close properly, and they can get in and out quicker.
- Are there any trash bins that you could take or dumpster dive? More on that in the next section.

Sometimes, nearby locations can reveal a great deal of information about your target organization. For example, you could try lost property in local train stations, visit local cafes or restaurants, and look for ID badges or business cards. In places with

FIGURE 5-5   This bank in Scotland has a B&B in the same building!

FIGURE 5-6   A ground floor window to this office is propped open with a cushion!

FIGURE 5-7 This offers a great opportunity to social engineers or burglars in the area.

public transport, like the Tube in London or the Metro in Paris, you can learn a lot by hanging around stations near your target organization when people are leaving work.

> **Tip** I always like to do a sweep of popular restaurants and cafés near my target organization and look out for the ones that have competitions where you leave your business card to enter a draw to win a meal, like the one in Figure 5-8. Business cards have several uses for the social engineer. First, they give you the name and contact details of potential targets within your organization. Second, you can use the business card to impersonate the real owner of the card. Third, you could copy the business card to make one of your own, with your name on it.

In some cases, it may be possible to go into the building you will be attempting to access. When I was targeting a sports stadium, I did some great reconnaissance

FIGURE 5-8 People can put cards in...or take them out!

by simply buying a ticket for their guided tour. In another test, the aim was to gain physical access to an insurance company's London headquarters and sniff ten minutes worth of network traffic. Coincidentally, a financial company phoned me to enquire if I would like to avail myself of their services; these calls drive me crazy so I usually decline, mostly in a polite manner. However, this particular company mentioned where they were based, and it turned out to be in the same building as the insurance company I was targeting. I couldn't believe it! I went in to meet with the financial company, and this gave me the opportunity I needed to do the reconnaissance both outside and inside the building. You never know what sources are going to come in handy during your reconnaissance phase.

Tip When it comes to physical testing, don't restrict it to headquarters. Local branches and regional offices can be just as interesting from a social engineer's point of view and often don't have the same level of defenses that a headquarters has.

Dumpster Diving

Dumpster diving, alternatively known as *trash picking or skipping*, isn't quite as necessary to social engineering as it used to be, thanks to the vast amounts of information that people are sharing online. Nevertheless, rubbish bins and dumpsters can be a really great source of information for social engineers. The kind of information I have retrieved when dumpster diving is listed in Table 5-3. If you are going to perform dumpster diving as part of your social engineering test, get it authorized in advance.

Dumpster diving is currently enjoying a resurgence in popularity, largely thanks to urban foraging communities such as the *freegans* who forage in bins for food and other items that can be recycled. Many of these groups have useful advice on the practicalities of dumpster diving. Because of its growing popularity with such groups, some organizations are taking additional steps to prevent dumpster diving (such as locking their rubbish bins and dumpsters, adding extra CCTV, or even destroying items to prevent them from being reused or resold). It also means that, if you get caught, some organizations may accuse you of being a "freeloader" who is going through their trash in the hope of making a buck or getting a free lunch. Alternatively, they may suspect you of illegal dumping. Either one can rub people the wrong way and is another reason why getting explicit sign-off for this activity is important if you are going to do any dumpster diving at any stage during your social engineering test.

When you are dumpster diving, wear appropriate clothing and equip yourself properly. Wear long sleeves and trousers and enclosed shoes or boots to protect yourself from dirt and cuts. Bring thick, waterproof gloves so you can rummage through the rubbish. Gardening gloves are good for this. In general, durable, nondescript clothes are

TABLE 5-3   What to Look Out for When Dumpster Diving

Bills and invoices	Documents with signatures (any document will do—that signature could be useful in spoofing documents later in your social engineering test)	Printouts of calendars
Business card rollers	Employee records	Printouts of source code
Company letterhead	Media such as disks and DVDs	Profit and loss accounts
Company phone books	Memos and emails	System manuals
Customer records	Organizational charts	Various hardware and even discarded PCs
Details about compensation packages for proposed redundancies		

best. Don't wear military clothing as people may see this as threatening. I find it useful to bring the following items on any dumpster-diving field trips:

- A friend or colleague to help, to give you a leg up, to watch out for security guards, in case of an emergency, or if you get injured
- A plain-looking bag that won't arouse suspicion, such as a gym bag, to put your loot in
- A pocket knife to cut open bags
- A "dive stick" to poke around with or even something with a grabbing apparatus on the end, such as fireplace tongs
- A flashlight if you are attempting it at night or, even better, a headlamp so you can work with both hands (easily obtainable at a camping or outdoors shop). A flashlight or headlight with a red light can't be seen from afar and doesn't interfere with night vision.
- A really clever tip that I heard for dumpster diving is to bring along a few cardboard boxes and leave them beside the dumpster. If you are challenged, explain that you are moving house and just looking to collect a few cardboard boxes for the move.
- Hand sanitizer and first aid kit, just in case...

> **Tip** When dumpster diving, grab your loot and get away as quickly as possible. Then you can go through it at your own leisure when you get back to the office. Remember: it's worth checking bins inside the office as well, once you get access to it—more on that in the next chapter.

Sometimes dumpster diving can be performed as a standalone activity. In some cases, you don't have to operate discreetly. The aim of the exercise may be to see what kinds of information you can retrieve from the rubbish on any particular day, in which case all you have to do is go and collect the trash (without having to sneak around), bring it back to your base, and go through it at your leisure. This test became popular in the UK a few years ago following the news that several leading banks were facing unlimited fines over allegations that they dumped confidential customer account details in bin bags on streets.

The practice of dumpster diving does have certain risks associated with it, apart from being caught! There are health risks—dumpsters are a breeding ground for bacteria. You could potentially injure yourself (even getting in or out of the dumpster) or cut yourself on disposed rubbish such as glass or even paper. One of the most important things to remember on a dumpster diving trip is to be aware of garbage collection vehicles. Be careful!

Telephone Reconnaissance

You can find out a lot by calling people and asking for information. Some social engineering tests are just this—performed entirely over the telephone. However, the telephone can also be used for information gathering for all types of social engineering tests. You can discover small pieces of information, such as the names of certain individuals and when they are in the office, that can help you to put together a social engineering scenario that is more likely to succeed.

A number of approaches seem to work for gathering information over the telephone. Usually, being friendly and chatty with the person who has answered the phone is helpful. Sometimes a more authoritative manner can be effective. Once or twice I have actually started crying and it has been quite effective—the person taking the call may not know how to act in this situation and may try to make you happy by giving you the information you require. Other times, being really grateful can throw people off course and get good results.

On the phone, as in any social engineering situation, people tend to correct you if you offer the wrong information. Giving a purposely erroneous statement has worked for me countless times. For example, to find out someone's room number in a hotel, ask reception to put you through. When the person answers, ask if this is < *wrong room number* >. A typical reaction is to say "no, it's < *right room number* >." Try it and see!

Caution   Don't forget to either spoof your number or simply block your phone number during telephone social engineering tests. It never ceases to amaze me that malicious scammers so often forget this seemingly basic step!

Here is a classic example from the Phone Losers of America (PLA), who have been placing prank calls since the 1990s. In one of their episodes recorded in February 2006 and dedicated to social engineering (available at www.phonelosers .org/2006/02/pla-radio-episode-2-social-engineering/), the caller rings the cellular phone company, SPRINT, pretending to be calling from collections department. The person who answers the call believes him and divulges all kinds of information relating to customers' accounts. One of the neat tricks that the PLA caller uses is to offer an incorrect piece of information, which the phone operator automatically corrects him on (I've included part of the transcript here). You can hear this at approximately 8.5 minutes into the recording, although the whole program is certainly worth listening to, to see how easily information can be obtained over the phone.

Call transcript:

Sprint Operator: Thanks for calling Sprint....How can I help today?
PLA Caller: Hello this is Brian from collections. I am transferring over a customer over to you.
Sprint Operator: OK can you give me the number?
PLA Caller: Sure it's 626 <bleep> 36 46 <bleep> 3
Sprint Operator: Thank you. And customer's name?
PLA Caller: Chris Tomkinson
Sprint Operator: And the name on the account?
PLA Caller: Ah, well he said it would be under his name, for Chris Tomkinson. Is it not coming up as that?
Sprint Operator: It's pulled up another account with this number.
PLA Caller: Oh what's the name of that one coming up then?

Sprint Operator: OK the account holder's name is *< bleep >* Thomas
PLA Caller: Thomas?
Sprint Operator: Yes, Thomas.
PLA Caller: Are you saying Thomas like T-H-O?
Sprint Operator: T-H-O. Yes. T-H-O-M-A-S.
PLA Caller: Could I check with her here, maybe she gave me a wrong number then.
Sprint Operator: Alright.
PLA Caller: Did it happen to be the 415 Beaumont Avenue for the billing address?
Sprint Operator: No. It's *< bleep >* 72 Sun Drive, *< bleep >* California.

Reconnaissance for Call Centers

If you are going to be social engineering a call center, you will need to find out how a standard call progresses, whether it's directly with a person on the other end or via an interactive voice response (IVR) system. It is useful to go through a call—or even a few dozen calls—until you have documented the call flow and all the available options.

If you are dealing directly with a person on the other end, don't try any social engineering techniques initially. Just walk through the call to identify how the script goes (unless, of course, you have been provided the script in advance), all the way through to call completion. Once you have the script documented, you can look for opportunities where you may be able to social engineer the call recipient.

IVR systems usually have several menus of prerecorded options that a caller can choose from. Map out the call flow, including each menu option. A typical call flow goes something like this:

- The IVR answers the call and plays a welcome message.
- The IVR presents a menu list (make a note of these) and asks the caller to select one of these options.
- If the caller selects an option that does not require talking directly to an individual, the IVR plays a message associated with that selection, for example, the caller selects the option to check her bank balance and this information is played back to her.
- If the caller selects an option that does require interacting with an individual on the other end of the call, the call is directed to the person who provides the relevant information and ends the call. This is where the social engineering happens.

Your call flow map should be much more detailed and show all the options available at each step of the call. You need to find the option that allows you to speak directly to a person on the other end of the call. Having this option mapped out will certainly speed up your future social engineering work.

> **Tip**   In any kind of telephone social engineering or reconnaissance, don't make too many calls over too short a period of time. Your voice or telephone number may be recognized, or your requests may arouse suspicion. Try to leave enough time between calls to avoid this.

Challenges During the Research and Reconnaissance Phase

We live in the information age. We are bombarded by information wherever we look. However, much of this is just noise rather than information that you need to know. Keep the goal of your social engineering test in mind during the research and reconnaissance phase and don't get caught up in things that are irrelevant. It's easy to get carried away gathering information and trying to find out everything about everything and everyone. For all the information you collect, consider how important that information is and how it could help you to achieve your goal. Evaluate the information you have collected according to the context of your social engineering test, its accuracy, credibility, and objectivity. Be as broad and deep as possible in your search, and consider how each nugget of information can be used to build your test scenario.

Final Thoughts

More information sources are available than can be covered in just one book, let alone in one chapter. The sources outlined in this chapter are a good place to start. The more preparation you do in the form of information gathering, the more successful your social engineering test scenario is likely to be. The information gathered will allow you to create a more convincing scenario. It will also give you increased confidence because you know you have a believable back story and will be better able to answer any questions thrown at you or to handle unplanned situations that may arise during your test.

You can sometimes find information in the most random places. On my way to one social engineering assignment, I took a cab from a cab company that turned out to be the preferred company for the organization I was targeting. The cab driver was chatty and started filling me in on everything that was going on at my target destination, from the fact that the CEO was about to resign and was flying in from abroad to announce it (he had just collected him from the airport!), to describing the culinary highlights of the company canteen, to telling me that the company always settled its accounts on time and was very friendly.

Social engineers have their own tricks or preferred sources for gathering information. One individual I met had an interest in genealogy and was able to use his research sources to gain access to all kinds of seemingly sensitive information, including mothers' maiden names and dates and places of birth. You never know where or when you are going to uncover information that will help you.

The next chapter explores how the information gathered in the research and reconnaissance phase can be used to build a plausible scenario that you can use for your social engineering test.

6 Creating the Scenario

Logic will get you from A to Z; imagination will get you everywhere.
—Albert Einstein

Those of you who have seen the movie *Argo* will be familiar with the story of the *Canadian Caper* where the CIA, with the help of the Canadian government, rescued six Americans from Tehran during the Iran Hostage Crisis. During the Iranian Revolution of 1979, the last Shah was overthrown, marking the end of 2,500 years of dynastic rule in Iran. The Shah left Iran and was eventually allowed to enter the US for a brief stay to undergo medical treatment. However, surgical complications resulted in a prolonged stay in the US, which was extremely unpopular with the revolutionary movement in Iran. Unhappy with the situation, protesters stormed the US embassy in Tehran and captured 52 embassy staff who were accused of being spies. Six staff managed to escape the embassy, avoiding capture. The six eventually ended up hiding in the home of the Canadian ambassador to Iran, Ken Taylor. The American authorities needed a way to sneak the six diplomats out of Iran. They could get six Canadian passports, but they needed a cover story.

The CIA brainstormed possible ideas. Could they pretend to be English teachers? No, all the English schools in Iran had been closed by the regime. Could they pretend to be agricultural experts? No, it was winter so there were no crops to inspect. The potential cover stories were discounted one by one until only one extremely unlikely option was left. Tony Mendez, the CIA's top exfiltration expert, proposed that the six diplomats pose as a Hollywood crew on a location scout for a science fiction film. With nothing else likely to work, the CIA reluctantly agreed to go with this fantastical option.

The cover story required a lot of background work prior to its execution to make it appear believable. Mendez set up a fake film production company called Studio Six Productions, which actually bought the rights to a science fiction movie script called "Argo." They printed fake business cards and took out ads in the media. They hosted a launch party in a Los Angeles nightclub. They enlisted the help of John Chambers, a well-known makeup artist who had done the costumes for the *Planet of the Apes* films.

Each of the six diplomats was assigned a cover identity within the fake film crew. Mendez traveled to Iran to train the diplomats in their cover identities. In the movie, Mendez drills the diplomats on their roles, repeatedly putting questions to them about their adopted identities. The cover story was a success. The six diplomats arrived home, via Switzerland, on January 30th, 1980.

The Canadian Caper took scenario creation to the extreme. It went against the standard practice of creating mundane, unassuming cover stories, but it was an extreme situation that called for such a scenario. The *Argo* movie demonstrates the scenario creation process perfectly, however, by detailing the following steps:

1. Brainstorm potential scenarios based on the information known to you (in social engineering, you get this information during the research and reconnaissance phase).
2. Validate the scenarios. Discount scenarios that won't work, and select the scenario that is most likely to work.
3. Add credibility to the scenario.
4. Identify possible pitfalls and how to deal with them.
5. Assign roles to individuals who will be involved in the scenario.
6. Assume the roles and practice, practice, practice.
7. Put the scenario into action (described in the next chapter).

We will explore each of these steps throughout the rest of this chapter.

Brainstorming Potential Scenarios

Now the fun starts! You create a scenario (sometimes called a *pretext*), or more likely you will create several scenarios, based on the information you have gathered in the research and reconnaissance phase (described in Chapter 5). Your scenario is the back story that explains who you are and why you need the information you are requesting; it even influences your attitude while executing the test. You will use your invented scenario to persuade your target individual to perform a certain action, such as revealing specific information or granting you physical access to a restricted area. You may or may not have to act out the scenario during the social engineering test, but you do need to keep your back story in mind throughout the test.

Based on the information gathered in the previous research and reconnaissance phase, brainstorm as many potential scenarios as possible. The more information you have gathered, the more scenario options you will have, allowing you to choose the best-fitting scenario for the actual attack. Each scenario has two key parts: a character, and a situation in which your character can request or attempt to access the information you are after. While in character, you will attempt to set up your ideal situation so you get access to the information you require. For example, if your chosen character is a reporter, why would you want to know about an organization's IT systems? If you decide to use the ever-popular survey cover story, why would you need to know the victim's password?

In the fake Microsoft calls that have become so ubiquitous, the malicious caller tells the recipient that he is calling from Microsoft and, by claiming the recipient's computer is at risk from viruses, asks for access to the target's computer or credit card details. To an unsuspecting computer user, this scenario may seem genuine, so she hands over her details. Chances are she probably has a Windows PC, so the role of Microsoft employee is believable, and most computer users realize viruses are a threat, so the situation is plausible as well.

Think about how sophisticated your scenario needs to be. More security-focused organizations, such as banks or governmental organizations, will usually require a more complex attack. On the other hand, tailgating often works just fine for less security-aware organizations. In this case, it is best to have a scenario prepared just in case you need it (for instance, if you are questioned or need to infiltrate the organization further). Consider the size of the organization you are targeting when developing your scenario. You can't pretend to be an employee in a small office. You also need to consider if your scenario is going to be directed at a particular individual or a group of people. Your scenario can get very specific and directed if you are targeting one individual in particular, but may need to stay more generic if you are targeting a whole group of people.

Both your character and your situation should appear natural and spontaneous. This can take a lot of work. I'll suggest a number of exercises throughout this chapter to help with this. You can choose to do as many or as few of them as you wish, or even none of them if the right scenario quickly presents itself.

Some of the scenarios that my team and I have used successfully in the past are presented in the following table. The first column lists the character we played and

Exercise: Identifying the People Who Have Regular Interaction with Your Target Organization

The first exercise is to make a list of the types of people who have regular interactions with your target organization, from all the various types of employees to customers and suppliers. Who does the cleaning? Does someone sell sandwiches in the office? Does the organization outsource secure waste disposal? Who does the catering? What kind of clients does the organization have? Could you play a character along these lines?

Try to be the sort of person people want to or feel obliged to help. Consider the type of individual your target might want to help, or feel obliged to help. The target may be more likely to help someone like herself (a fellow employee, another new person on the job); someone it would be profitable to help (a survey person offering a prize, a Nigerian prince offering $1m); someone she might feel sorry for (a co-worker who is crying or upset or in trouble with her boss); or someone she is afraid of (perhaps a more senior person in the office or an important client). Make a list of these people and think about using a similar identity for your scenario.

the second column describes the situation we contrived. Remember that it may be illegal to impersonate real people or organizations.

Character	Situation
Graduate or final-year university student	Seeking employment at the target organization
Temp worker/employee	Working at target organization
Internal IT support	Looking to test a new system
Tourist	Being completely lost or taking a tour
School teacher	Looking to organize a school tour to the venue
Girlfriend/boyfriend	Delivering flowers
Fire warden/fire extinguisher inspector	Doing an inspection
Engineer/customer support personnel	Fixing a problem, real or fictional, such as broken printers
Pest control	Laying traps for mice—giving you a great excuse to look for network points on the office floor!
Delivery person	Making a delivery—pizza, courier, and so on
Internet service provider (ISP) abuse team member	Willing to scrub the culprit's history if he hands over his credentials
Potential customer	Seeking information about a product
Supplier	Introducing a new account manager
Remote worker	Having trouble connecting to the network
Salesperson	New account manager looking to introduce himself and set up a meeting
Journalist	Writing an article on the latest technology
Recruiter	Looking to fill a well-paid position
Cleaner/security/maintenance	Cleaning/securing/maintaining office

Scenarios can play on human emotions such as fear, guilt, sympathy, confusion, intimidation, flattery, and friendship. If you are stuck for a scenario, think of scenarios that would fall into each of these categories. For example, if you are phoning a call center, consider how you could use each of these emotions to drive your scenario. Let's take a banking call center as an example. The following table lists some of the emotions that you could try to work into your scenarios and an example of how you could use each one.

Emotion	Example
Fear	Act unhappy with the call center agent. Threaten to complain to his manager.
Sympathy	Give the call center agent a sob story. Try crying! You had promised your daughter a really great Christmas present after she had such a hard year, but because your credit card has been cut off you can't fulfill your promise.
Confusion	Give him the wrong account number but insist it is correct and you had to change it for security reasons.
Flattery	Tell him what a great job he is doing and try to break out of the standard call center script.
Friendship	Call on a Friday evening and start chatting about the weekend. Act chummy.

Many emotions involve using negative feelings. Inducing negative emotions, whether fear, confusion, disappointment, or something else, can be quite useful (and manipulative) in social engineering. A friend of mine purposefully forgets the names of people who annoy him repeatedly, thus annoying them in return and gently pushing them away. However, because using negative emotions can verge on being manipulative, it must be done sensitively as part of an ethical social engineering test.

If you are really stuck for an idea when creating your scenario, you could always apply for a job with your target organization, or at least go for an interview. I did this for a financial organization I was testing. The firm was recruiting for an audit position. As a security professional, I figured I could talk my way through that one with some research. I faked a CV and ran it past an auditor. The CV was impressive but not too much, so I was reasonably confident I would be called in for an interview, and I was. I attended the interview but didn't do that great. Of course, I had my laptop with me, and nobody objected or even seemed to notice when I plugged it into the organization's network.

Don't forget to think about how to exit or close your scenario, whether your scenario is successful or unsuccessful. If your scenario has worked fine, closing it should be easy. Think about how to leave it with the person(s) you have targeted. Ideally, you don't want the person to realize she has been targeted, so you can either approach the individual again or approach her colleagues without wondering if she has raised the alarm. You don't want your target to become suspicious or, indeed, upset that he has been targeted. I have heard this referred to as the *Tyson Effect* as the target does not even know he or she has been hit!

I once performed a very successful test where I played the role of a fire extinguisher inspector looking to inspect every fire extinguisher in the building, such a long and arduous task that the company finally gave up on having someone escort me around the building. I did have to ask to be escorted into the server room, but once inside they didn't pay too much attention to me. I requested certain fire safety documents that the company didn't have on hand. Someone tried to contact me later but was unable to track me down. The company eventually realized it had been a hoax and rang the police. Luckily I had my Get Out of Jail Free card. However, if I had done more preparation in setting up a fake fire company with phone numbers that really worked (as in *Argo*), it might not have come to that.

You also need to think about what to do if your scenario fails. If it fails and your attack has not been identified, as long as it is within budget, you can probably continue with your scenario using a different target victim. If it fails and you have been identified as the social engineer, consider whether to continue or to call off the test. If you choose to continue, will you need to use a different scenario or is there some way to work around it?

Your scenarios should be realistic and reflect events that could potentially happen in real life. The reason for this is twofold: First, it gives a more accurate reflection of whether a real attack would be successful. Second, it gives employees practice at identifying techniques that might be used against them by malicious social engineers. There are a couple of exceptions to this. For example, once I was asked to open a sales conference by posing as the newly appointed CEO. The previous CEO had resigned days before the conference, and it was widely expected that the new CEO would be unveiled during the conference. I can't imagine any malicious social engineer using a scenario like this; it would be too brazen and the ruse would be uncovered too quickly. However, as an awareness-raising exercise, it was perfect. Then you'll have tests where you have been given a ridiculously low budget or short timeframe. Of course, you can choose not to accept these jobs, but business is business after all. Such tests are mostly restricted to tailgating or using the first scenario you come up with, regardless of how realistic or achievable it may be. These sorts of tests do not give an accurate reflection of the organization's susceptibility to social engineering. Neither do they give staff good practice at identifying the techniques that would be used by a malicious social engineer. They are just check-off-the-box tests and are often money badly spent.

Validating Scenarios

Next you need to validate each of the scenarios on your shortlist. Discount the scenarios that won't work for various reasons. For each scenario, consider if it meets the following requirements:

- Is it legal?
- Does it achieve the goal?
- Is it within budget?
- Can it be achieved within your timeframe?
- Is it achievable by your team members?
- It is believable?
- Would it happen in a real-life situation?

Of the remaining scenarios, select the scenario that is most likely to achieve your goal. You might have the perfect scenario that would allow you to compromise the CEO's computer, gaining access to restricted information about the next product launch, but if your purpose is to get usernames and passwords from a handful of employees in HR, this scenario is irrelevant as it will not achieve your goal.

Most of the time, the simpler the scenario, the more effective it is. Straightforward scenarios involving as few people and as little setup as possible are often most effective. Elaborate scenarios are less credible and much harder to act out. Complex scenarios can get overly complicated and trip you up a lot easier than a less sophisticated scenario. Simple scenarios are more flexible and can be more quickly adapted as the social engineering test progresses.

Adding Credibility

If your scenario lacks credibility or has holes in it, it will be less likely to work. A credible scenario can disarm the target's suspicions and establishes a sense of legitimacy in the mind of the target victim. So how do you make your scenario more credible? The devil is in the details. In Malcolm Gladwell's book, *Blink* (Little, Brown and Company, 2005), he talks about the kind of conclusions we make in the blink of an eye, our gut feelings when we meet people for the first time, and the power of first impressions. First impressions are very important to a social engineer. Our targets will immediately recognize if something seems a bit fishy or out of place. For this reason, we need to play the part to perfection. The social engineer needs to know the character she is playing inside out. She must look the part, act the part, and have all the props that her character would have in real life. Name dropping without it appearing forced can be a useful way to establish credibility.

You may find it helpful to create social media accounts, websites, and email addresses to make your scenario more believable. You may even have to set up a fake physical organization for the duration of the attack (think of the fake gambling shop in *The Sting*, mentioned in Chapter 2), depending on how sophisticated your scenario is and how extensive your budget is.

Every action the character you are playing makes must have a "motivation." Why do you need to see the CEO *today*? Why does the fire inspector need to examine *every* fire extinguisher? Consider the motivations for each action and be able to explain, but not over explain, them. This information should be on the tip of your tongue when questioned. Your motivations must be transferrable to your target with minimal questioning from them and explaining by you.

Character Development

Your research and brainstorming will give you a character profile. To build a believable character, however, you must know your character and *become* the character you have selected. It's very much like method acting. The social engineer is an actor who is aiming to break the security of a system. How would your character think? How would he talk? What kind of language would he use (this is why researching company jargon can come in handy)? How would he act? For this reason, I find it easier to play the role of something I have had experience being: a temp worker, a graduate student, a new person on the job. I know how these people would act because I have been in that situation myself and can call on it during the course of the test. This is more of a half-truth, and for a non-actor like myself is easier to work with. The more complex your scenario gets and the further removed from your normal day-to-day life, the better an actor you need to be.

If you are prone to embarrassment or blushing or stumbling over your words, build this into your character. What kind of character would exhibit these characteristics? When I was starting out in social engineering, I found it quite nerve-wracking. I would go red in the face from a combination of adrenaline and nervousness. So I chose a character that this would suit. I often played the role of a graduate either new to the job or looking for a job. Eventually I got over it. Don't get me wrong—I still find each and every test nerve-wracking but experience has brought me confidence.

> **Tip**
>
> What name should you choose? I generally like to stick with my own first name and then a fake surname. People generally use first names nowadays, and if someone uses my real first name, I am far more likely to respond! Imagine if you are walking through an office unescorted and someone shouts, "Hey <*not real name*>," and you don't respond. It will look fishy straightaway. When I started social engineering initially, I would also use a surname that sounded like my own surname, for exactly this reason—I was far more likely to respond to it.

Don't be afraid to use what you've got. If you understand how other people potentially stereotype you, you can use this to your advantage. For example, a guy with long hair may not find it easy to pass himself off as the CEO of a Fortune 500 company; however, he may be very convincing at playing the CEO of a small tech startup or of a delivery guy. A female associate of mine had great success in physical social engineering tests while she was pregnant. No one could say no to a pregnant woman. She would walk into a building, ask to use the toilets, and they would let her walk straight in!

Many character development worksheets are available online, generally geared toward authors or actors; I've provided a sample in the upcoming sidebar. These worksheets really go into detail on the characters, from your character's favorite color to her happiest memory to what she had for breakfast this morning. You are unlikely to have the luxury of developing your character quite this far! However, it is useful to run through some background questions and, at least, think about the answers, if not write them down.

Costumes

Looking the part is important for a social engineer. Is there any particular costume or prop that your character would be likely to wear or use? If you are attempting to gain access to an office environment where everybody is wearing a suit, you are more likely to blend in if you wear a suit also. If most people in your target organization wear jeans and a T-shirt, you should consider wearing this "uniform" too. (In this case, a suit may imply you are higher up the corporate ladder, but if you go for this option, you need to be able to back it up.) Would a T-shirt with the company logo be useful?

Sample Character Development Worksheet

- What's your character's name?
- Write a physical description. What kind of posture does your character have? How do they walk?
- Describe your character's appearance and dress. What kind of clothes does your character wear? Expensive or inexpensive?
- Describe your character's grooming habits.
- Describe your character's speech:
  - Speed of talking: fast, average, slow
  - Accent/dialect
  - Frequently used words or phrases
  - Vocabulary (educated, pretentious, average, uneducated)
- Describe your character's mannerisms (cool/confident/nervous/shy/other).
- What are some common gestures (bites nails, drums fingers, plays with hair)?
- Where is your character from?
- What is your character's occupation and where does he or she work?
- What are your character's interests?
- What are some of the most important images or props associated with your character?
- How is this character different from you?
- How is this character similar to you?
- Provide a short character history.
- What kind of person do other people think your character is?
- Why do people like/dislike this character?
- Characters that your character frequently comes into contact with (home and work)
- What is the character's level of job satisfaction?
- Is your character a smoker (this can be useful in social engineering)?

Any kind of uniform is like an invisibility cloak when it comes to physical social engineering. A great example of this was in the movie, *Catch Me If You Can*, where Leonardo DiCaprio, playing Frank Abagnale, Jr., dresses as a security guard, puts an out-of-order sign on a bank's night deposit box, and simply stands beside it and lets people hand him the money that was destined for the box! In another real-life example, a man in Monroe, Washington, placed an ad on Craigslist seeking workers for a road maintenance project. He told interested parties to meet near the Bank of America at 11 A.M. the following Tuesday morning and to wear a blue shirt and a dust mask. On that Tuesday morning, the perpetrator robbed an armored-car guard leaving the Bank of America in question and fled with the money, supposedly using an inner tube to float down a nearby creek. The suspect was reported to be wearing a blue shirt and a dust mask. There were least a dozen individuals outside the bank at the time of the robbery who matched this description!

This is a good example of life reflecting art. There is a great scene in the art heist movie, *The Thomas Crown Affair*, where the museum security are closing in on the

Exercise: What Clothing or Uniforms Are Worn Within Your Target Organization?

Make a list of the types of clothing or uniforms that different individuals within your target organization or those who deal with your target organization might wear. What does your target wear to the office? What does the receptionist wear? What about the security guard? What about the copier repair technician, the CEO, the bike messenger. Consider all the individuals with whom your target comes in contact during a typical day at the office.

art thief. He has stolen the artwork and is still within the premises. Security identifies him on CCTV. The thief is wearing a distinguishable outfit, consisting of a bowler hat, a black coat, a business suit, and a red tie. In fact, he is wearing the same outfit as is depicted in René Magritte's *The Son of Man* painting, which is featured several times in the film. Security puts a call out to the guards on the floor to apprehend the man in the bowler hat. It turns out that there are dozens of men in the museum who are wearing the exact same outfit as the thief. (Spoiler alert: The art thief gets away.)

You can purchase many uniforms on the Internet. eBay is a great resource for this—just do a search on "Dominos Pizza" to get an idea, as shown in Figure 6-1! Alternatively, you can print your own iron-on transfers and iron them on to a T-shirt. I sometimes pick up T-shirts at tradeshows that myself or my team can use to add credibility to our scenarios.

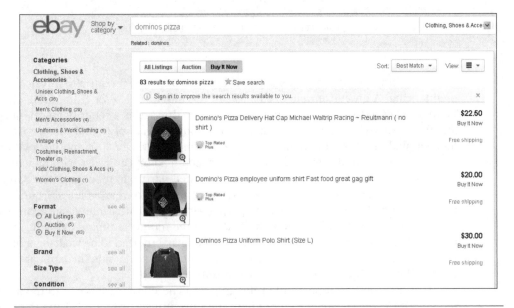

FIGURE 6-1   A search on eBay gives you a lot of options for Domino's Pizza T-shirts.

eBay is a treasure trove of potential costumes for social engineers. You can buy anything from a security jacket to a chef's uniform to a FedEx uniform, as shown in Figure 6-2 or, rather worryingly, airline clothing, as shown in Figure 6-3. Do a search online and you will find plenty of stories about people masquerading as airline pilots. Now we know where they get their uniforms! In 2007, it was reported that a 23-year-old Chinese man, Shu Shi, boarded an airplane in Beijing International Airport disguised as a pilot so he could get a free flight home. He reportedly bought his uniform on the Internet and downloaded fake identification online.

> **Tip**   Stories like Shu Shi's are quite common. We hear about fake pilots, doctors, and lawyers regularly. If you work for an organization whose employees are required to wear uniforms, ensure that they hand them in once their employment finishes.

Props

Props can also go a long way toward establishing credibility during your social engineering test, whether it's arriving in a branded delivery van, actually bringing a pizza to deliver (who could resist a freshly made pizza), or simply using a fake business card. Here are some of the props my team has used throughout the years:

- Cell phones. Cell phones are my number one prop when it comes to social engineering. People are a lot less likely to question you or challenge you if you are on the phone. Just remember to set it to silent so it doesn't ring while you are talking on it!

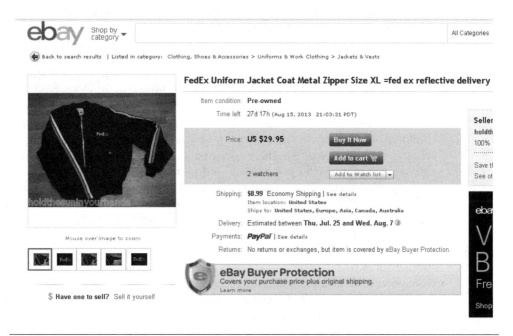

FIGURE 6-2   FedEx uniforms are widely available on eBay.

FIGURE 6-3   A flight attendant uniform for sale

- ID cards. Real or fake ID cards can get you a long way. You can try to procure a real ID card, print a fake one yourself, or just use a standard magnetic stripe card turned backward, as shown in Figure 6-4. I often carry a blank magnetic stripe card and hang it around my neck, making sure it is turned backward. It looks like any standard generic ID card.
- Cups of coffee, boxes, suitcases, or anything that means your hands aren't free. This way, people more often than not will open the door for you to be polite.
- Folders or official-looking documents just make you look the part, especially if they have any kind of corporate branding or logos on them. They also make you look like you belong and appear to give you a sense of purpose. For this reason, I always grab some documents the minute I get into a building.
- Boxes, pizza, flowers, something to deliver, ideally by you directly to the person who they are intended for—perhaps to get you past reception so you can roam the building. You might consider bringing a change of clothes for this so that you can change roles (e.g. to an employee dressed in a suit) when you get past reception, if it doesn't matter who you deliver your pizza or flowers to. Or, if, alternatively, the intended recipient is your target, you will want to deliver your pizza, etc., directly to that person. Even so, in this scenario, bringing a change of clothes so you can quickly change out of your delivery role can be handy.
- As mentioned in the previous chapter, I take a handful of business cards whenever I see a competition that says "drop your business card here for a chance to win dinner for two."
- A clipboard. Who doesn't look important carrying a clipboard? A clipboard is a good prop for any kind of inspector, such as a fire extinguisher inspector, health and safety inspector, property appraiser, or loss adjuster.

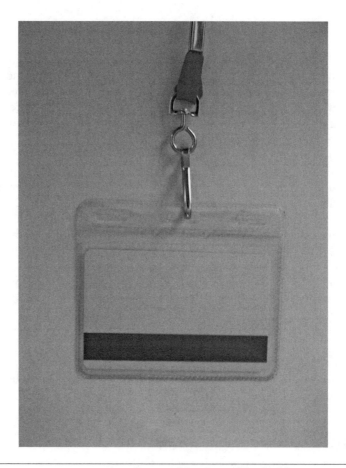

FIGURE 6-4   A magnetic stripe card turned backward looks like any generic ID card.

Identifying Possible Pitfalls

Role playing and drilling your scenario can help you to identify possible pitfalls in your chosen scenario and consider how to deal with them. Think through the disadvantages or possible complications of the role you are playing. If you are impersonating a real employee from another office, is that employee well known? Is there a photo ID system that the person can be looked up on? Will the employee be in the office during the attack? If you are playing a fictional character, what background work do you need to do to make your character seem more real? Should you set up a website, social media account, email account?

In my experience, things that can go wrong include

- Your target blocks your attack by refusing to give information. In this case, should you continue pursuing the scenario with the same target individual, try the scenario on a different target individual, or change your tactics?
- You are identified as a social engineer. Do you call off the test, ask the person who has identified you to keep this information to him- or herself, or have somebody else on your team try another scenario?
- You are recognized.
- The target raises the alarm, alerting other people to your techniques. For example, you try a certain scenario with an individual in the call center and she tells her colleagues about the attempted scenario.
- The target doesn't know what you are talking about. You've asked for a certain piece of information but she really doesn't know it. In one test, I asked for a print out from the ticketing system of case EPD-782-C. It turned out that this code was for a different system altogether, so the person I was requesting the information from didn't know what I was talking about and got suspicious.
- The target calls the police. This is where your Get Out of Jail Free card comes in useful!
- You can't get past the physical perimeter or reception. What should you do then?

Consider how to deal with each situation. In some cases, you may choose to discuss this with your client. For example, how many people should you target unsuccessfully before you decide to call off your social engineering test?

Assigning Roles

The next step involves assigning roles to the team members who will be involved in the scenario. Acting out the scenario can be hard. The person(s) who will execute the scenario needs to be confident, good at acting, able to think on his or her feet, good at bullshitting (which is easier when you have done all the research and reconnaissance), and finally, good with people (or can at least fake being good with people). Remember—you don't need to execute the scenario yourself. Security professionals are not necessarily good actors, so you can always recruit an actor for the course of the test (as long as subcontracting is permitted by your client). Nevertheless, the more social engineering tests you do, the better you get. In the meantime, acting and improvisation classes or workshops can help you to improve.

There are three categories of social engineering: remote social engineering where there is no physical or vocal interaction (phishing, social media, and so on), social engineering by phone, and physical social engineering conducted onsite. In the first case, remote social engineering, if there is no required physical or vocal interaction, you can be whoever you choose, regardless of gender, age, nationality, or any other physical characteristic. You can be a Nigerian prince or a beautiful lady called Robin Sage. You can play several roles, or several of you can play one role.

The only limit is your imagination. You may be slightly more limited in a telephone test, where you have to speak to your target. In this case, you are better off playing something suited to your voice and accent. Unless you are a really good actor, forget about using fake accents. You will already have so much to think about and be running on adrenaline—you may even have a fake name—don't add anything else into the mix. You could potentially use a voice changer, but make sure it sounds realistic.

If you are doing a physical social engineering test, it is important to take on a believable role that is physically suited to you. If you are not believable, your test attack will fall flat. If you are 21 and you are playing the role of a CEO and sporting a Rolex watch, your scenario is highly unlikely to work. Similarly, if you are 50 and playing the role of a graduate, the chances of that working are slim.

When it comes to physical social engineering, consider your physical characteristics and how these will affect the role you are going to play. These can include gender, nationality, physical build, age, and more superficial characteristics such as clothes and manner. Build your scenario around these characteristics. Use them to make your scenarios more plausible, even if it means playing up to stereotypes (say, a damsel in distress). For example, I am female, with a petite build; I'm Irish; and I smile a lot. This means that

- Guys open doors for me, especially in the UK where people are very polite.
- People don't get worried or necessarily notice when I tailgate them.
- I am good at hiding in small spaces, in cupboards, under desks, even in boxes. If I am caught, I can say I dropped an earring. Once I was caught by a security guard hiding under a desk in an office with all the lights switched off. I had my laptop out and was sniffing network traffic. I heard the security guard come in and switch on the lights. I dived under the desk but it was too late—he saw me. He came over to question me. I noticed a box of Pringles under the desk and rather cheekily offered him one. He took one, and we started chatting. He left. I continued my probing of the network.
- I know I don't look threatening or malicious (unless you know me). No one expects me to be a social engineer, sometimes even when forewarned that a social engineering test is going to take place.

I have played authoritative roles in the past, but they never seem to be as convincing as when I play friendlier, "softer" roles, in spite of me being quite bossy in real life—I guess my physical characteristics are not necessarily associated with an authoritative character. Given my physical characteristics, which of the following character roles do you think are likely to work for me?

- IT department
- Teacher
- Telecoms engineer
- Waitress/catering
- Construction worker
- Cleaner

- Pizza delivery
- Fire inspection officer

Consider what impact your physical characteristics will have on your scenario and if you are best suited to play the role.

Practicing Again and Again

Role-play your chosen scenario with your colleagues prior to executing the test. Get them to throw random questions at you and think through how the scenario will play out during the test, giving consideration to what may go wrong. The social engineer should prepare answers to questions that might be asked while playing out the scenario. For example, questions that I have been asked in the past while executing a social engineering scenario include

- Who are you?
- Why do you need this information (so urgently)?
- Can I see some ID?
- Do you work here?
- Who are you looking for?
- What are you looking for?
- What are you doing?
- How can I help you?
- Are you lost?
- What's your email address/telephone number?
- Who do you work for?
- Do you have an appointment?
- What are you doing (when plugging into network or generally looking suspicious!)?
- Who are you here to see?
- Are you here for the social engineering test?
- Are you here to fix the telephones/printers/air conditioning?
- What's your account number?
- Are you here to give blood? I was actually asked this once! It gave me a great excuse to be onsite but left me feeling a bit squeamish... You just don't know what social engineering tests will throw at you.

You can use these answers to help develop a script. Unless I'm social engineering a call center, which has standard scripts that they use, I don't develop a script in case it sounds over-practiced or forced. Instead, I perform an exercise where my colleagues ask me as many questions as possible. This is a fun exercise to get you thinking about your character and your scenario. Make note of your answers or even consider recording this session, so you can remember what you said!

Social engineering scenarios are, by their very nature, fluid. They can change as you go along. You will most likely need to ad lib during the actual test. This is where role-playing and practicing in advance will pay off. Stick to your story line but improvise, based on your research.

An Improvisation Exercise

We improvise all the time in our day-to-day lives and it comes perfectly naturally to us. We make up our dialogue with people we are talking to, whether with friends, family, colleagues, or complete strangers. This kind of improvisation doesn't necessarily come that naturally in social engineering, however. In this case, we can take a lead from performers who specialize in stage improvisation. Many comedians improvise, for example. Typically, at an improvised comedy gig, the master of ceremonies will ask the audience to suggest film or theater styles for the improvised scene—sci-fi, a musical, a Western. Then the audience is asked to suggest a location where the scene takes place (at a launderette, on the moon...). The resulting improvisation is often hilarious. Improvisation performers have many games and drills that they do to hone their improvisation skills. A classic theater improvisation exercise involves two characters improvising a scene until a third party shouts "freeze," at which point the third party enters the scene and replaces one of the original actors. Other improvisation exercises are more story-telling based, for example, participants tell a made-up story by each saying only one word of the story. Yet another exercise involves two participants improvising dialogue where the first word each one speaks must begin with the next letter of the alphabet: "Are you here to fix the computer?" "Broken, is it?" "Course it is." "Do explain what seems to be the problem."

Improvisers view any situation, action, or dialogue as "an offer" that can advance a scene. They choose how to accept that offer, either accepting or rejecting it. In good stage improvisation, the offer is always accepted and the improviser does his best to work with what he has been given. In social engineering, it doesn't always work that way. Your offer may be accepted or rejected by the person you are dealing with, so you should think about both situations. Here are a couple of exercises that you can do to help.

In the first improvisation exercise that you can practice, you accept every offer that is thrown at you. So, on stage this might translate as the following:

Improviser A: Hi, my name is Sam. Welcome to my café.
Improviser B: Hi Sam. Lovely café. Please can I order a coffee?
Improviser A: Sure, what kind of coffee can I get you?
Improviser B: An espresso please. How much will that be?

Improviser B goes along with whatever situation she is faced with, accepting the offer, and saying yes where possible. Try doing this with your devised scenario. It might look something like this:

Social Engineer: Hi, my name is Sharon. I'm here to do an article on the latest technology and would like to take some photos of the technology you are using.
Colleague: Hi Sharon. No problem. Let me find someone to show you around. What are you interested in exactly?

(continued)

> *Social Engineer:* I'd love to see your server room and have someone explain a bit about what you do.
>
> What a dream scenario!
>
> In the second exercise, the second person rejects each offer, acting negatively and saying no where possible. The improviser has to work around this. In a stage situation, it might look like this:
>
> *Improviser A:* Hi, my name is Sam. Welcome to my café.
> *Improviser B:* Your name is Michael, not Sam and this isn't your café.
>
> In a social engineering exercise, it could look like this:
>
> *Social Engineer:* Hi, my name is Sharon. I'm here to do an article on the latest technology and would like to take some photos of the technology you are using.
> *Colleague:* Your name is not Sharon, and I don't believe you are here to take some photos.
> *Social Engineer:* Yes, my name is Sharon and here's my ID. I called earlier to say I would be coming in and they said it would be fine.
> *Colleague:* I don't recognize your ID. Nobody here spoke to you earlier.
> *Social Engineer:* I'm sorry. You can call my boss to confirm. Their number is on the back of the card. I spoke to Jack earlier.

Final Thoughts

Good research and reconnaissance is the key to creating a plausible and solid scenario. Your scenario should allow you to create a situation in which the target is comfortable with releasing information that he or she normally would not release. Your scenario should include enough information for it to be validated, which you can drip feed to the target as and when necessary. You don't want to bombard the target with too much information and too many excuses straightaway, as it can appear unnatural. You need a detailed scenario, but you don't necessarily need to use all those details during the test execution.

There is no one-size-fits-all solution when it comes to creating your scenario. Each test is different. A social engineer will develop many different scenarios or pretexts over the course of her career. You can grow out of them, become known for them, or they just become outdated. You can only get away with playing a university graduate for so long, regardless of the fact that more mature students are returning to school. Calling people and asking straight out for their password doesn't work as well as it used to because people are just more clued in than before.

The best scenarios are boringly mundane but solid. If you have a good solid scenario, you can take your social engineering test further, confident in the knowledge that if you are apprehended or questioned, you may be able to use your back story to get out of it, or at least to buy you more time. You won't have to show your Get Out of

Jail Free card as quickly as someone who has not taken the time to do her research and plan a scenario.

Accept that your scenario may need to change throughout your assignment, and sometimes even while you are executing it. You can never predict how the test is going to turn out, so you need to be ready to adapt your scenario as you go along.

The story line is important. Your scenario should be based on a credible role and a plausible situation. Using your research and reconnaissance, create a good scenario and practice it as much as possible before executing your test.

The next chapter looks at putting your chosen scenario(s) into play and actually executing the social engineering test.

7

Executing the Social Engineering Test

The game is afoot. Not a word! Into your clothes and come!
—Sherlock Holmes to Dr. Watson, *Adventure of the Abbey Grange*, by Sir Arthur Conan Doyle

At this point, you have done the research and reconnaissance and created a scenario, now it's time to execute your plan. Performing a social engineering test is both stressful and fun and will get your adrenaline pumping—to varying levels depending on the type of test.

Executing an email or phishing test is straightforward and usually the least stressful of any kind of social engineering test. You send the email and then wait for an agreed-upon period of time for responses to flow in, whether the response is a return email, inadvertently running some program or other, or visiting a website of your choosing. Your plan may include subsequent steps once someone responds to your email, opens an attachment, or clicks a link. As this type of test does not necessitate immediate interaction with your target, you can plan the execution carefully. You have time to consider each step you will take along the way and how you will respond to each interaction.

Performing social engineering activities over the phone can be more exciting because the test is (mostly) live. You are talking to another person, someone who could identify your attack and call you out at any moment. Executing the social engineering test does not normally take long, depending on the length of your phone call, but it can be very effective. People may disclose information over the phone because they are trying to be helpful or friendly or simply because they have been asked for it.

However, by far the most exciting—and stressful—type of test is the onsite social engineering test. You risk being discovered at any point during the exercise. You are "playing" so many people. You may be trying to avoid CCTV cameras or attempting to compromise other physical security controls. You may be using suspicious-looking techniques such as lock picking or waiting to tailgate someone through a door. During face-to-face interactions, you can't give the game away. Everything you say and do must be consistent with your back story: the way you act, the way you dress, the things you say, your attitude, and your requests for information.

What most people don't tell you about onsite social engineering tests is that your adrenaline pumps so hard that afterward you are completely exhausted. It almost gives you a social engineering hangover! You might find it hard to remember exactly what happened and when, so note taking or recording your actions becomes particularly important. Once I have executed my attack, I immediately run through what has happened with my colleagues (partly as an informative exercise and partly to show off) and then I get a blinding headache and zone out for the rest of the day!

In this chapter, we'll look at how to execute each of the following types of social engineering tests:

- A phishing test
- A telephone test
- An onsite test

Executing a Phishing Test

A phishing test is a good example of a bait-and-hook attack. The bait is the email contents and/or email subject line that will entice your target into opening the message. At this stage, you will have already thought about your bait, or back story. Now you just need to design it effectively. The email has to look realistic. Base it on real examples of legitimate emails that you have seen. Make sure there are no spelling mistakes that can make the email look unprofessional. Craft the email so it looks like it has come from a valid and relevant email address. You may wish to consider purchasing a realistic-sounding domain name for this purpose, perhaps something similar to the organization you are testing or another domain name that sounds equally official. If you do this, you and your client need to decide what to do with the domain name when you have finished the test—especially if it sounds like one of theirs. Finally, place a hook somewhere in the email. This hook could be an attachment you want the target to open, a URL you want them to visit, or maybe even a telephone number you want them to call.

Phishing emails should be designed to test the many security controls encountered within the target network. Many technical controls can potentially stop your phishing test from being successful, from email gateway spam filters to antivirus, egress filtering, intrusion prevention, or junk email filters. If you know what kind of technical controls are in place, you can design a payload to bypass these controls. You may be able to discover this information through social engineering your target organization's staff ("Hi, I'm doing a survey on popular antivirus software. Please could you tell me which antivirus you use?"). Alternatively, you can always just ask the person who has commissioned the SE test to provide this information in advance. Otherwise it's a question of trial and error until your test attack gets through.

A Non–Social Engineering Phishing Test

A phishing test is essentially composed of two components:

- The social engineering aspect where you lure people into opening the email and performing a certain action
- Penetration testing activities that test the technical security controls in place

The two activities do not necessarily need to be performed together. You can more or less assume that you will eventually come up with a good enough phish to catch an unsuspecting user in your target organization. The real question is whether your payload will execute within the organization's network.

My team has performed several tests in which the company we are testing has assumed that someone will fall for the phishing attack, so they have skipped straight to the technical side of the test. We sent a number of emails to a designated recipient at an agreed-upon time with a selection of payloads. He clicked each payload to determine if it would successfully execute or be blocked by the various security controls the company had in place.

Of course, this setup doesn't test whether users would click a link and enter their user credentials, but it does go some way toward determining whether or not certain technical anti-phishing controls are effective.

Executing a Telephone Social Engineering Test

A lot of social engineering takes place over the phone, sometimes as part of a wider attack and sometimes as the sole focus of the attack itself. It helps to have a good telephone manner. Most of us are not particularly good on the telephone. We use the phone all the time but rarely think about how to use it effectively. Telephone communication skills are some of the most crucial skills that are needed not only in social engineering but also in business in general.

Here are a number of tips for cultivating a good telephone manner that you can use (if appropriate) during your telephone social engineering exercise:

- *Plan what you are going to say before the call.* Make a list of questions you want to ask and information you want to obtain. Think about questions that the person you have called may ask you and plan your answers in advance.
- *In your call opener, you should identify yourself and the purpose of your call.* "Hello, this is Sharon from City Dry Cleaners. I'm calling to let you know that your dry cleaning is ready for pickup." If you don't already know the name of the person you are speaking to, make an effort to find out and use it from time to time throughout the conversation.

- *Be aware of the tone of your voice.* Try to make your tone as natural as possible. You are mostly seeking to sound authoritative and confident, speaking in a low and even tone of voice, although this does depend on your chosen scenario. It may be that you are pretending to get angry or worked up, in which case you are probably going to opt to speak loudly, in a high pitch, or even start crying. The tone of voice you use should be in line with your scenario.

- *Articulate clearly and slowly.* Your social engineering test is not going to be very effective if the person you are calling cannot understand you (unless it's a mumble attack!). Sit up straight in your chair or stand during the telephone call to generate energy in your body and to help project your voice.

- *Be friendly (but not overly so).* Take opportunities to make a little small talk. Look for clues as to what is relevant to the person you are calling. "I love your accent—where are you from?" "Thank goodness it's Friday; I can't wait for the weekend." "Where are you based? New York? I love New York!"

- *If you are adopting a friendly persona, use the smile rule.* Smile when you are on the phone, so your voice has a positive inflection, conveying a positive attitude and even making you come across as more likeable. This puts the person you have called at ease and lays the foundation for a positive telephone conversation, making it more likely that the person you have called will volunteer useful information.

- *Think about what time you place the call.* Does your target organization send calls over to a call center after hours? What time do staff go home? If you call them just before they leave the office, will they be more or less helpful than usual? If you are calling a foreign country, be sensitive to the time difference, although you can use this to your advantage as well. On several occasions, I have social engineered European offices first thing in the morning, claiming to be based in a US office and knowing that I have a couple of hours before people start arriving to work in the US and my ruse is up.

- *Be aware of background sounds and make the phone call from an appropriate location.* Ensure that you will not be disturbed during the course of the call.

> **Tip**   If you get an Interactive Voice Response (IVR) where you can respond via voice or keypad and want to skip directly to a human operator, some IVRs listen out for bad language and put you through when they hear it. Use this information how you will—just be aware of who is around you when you start cursing on the phone!

- *Have a pen and paper nearby so you can make notes throughout the call.* Jot down key words and jargon that the person you are speaking to uses. Note project names, internal department names, staff names, and so on. You may be able to record the phone call, but this very much depends on local jurisdiction and whether you have specific authorization to do so. (Recording yourself speaking on the phone can also help you to improve your telephone skills.) In many jurisdictions, you have to tell people the call is being recorded, so often you will get a recording along the lines of "this call may be recorded for quality assurance purposes" before the real person comes online.

The key challenge in social engineering over the phone is engaging the person you have called so that she will willingly share information without any sense of suspicion. Ideally, you will close the call in a way that allows you to call her back at a later time or date. To do this, you need to have a smooth telephone call, come across professionally, and connect with the person you are talking to.

Executing an Onsite Social Engineering Test

Depending on your scenario, the organization that you are social engineering may or may not be expecting you. If the organization is expecting you, that's great. Getting past the perimeter security, such as reception, security guards, and turnstiles, should be relatively straightforward. You can progress with your social engineering test as planned. If the company is not expecting you, and you have managed to get past the perimeter security, maybe through tailgating or by social engineering, what do you do next?

The Basic Routine

I find it useful to have a basic routine that I can use once I get unauthorized access to a building. My routine contains two simple steps:

1. Find the bathroom.
2. Pick up some official-looking documents to hold.

If you perform physical social engineering tests regularly, you may build your own fallback routine. In my routine, step 1, locating the bathroom, has several advantages in addition to actually using the facilities... If I have entered a building without having organized a meeting with a staff member, the first thing I like to do once I get in is to take five minutes and reconsider my course of action; the restroom is a good place to do this. You will likely be relieved that you have made it through the perimeter security. Pausing for a moment at this stage to collect your thoughts and think through your next steps is useful. Will they still work? Is there anything you need to change based on your experience so far? The bathroom is also a good place to go through documents or information you have obtained. If you need to disappear for a while—for example, if you are worried that someone has identified you as a social engineer—you can hide out there or you can always walk with a sense of purpose toward the restroom!

Earlier in this chapter, I mentioned that physical social engineering is the most exciting form of social engineering. It can also be the most boring. I've spent hours in the freezing cold outside a building, casing the joint or waiting for someone to let me in. I've been stranded on stairwells. I've spent ages hidden away in buildings waiting for staff to go home so I can roam their offices. Most of the time I wait in the bathroom, where I generally go unnoticed. The four most important lessons I have learned from this are

- The toilets for the disabled have the most space and are, therefore, the most comfortable if you are camping out for a couple of hours. You'll want to free up the disabled stall from time to time in case a disabled person needs to use it.
- Change stalls periodically or the cleaners will begin to wonder why one stall has been locked all day. Maybe also flush once in a while...

- Bathrooms can be chilly. Dress warmly if you think you will be in there for long stretches of time.
- Bring reading material. Waiting for the office to clear out can be boring.

Once I have taken a moment to gather my thoughts, I move on to the second step of finding some important-looking documents to carry. I usually pick these up at photocopiers, printers, or from inboxes or the mail room. I find that the process of both looking for them and holding them gives me a sense of purpose and can make it seem like I work in the organization. Internal mail envelopes, such as that shown in Figure 7-1, are good because they make it look like you must be internal to the organization!

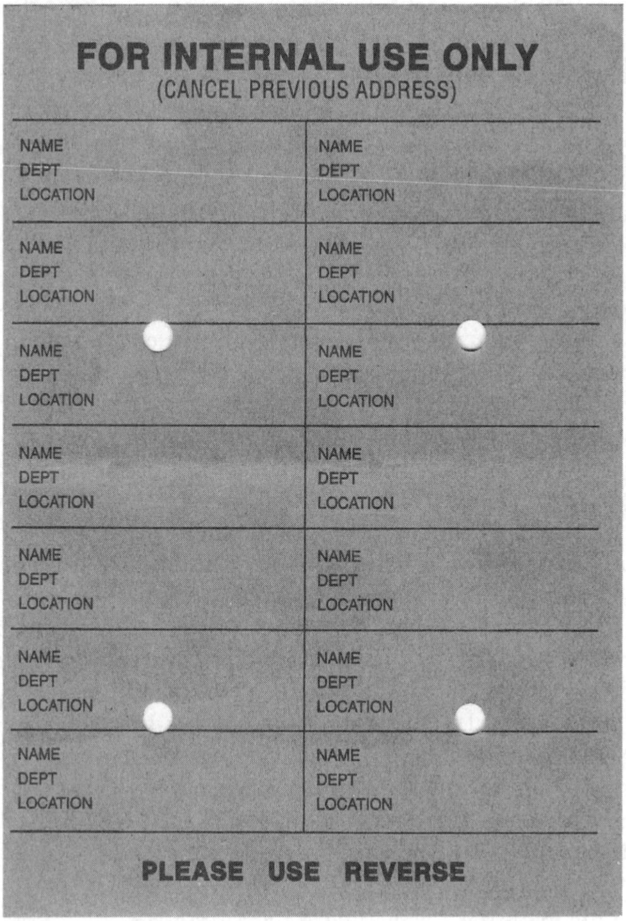

FOR INTERNAL USE ONLY
(CANCEL PREVIOUS ADDRESS)

NAME	NAME
DEPT	DEPT
LOCATION	LOCATION

PLEASE USE REVERSE

FIGURE 7-1   Carrying an internal mail envelope like this one can make you look like an employee.

Common Actions Once Inside

The most common actions I have taken once inside a building include

- Leaving a business card or some kind of calling card to prove I have accessed the area. I like to leave a calling card with the date of the test on it so clients don't suspect me of re-entering the premises at a later date, if they don't find all the calling cards straightaway. Keep a note of how many cards you've left and where you left them for this same reason—so you can retrieve them shortly after the test and they won't confuse people at a later date. If possible and if it doesn't attract too much attention, take a photo showing where you have left each calling card.
- Connecting to the network and getting an IP address. Take a screenshot of the IP address as proof that you connected to the internal network.
- Trying to gain access to more secure areas such as the server room, CEO's office, HR area, and so on.
- Calling the person who has commissioned the test. This is cheeky but effective and, above all, gives you a chance to show off your ninja social engineering skills.
- Looking for ID cards that people have left on their desks. On one occasion, I accessed a financial organization where people clocked in using their ID cards, but actually had to leave them in the clocking-in machine for as long as they were in the office. I could have picked up any of these cards and used them for malicious purposes. I didn't do this because I didn't know how it would impact the person whose card I had taken and if it would affect his or her logged working hours. A photograph of the machine sufficed to prove my point.
- Asking to borrow ID cards. People have willingly handed over their ID cards to me, usually when I ask to borrow them to pop out for a cigarette or to use the ladies room. I use excuses such as "I've forgotten my access card," "I'm new and don't have a card yet," or "I'm a temp/contractor so haven't been issued a card." I take the card for a couple of minutes, take a photo of it, and return it.
- Identifying sensitive documents within the organization. You hopefully will have established in advance whether you can take these off the premises. If not, make a note of what the documents are and where you found them, or even take a photograph as evidence.
- Checking photocopiers, mail boxes, fax machines, and so on, for interesting documents. Also perform desktop snooping, if legally permissible and within the scope of the test.
- Shoulder surfing to identify passwords, access codes, and so on. If you are authorized to hold or wear any kind of recording device, make sure it is pointing in the right direction while people are logging in or entering access codes. If you have a terrible memory, at least you can replay the key strokes afterward.
- Looking for passwords written on post-it notes, whiteboards, hidden under keyboards, in the top drawers of desks, and so on. It never ceases to amaze me how often I discover written passwords.
- Dropping road apples in strategic locations around the building.

Occasionally, I have had to do the following:

- Connect my laptop to the internal network and perform an internal penetration test. Be sure to establish if penetration-testing activities are authorized and have been explicitly agreed on in the scope of work *before* doing this. Don't attempt any penetration-testing activities without written permission.
- Perform a scan of the network to ascertain how long it would take for the security team to identify the scan and track me down within the building. For one organization where I did this, I changed rooms three times. It took about half a day for them to discover me. If you are doing a test where your target is going to try to track you down, this may influence the type of scan you choose to run and how stealthy you are going to make it.
- Convince someone to give me a laptop. Usually I give it back before going offsite, having photographed it or presented it to a security manager or to the person who has commissioned the test.
- Install a keystroke logger. More frequently, I have simply placed a sticker near a USB port or near a cable connector to indicate that I would have been able to install a keystroke logger. A sticker proves you've been there and is lower risk than actually installing a keystroke logger—and has been the preferred option of many of my clients.
- Obtain an access card for the building by convincing security or facilities to issue you your own card.
- Connect a wireless access point to the network, which my team can access from outside the building and potentially conduct technical penetration-testing activities, if permitted within the scope of the test.

In one case, I ended up on a tour of the canteen learning how to cook fish and chips. You never know where your social engineering test will take you!

During one of my favorite social engineering tests of an insurance company, I found an empty office room with about six desk spaces. A number of these had desktop PCs and the rest were empty. I sat in the room and unplugged the network cable from one of the PCs so that I could use it to connect my laptop to the network and sniff some network traffic. It was lunchtime, so I assumed the PC users were on their lunch break. They arrived back shortly after I sat down, however, and proceeded to have their team meeting. They didn't so much as ask who I was or what I was doing there. They just had the team meeting around me! At one point, one of the guys tried to present a financial spreadsheet to the others in the group, but had trouble accessing it as he didn't appear to have a network connection. I interrupted to say "I'm sorry—I think I am using your network cable," and passed the cable back to him. He said thanks, and they continued with their meeting. I typed documents randomly and listened in. The meeting lasted almost an hour. At no point was I challenged!

Remember that throughout your onsite social engineering test, the emotions you express and your manner will determine how other people react to you. If you look uncomfortable or don't appear confident in what you are doing, people may become suspicious. If you are embarrassed and don't want other people to laugh at you, keep a blank face and no one will laugh. One of the best examples I ever saw of controlling people's reactions was seeing a woman tripping (not badly!) while walking down the street. She calmly got up and announced to the passersby that "that never happened. It was all a figment of your imagination!" The woman appeared confident and really cool. She turned a potentially embarrassing moment into a funny moment in one deft move.

Another important thing to remember in physical social engineering is that it's not just about getting through the front door. You have to plan what you are going to do when you are inside and consider how you are going to get out again. Hopefully, both of these will be covered by your test plan and agreed-on in advance with your client. Whatever you do once you are on the grounds of an organization, do it calmly and with confidence.

Recording the Test

As mentioned earlier in the chapter, recording all your activities throughout the course of the social engineering test is important. It becomes particularly important in physical social engineering as it can be difficult to remember exactly what you did once you have exited the scenario. If possible (and if allowed under local jurisdiction and specifically authorized by your target organization), you can use a recording device to record the entire test execution. I have a spy handbag especially for this purpose. If I see someone logging in, I point my handbag in the right direction and try to decipher the keystrokes when I have exited the building. My colleagues have used pinhole cameras attached to their ties. You can record sound or video or both. If your recording device can timestamp the proceedings, it's better still.

If you are not allowed to use a recording device (which has rarely been permitted in any of the European-based tests I have done), you need to make notes as you go along. I use a combination of things: I take notes, take photos on my cell phone, and leave myself or a colleague voicemails describing what I have done—obviously out of earshot of any staff in my target organization. The advantage of making notes, taking photos, or leaving voicemails on your cell phone is that you have a timestamp to tell you at exactly what time you performed the activity in question.

Trophy Gathering

If you are going to gather evidence or trophies and bring them offsite, make sure you and the client have agreed on this in advance. If you are taking any items offsite, whether it's information assets, product prototypes, physical files, or anything else, make sure you securely store those items. Even better—call your client and give it back before you exit the building. Trophies I have been authorized to collect in the past include

- Internal sales material, flyers, brochures, and so on
- Projected plans/figures for the next year's business
- ID cards
- A fake HR file set up specifically for the test
- A laptop
- A server (the security guard helped me to carry it out as it was a little too heavy for me to manage on my own!)

Occasionally you get free reign to remove anything you like, but it is always best to check this out first.

Helpdesk Ticket Test

I performed a social engineering test of a professional services company in which the aim of the test was to get a printout of a particular ticket from the helpdesk, for which I was given the ticketing number. The ticket, which was prepared by the security team, was completely fabricated. All the details looked real, and most employees wouldn't have been able to tell that it was a fake ticket on the system. Because of this, there was no breach of data protection. None of the information I saw was real, but it still proved that I could have gotten access to sensitive data.

I arrived at the office a little earlier than most employees. It was a European office, and I claimed to be from an American branch. I told the receptionist that I needed a place to work for the day as my flight home had been delayed. I used the name of a real staff member who was based in the American branch. I knew that, with the time difference, I had a few hours before the American employees arrived to work. The receptionist looked up the name on the system to verify that I worked for her company. Luckily for me, there was no photo on the system, so she let me into the office.

I found the break area, and, as employees arrived in the morning, they started coming over to grab a cup of coffee. I made a bit of small talk with the friendlier-looking employees. I asked one particularly chatty employee to point me in the direction of the helpdesk. As I expected, she escorted me over and introduced me: "This is Sharon, from our US office." The introduction from a fellow employee made me look more legitimate.

I asked one of the guys on the helpdesk to print the ticket for me. He immediately became suspicious. No one ever asked for a ticket to be printed and very few people had access to this particular system. He quizzed me on who I was and why I needed it. I stuck to my story that I found myself unexpectedly in the European office for the day and didn't have my laptop or any of my working documents with me. I explained that I had signed in at reception, and he could check this with the receptionist.

This individual was reasonably security aware. He marched me out to reception. The receptionist was on the phone. We waited a couple of minutes for the phone call to finish, with me keeping my fingers crossed the entire time. I didn't make small talk. I just tried to look relaxed and a tad put out that this guy was stopping me from doing my job. When the receptionist hung up, the guy explained that he found the whole situation suspicious and asked the receptionist if I worked in the organization. Note that the "security-aware" individual did some "authorization transference" to the receptionist. She told him that I worked in the US office and I had signed in that morning. She asked him to print out my documents as soon as possible. She looked embarrassed and apologized to me for the "bad" treatment.

Afterward, the receptionist couldn't believe she had been duped. She vowed to try to be more security aware in future. The point of this story is that I performed the whole assignment without having to access any real sensitive information. It was a mock ticket and was more than enough to prove the point. The second point is that the more social engineering you do, the braver you'll be. You'll know that the worst that can happen is you'll have to present your Get Out of Jail Free card and call your contact!

Creating a Good Road Apple/Physical Bait

Sometimes rather than taking something from an organization, you might want to leave something there instead. You could leave a calling card or sticker as proof that you were inside the building, or you could leave a road apple that can further your attack. DarkReading reported on a classic road apple story in 2006 that involved performing a social engineering test of a credit union[1]. Early one morning, the social engineers scattered 20 USB keys in the credit union's parking lot. The USB keys had programs on them that, when run, collected passwords, logins, and machine-specific information from the user's computer and emailed them back to the tester. After three days, 15 out of 20 of the USB keys had been plugged into company computers. The information relayed back by these USB keys helped the testers to compromise additional systems. It was an extremely successful attack, with a low risk of being caught.

The key to creating a good road apple is to make people want to see what is on the storage device. You're relying on the victim's curiosity. You want the victim to plug in the device to figure out who the device belongs to, to find out what is on the device, or to use it for the victim's own purposes ("yay—free USB key!"). So put an interesting label on the road apple or on the files stored on it. Maybe it could be one of the following:

- **Salary information**   Most people have no idea how much money their colleagues are making and would love an opportunity to find out.
- **Redundancy information**   In challenging economic climates, redundancy is a constant worry for many people. It may affect them personally or affect colleagues and friends within their organization. Who wouldn't want an opportunity to see what information such a storage device held?
- **Quarterly results**   Any kind of financial information is potentially interesting, especially if it hasn't been published yet.
- **Photos**   Christmas party photos are a good one. People want to see if there is anything incriminating. Wedding/honeymoon photos are also good, as the thought of someone losing these photos is unbearable to most people and the natural inclination is to want to return the device, so they are more likely to plug it in to determine who it belongs to.
- **Porn**   What can I say? More likely to be plugged in by a guy than a gal, but you never know! Also more likely to be inserted into personal devices rather than company machines.

You can make road apples targeted at specific individuals or groups. You could even send a road apple in the post, avoiding the requirement to gain physical access to the office in the first place. MicroSolved, a security testing company, used this technique in 2009, although it had some unexpected consequences. The company was engaged to perform a security test of a credit union. The tester mailed letters claiming to be from the National Credit Union Association (NCUA) with an accompanying CD of supposed training material. One member of the staff in the targeted credit union became suspicious and notified the NCUA, resulting in the association issuing a fraud

---

[1]www.darkreading.com/attacks-breaches/social-engineering-the-usb-way/d/d-id/1128081?

alert to all federally insured credit unions across the country! MicroSolved published a detailed explanation of the test on their blog at http://stateofsecurity.com/?p=766.

> **Note** Be careful of using real logos and signatures in your social engineering test without obtaining permission first. In an update to its fraud alert, the NCUA said of the social engineering test that it was an unauthorized and improper use of the NCUA logo and that credit unions are not authorized to use NCUA logos or signatures, even as part of a security assessment.

You can make your road apple look more legitimate (if this is relevant to your scenario) by printing your target organization's logo on it (with permission) or by using one of its own devices. If it's an internal device, it must be okay to plug it in, right? Many organizations give out free USB keys at conferences. Try to collect as many as you can every time you attend an industry gathering. Alternatively, you could also ask your client contact to provide you with some, in the interest of saving time.

You want to leave your road apple in a location where people will see it and be likely to pick it up. The best areas for this, in my experience, are in restrooms and around the photocopier. Anywhere people gather and there is a lot of foot traffic are good places, so car parks, reception areas, canteens, elevators, and so on, are also effective. I have had more success leaving road apples within the physical perimeter of the organization as opposed to outside the building or in shared areas such as reception if there is more than one organization based in the building I am targeting. This setup is also less risky; you don't want people who do not work for your target organization to pick up the device and plug it in.

Think about what you want your road apple to do when it is connected to the network. Malicious road apples typically run some kind of malware when plugged in, which is unlikely to be within the scope of your test. You are far more likely to have to design a more benign road apple. Maybe you want to run a program to phone home to your own computer to alert you if and when your road apple has been connected to a corporate system. Maybe there is a program on the USB key that directs the user to an internal security awareness website to explain to the recipient why plugging in unknown devices is dangerous. Alternatively, the road apple might simply have a file asking for it to be returned to a certain individual, maybe in the security department. In my experience, this option has not been particularly successful, as once people are asked to return the device to someone—especially if that someone works in the security department, they know they have done something wrong and just say nothing.

The key advantages to dropping road apples are

- You can get in and out of your target organization as quickly as possible. If you can get the road apple inside the building without physically entering the building yourself, all the better. If you do need to drop it off yourself, however, you just need enough time to drop off a selection of road apples and get out.
- You don't necessarily have to talk to anyone during your physical visit.

Of course, the danger of road apples is that they may be plugged into a network other than that of your target organization. For example, staff members may plug the device into their personal laptop when they get home. If the organization you are targeting is in a shared building, someone working for a different organization could potentially pick up the USB key, inadvertently falling for your social engineering test, but unfortunately they are outside the scope of the test.

The road apple exercise does not necessarily need to be performed as part of a wider social engineering test (for example, where you have to gain physical access to a location and leave road apples in various locations throughout the building). Instead, you can perform this test as a stand-alone activity to get an idea of whether people will connect unidentified devices to the network.

Walking Through Doors: Access Codes and Tailgating

Doors pose a great temptation for social engineers. I love doors that are marked "Private," "Staff Only," or "Do not enter." They challenge me, like a red rag to a bull! I want to get through that door and find out what is on the other side. Sometimes you can just open the door and walk through. Sometimes the door is locked. You may be able to lock pick, if it's within the scope of the test. Sometimes doors are (supposedly) protected by an access code. Other times, you can tailgate your way through a door.

Access Codes

Access codes don't do much to keep out social engineers effectively. Most door access codes are four-digits long. All staff members generally use the same code. Keypads tend to be placed at eye level, which is very convenient for shoulder surfing. Employees aren't usually particularly secretive about the code they enter, especially first thing in the morning! At peak times, shoulder surfing works well. Dress like an employee and look over someone's shoulder to learn the code.

You could also try wiping a clean cloth over the keypad and then ensure it is dry and free from fingerprints. The next time someone enters the code, his or her fingerprints will be visible. A light sprinkle of flour or chalk dust achieves the same effect. You will have the four digits. Next, you just have to get them in the right order—although some keypads accept the digits in any order. Sometimes you don't even have to work that hard to figure the numbers out. I have seen keypads, as in Figure 7-2, where the combination numbers have been so worn down that you can spot them straightaway.

You can take a leaf out of the book of ATM thieves and use a recording device to get the access code. You could simply install an official-looking camera near the keypad and write "diagnostic test" on it, or you could use a long-range device. Binoculars are old school but still useful!

Tailgating

In 2010, *The Atlantic* reported on a series of thefts from government offices in North Virginia, some of which contained classified materials[2]. According to a Department of Defense memo, the thieves appeared wearing laminated badges on lanyards, loitered

---

[2]www.theatlantic.com/politics/archive/2010/06/theft-ring-targets-government-offices/58121/

FIGURE 7-2 No prizes for guessing the four-digit code for this keypad! Can you see the smudge marks around 1, 2, 5 and 9?

near building entrances that required card key or fob access, and followed authorized employees in the door. Armed with only a homemade badge and by simply tailgating their way in, the thieves managed to steal credit cards and cash and had a Pentagon official call it a "major counter-intelligence problem."

Tailgating is a common security problem and is one of the most useful skills in physical social engineering. On some social engineering tests, you can tailgate right in through the front door. If you are really lucky, you won't even have to talk to anyone during your social engineering test—you can tailgate your way in, plant some road apples, and get out as quickly as possible. On other occasions, you will tailgate people through internal doors to get further into an organization. To date, I've never been challenged while tailgating. But I do it sensibly. I try to tailgate groups of people rather than individuals, and, where possible, I try not to follow the same people through more than one door.

Tailgating someone means you are following someone through a door without their consent. *Piggybacking*, on the other hand, implies that you have the consent of the person you are following to go through the entrance with them. Malicious individuals may bribe or blackmail employees into allowing them to piggyback into their office building. However, this distinction is not as relevant in an ethical social engineering test, unless you are following a social engineer on your team who already has access to the target location.

Tailgating works because of three factors. First, common courtesy dictates that you open the door for colleagues and visitors, or at least you don't close the door in their face when they are following you. Second, it works because of the security culture, or lack of security culture, within an organization. If people don't realize tailgating is a risk or are reluctant to challenge people they don't recognize, tailgaters will succeed. Third, tailgating works in places where there are no physical security controls in place to prevent it. It's easy to follow someone through a standard door accessed through swiping an access card—it's really rather difficult (although not impossible) to barge into a turnstile with them!

Most people are polite and will open the door for those who come in directly after them, especially if that person is carrying something. Here are some useful tips for tailgating:

- Carry something, for instance, coffee (two cups so you can't open the door yourself and need assistance to do so) or bags or boxes.
- Talk on your cell phone near a door.
- Follow groups of people. Get out of the elevators with them on random floors.
- Don't follow the same individual through multiple doors.
- Dress like everyone else.
- Wear an ID card backward.
- Find smokers and tailgate them back in. Make sure you are not wearing a jacket and roll up your sleeves, so it looks like you have come out of the office for a quick break.

You can even ask people to hold the door for you, as long as you are carrying something that makes it difficult to open the door yourself unassisted.

The best time to tailgate is when the entrance you are trying to get through is busy. For an office building, this is typically at the beginning or end of the day when people are arriving or leaving work and at lunch time and during coffee breaks. You should aim to collect this information when you do your physical reconnaissance. For example, if everyone goes to the local coffee shop at 11 A.M., arrive at the office at 11:10 A.M. carrying two cups of coffee in the local coffee shop–branded cups. And don't wear a coat, so it looks like you have just popped out for a break.

Tailgating is obviously going to be most successful when going through entrances with the most foot traffic. Doors that aren't used as frequently are more difficult to tailgate your way through, as you are more likely to have to follow individuals rather than groups and may have to wait around for someone to tailgate. Unless you can fabricate a valid reason for hanging around a doorway (you are speaking on your cell phone and appear to be a bit distracted), hanging around is going to look suspicious.

Tailgating is unlikely to work in small organizations where all the staff know each other. Neither is it likely to work in more security-aware organizations where physical controls are in place to protect against it, such as mantraps (a small entrance room to a secure area with an entry door on one side and an exit door on the other side where only one door can be unlocked at a time) or turnstiles that only allow access to one person at a time. However, most physical security barriers are in place at the perimeter of an organization and are less likely to be found once you get inside a building, so tailgating may still be possible.

Coffee/Smoking Break Analysis

If you want to talk to staff, either to blend in or to elicit information from them, useful places to target inside the building include any kind of break room, such as coffee/refreshment areas or smokers' areas. The latter are almost always located outside a building. Take off your jacket, roll up your shirt sleeves, and make your way over. Bum a cigarette off someone—or even better—if you can engineer it to offer a cigarette yourself, you can ingratiate yourself and play the reciprocity game.

People let down their guard when they are relaxing or on a break from work. The coffee pot is a very sociable area. Staff hanging around the coffee pot are often up for having a chat. Engaging in some small talk with these people can pay dividends. They may reveal project information, colleagues' names, or even introduce you to other colleagues—which makes it look like you have been validated or vetted by someone within the organization. Don't be afraid to ask people to introduce you to other staff members. Tell them you are looking for a certain individual and ask them to point you in the right direction—often they will introduce you directly. Say that you need to find the person in charge of granting access to a particular system. Basically, you're trying to build rapport as quickly as possible.

Building Rapport

Personal interaction and rapport building can, at times, be overrated when it comes to social engineering. You want as little direct interaction as possible with as few people as possible, so you are less likely to be challenged and less likely to be remembered after the event. However, social engineering tests typically do involve some level of person-to-person interaction (otherwise it wouldn't be *social* engineering), so the social engineer should have some level of *soft skills*. These include getting along with people, blending in, and generally being sociable. If you don't do this naturally or can't "turn it on," then adjust your role to suit your personality better. For example, you could play the role of someone working in IT as people often don't expect IT professionals to have soft skills. A good role to play if you want people to stay away from you is that of a pest control worker.

As soon as you have any kind of direct interaction with target individuals, however, whether it's in person, over the phone, via email, or on social networks, building rapport quickly becomes of the utmost importance. Some people have a knack for building rapport, but the good news is this skill can be learned and improved upon. There are hundreds, if not thousands, of books and training courses available on building rapport that you can consult. Here are some pointers on building a good rapport with someone:

- Smile so you appear friendly and confident.
- Look people in the eye, but don't creep them out or have a staring match. Do not eyeball them in an aggressive manner. Try to maintain eye contact in a nonthreatening manner and without looking like a psychopath. Experts say eye contact should be for around 60 percent to 70 percent of the time, so don't forget to blink!

> **Note**
>
> A study done by Quantified Impressions, a company specializing in communications-analytics, analyzed 3,000 people speaking to individuals and groups and found that people should make eye contact 60 to 70 percent of the time to create a sense of emotional connection. Interestingly, adults currently only make eye contact between 30 and 60 percent of the time in an average conversation. Multitasking plays a big factor in this—glancing at your phone or checking your email during a conversation has become more socially acceptable.

- Be aware of your body language as well as the body language of your target. Your body language should match what you are saying verbally. Many people suggest using mirroring, where you copy movements made by the person you are speaking to. For example, if the person leans forward, you lean forward; if she crosses her legs, you cross your legs. I find this really irritating unless it is completely natural, however.
- Ask open-ended questions. Be interested in what the person you are talking to is saying. Do your best to be sincere.
- Be aware of your tone of voice and the language you are using. When we are nervous, as is often the case in a social engineering test, we tend to talk faster, which can make us sound tense and sometimes even aggressive. Try using a lower tone, and speak more slowly and softly. Take a deep breath before you make your call!
- React to your conversation partner's comment in the spirit in which it was intended. If he makes a joke, laugh. If he sounds serious, match his tone.

The best way to build rapport is to find something you have in common with the person you are talking to and talk about it. Maybe you have a hobby in common; maybe you share colleagues or friends, went to the same school, or vacation in the same place. You need to find that common ground, and this area is where your background research can pay dividends. If you need to find common ground on the fly, you can try doing it through idle chit chat or simply by being observant. If the person you are talking to is wearing a T-shirt or a cap from a certain sports team, maybe you can pick up on that. If she is reading a book that you are familiar with, talk about that. I've used this latter example in several physical social engineering tests where I was looking to build rapport or blend in quickly. In one case, a guy in the elevator was reading Neil Strauss' pickup artist book, *The Game* (Harper Collins, 2005), which, incidentally, makes an interesting read for aspiring social engineers. I picked up on it and asked him if he liked it, saying that I had read it myself (therefore we had something in common). The conversation that ensued was quite entertaining. He was more than happy to introduce me to someone in his organization's IT department. And no, he didn't work in IT himself in spite of his chosen reading material!

Who was the last person you met who you really clicked with? Think about why you hit it off. What was it that made you feel comfortable and relaxed with that person? Is there anything that you can learn from that individual that you can apply in your social engineering exercises? Someone I really clicked with is Chris Hadnagy of the social-engineer.org podcast. The first time I met Chris face to face I felt like I could have talked to him for days. We talked for hours and the time just flew by. I was sorry when we had to part company and always look forward to catching up with him again. So why did I like Chris so much the very first time I met him? It's likely because of the following reasons:

- We have a lot of common ground. We are both professional, ethical social engineers and have war stories that the other person finds interesting. We face many of the same challenges and find the same things fascinating.
- As anyone who listens to the social-engineer.org podcast will almost certainly agree, Chris has got a good sense of humor. We laughed a lot.
- Chris seemed to have struck the right balance between asking questions and listening, offering information about himself and asking me questions about myself.
- Chris seemed to be sincere and open. He was friendly.

Of course, it is possible (maybe even likely) that Chris faked all of this and had me totally social engineered. Who knows? Ethical social engineers can become very paranoid!

Conversely, picture someone you've met who you didn't like or didn't feel comfortable with and explore why. These exercises can identify traits that would be useful to a social engineer. In a social engineering assignment, you can take a friendly approach or a more authoritative, unfriendly position. In my experience of social engineering, the friendly, softer approach seems to work better. However, it's good to be able to do both, playing good cop or bad cop as necessary.

How to Make Small Talk

Sometimes just starting to talk to people in your target organization can be incredibly difficult. Even if you are usually quite a social person and good at small talk, your mind can go blank when you are under pressure in a social engineering scenario. On one of the first social engineering tests I did, I gained access to the building I was targeting. I ran around the building for about 30 minutes and then realized I needed to exit the building. I jumped into the elevator with a group of people, knowing that I needed to befriend them so I could exit with them. I had to say something to start the conversation and make it look like I was part of the crowd. All I could think of to say was does this lift go up or down! I realized that I had to work on my "small talking under pressure" skills!

In my social engineering experience, good topics for small talk include

- *The weather*. This is certainly a great topic in the UK or Ireland and in certain parts of the US, where people are obsessed with the weather. "What a beautiful day!" "It's so cold today." Sneeze and then say, "I always get hay fever around this time of the year." You never know. Maybe the person you are talking to is a fellow hay-fever sufferer. Unusual weather in other countries can be a good conversation starter too.
- *Current affairs*. Know what's in the news around the time you execute your social engineering test. Are there any talking points you can discuss? Stay away from politics as it can polarize people, but most other things are fair game. Stay on top of popular culture—what are people watching on TV, what music are people listening to? Popular TV shows, newly released movies, or what's on top of the music charts can make great topics for small talk. "Oh my God—did you see the *Breaking Bad* finale?" "Have you seen the new Batman movie?"
- *Weekends or upcoming holidays*. "Great, it's Friday. Roll on the weekend." See if you get a response. Or on Mondays, "Did you have a good weekend?" If a public holiday is coming up, "I can't wait for the long weekend."
- *Complaining about pretty much anything innocuous*. For example, anything to do with your commute to work ("The traffic was terrible today") to not feeling well ("I am so tired. I hope I am not coming down with something"), how expensive things are ("The coffee in the café is so expensive"), and ideally to network problems ("Have you had network problems today? It's been really slow for me"). Showing frustration about some event, especially if it's an event that your target has likely encountered, can be a great conversation starter. "I can't believe the weather today—I forgot my umbrella and got soaked on the way into the office." Expressing the same thoughts as the person you are talking to can draw them closer to you.

> **Note** Topics for small talk can be culturally specific, so make sure the subject you are talking about is appropriate or common in the region where you are executing your test.

Try to introduce an element of humor, if appropriate, and if it comes naturally to you. Laughing together creates a bond and draws people together. Make a humorous comment rather than telling a joke. A friend of mine likes to use a one liner about the weather: "Everyone complains about the weather, but no one ever does anything about it!" It is good because it is reasonably funny but not hilarious. It is so completely innocuous and vanilla that it never polarizes the audience. You can laugh about yourself or the situation you are in, but never laugh at other people, especially not at the people you are talking to. However, if you are not gifted in the humor department, or your humor verges more toward the caustic or sarcastic, forget about it. Nobody wants to hear a bad joke or to feel uncomfortable.

Remember people's names and make an effort to use them occasionally in conversation. Using people's names makes them feel appreciated. As Dale Carnegie said in his 1936 book *How to Win Friends and Influence People*—"remember that a man's name is to him the sweetest and most important sound in any language." However, be careful of overusing names as it sounds unnatural and, to my mind, like a bad salesperson. Using someone's name should sound natural and friendly, not forced.

Offer a compliment (without being too sleazy!). Try to be genuine—if it isn't real, people know. Look for something real that you can compliment so it sounds sincere. It doesn't matter how small it is. Appropriate compliments could be

- What an impressive office!
- What a lovely photo!
- Nice shoes!

Tip Try practicing your small talk whenever you can. Taxi drivers and hairdressers are great for this.

The FORD or FAWN Technique for Making Small Talk

If you are stuck for small talk, keep in mind the FORD technique. FORD is an acronym that stands for:

- Family
- Occupation
- Recreation
- Dreams

Think of a couple of questions for each category and commit them to memory. When you are stuck for small talk, refer back to these questions and use them, where appropriate.

Apparently, there is a UK-specific acronym, which is FAWN:

- Football
- Ale
- Weather
- Nothing

A wonderful example of this occurs in an episode of the television series, *The IT Crowd*, where one of the really geeky characters makes a whole load of new friends by pretending to be a football fan. He signs up for a service called Bluffball, which gives users daily updates on key football phrases to use, along with a pronunciation guide. By making comments such as, "Did you see that ludicrous display last night?" the character convinces bonafide football fans that he knows what he is talking about and is accepted into their gang, with rather hilarious consequences.

What to Do If You Are Challenged

Not every social engineering test goes entirely smoothly. Sometimes you will be challenged. If you're performing a remote test with no real-time interaction (a phishing attack), it's no big deal. You simply discontinue the test. If the test is over the telephone, it's a little trickier, but you need to exit graciously, preferably without the person you are speaking to raising the alarm or alerting his or her colleagues. However, if you are onsite and someone challenges you, it can be a lot more difficult.

People are usually satisfied if you give some kind of passable excuse, so this is the moment your cover story, developed in the previous stage (and chapter), comes in handy. Use your cover story and bluff. Your excuse doesn't need to be overly complicated or even particularly good. Psychologist Ellen Langer performed a famous study in 1978 to see if her volunteers could convince people queuing to use a photocopier to let them cut the queue and go first.[3] They told the people in line that they had either 5 or 20 copies to make and made one of the following three requests.

- **Request only**   Excuse me, I have 5/20 pages. May I use the Xerox machine?
- **Placebo information**   Excuse me, I have 5/20 pages. May I use the Xerox machine, because I have to make copies?
- **Real information**   Excuse me, I have 5/20 pages. May I use the Xerox machine, because I'm in a rush?

In the first request, the volunteers simply ask to skip the queue. In the second request, they give an empty reason—of course, they have to make copies; that's what everyone using a photocopier is there to do. In the third request, they give a valid reason. The study found that it's not the reason that matters. It's the structure of the sentence; it's because you said the word "because." Even if the reason is empty, the point is you have given a reason and often that's good enough. Think about this when you are doing your social engineering test, and don't get too put out if you are challenged. Sometimes a pointless excuse can do the trick.

If you are challenged, you can try acting annoyed, depending on what role you are playing. If you are playing an authoritative role and someone questions you, acting annoyed would be in character. If you are playing the role of a cleaner and someone questions you, you could potentially act annoyed because the person is not letting you do your job. But if you are going in as a softer character, maybe a new employee or a temp, being annoyed might not be such a good option. Only act that way if it would be plausible for your character to act annoyed in that situation. Ensure that the rest of your character's traits stay in line with this. You can't act annoyed one minute and then be really friendly the next.

Sometimes your challenge may be helpful. I know some social engineers who like to use the "yes rule." If someone challenges them by saying something along the lines of, "You must be here to fix the telephones," they say, "Yes I am," and play along

---

[3]E. Langer, A. Blank, and B. Chanowitz, "The Mindlessness of Ostensibly Thoughtful Action: The Role of 'Placebic' Information in Interpersonal Interaction," *Journal of Personality and Social Psychology* 36,6 (1978): 635–642.

with it. The advantage of this challenge is that the challenger has given you a reason for being there; you just need to fall in line with it. The disadvantage is that the role that the challenger has assigned you is unlikely to be a scenario or role that you have prepared in advance—unless you have set up a reverse social engineer where you have, for example, taken down the phones in advance and your target organization has asked for your help in restoring them (this runs the risk of being a denial of service attack so is not one I have ever done). Another consideration if you are using the yes rule is if the person who is really supposed to come in to fix the telephones arrives, then it will look very suspicious.

Finally, if you are challenged and you cannot see a way out of it, show your Get Out of Jail Free card. That's what it is for, after all. Some social engineers try using a fake Get Out of Jail free card, although I prefer not to do this. This could create a Boy Who Cried Wolf–type situation where your challenger does not trust your real Get Out of Jail Free card. When challenged on one particular test, Alex Bayly, a social engineering friend of mine, congratulated the challenger on identifying the security test and then brazenly continued on. That takes droves of confidence! Learn to enjoy the challenges. The more practice you get in dealing with them, the better social engineer you will become.

What Else Can Go Wrong

Things can go wrong on a social engineering test so you need to be as prepared as possible. Hopefully you will have brainstormed some scenarios in which things go wrong, so you have some ideas on how to deal with them if they happen. You will have planned for some of these occasions when you tried to identify possible pitfalls with your scenarios, as discussed in Chapter 6. Apart from being challenged, there are other things that can go wrong during the test execution, for example:

- You may be recognized. On one test, while my target individual was fetching me a cup of coffee, an Irish guy came over to chat to me. He seemed to know me and even knew my name. I was close to panicking, thinking that the guy knew me and would give the game away! It turned out that my target individual had told his colleague that an Irish university graduate was coming in to see him, so the Irish colleague decided to be friendly and come down to say hello.
- If you are playing an authoritative role, this could rub your target individual the wrong way. If you are too demanding or unlikeable, your target could just decide not to help you because of your attitude.
- If you are starting out as a social engineer, you may give too much information away if you are challenged, making your back story appear unnatural and suspicious.
- You could potentially break any number of laws, in particular laws relating to trespass, breaking and entering, deception, impersonation, going equipped (i.e. carrying an object that could be used for burglary or theft, such as lockpicks), or even theft. Consult a lawyer to make sure everything you do is legal and has been appropriately authorized by your client.

Final Thoughts

Executing the social engineering test is the best part of the social engineering process. You have done a lot of preparation to get to this point. Enjoy it! Once you have performed one or two social engineering assignments, you will get used to the process. Each test is different and gets your adrenaline pumping on each occasion. It's a constant challenge, especially in the physical domain, but it's exciting and fun.

Don't get too carried away during the course of your social engineering test. Don't push your luck. You are not a malicious social engineer, and you are not seeking to upset anyone or interrupt business. Don't get overly excited with your success—keep the gloating and the cheering for after the event when you have successfully closed the social engineering test. You can even plan for this and hold a debrief with your team, or hang out with a friend who loves to hear about your exploits and is primed for a good storytelling session later that day or week. This aspect is an important part of the procedure to conquer the adrenaline rushes eventually. Just keep calm and carry on!

You have executed your social engineering test and hopefully identified some useful recommendations for your client. You just have one more hurdle until the assignment is complete: writing the report.

8 Writing the Social Engineering Report

(News) reporting is a cycle: No matter how much you work at sending a message, it's only successful if it's received.
—Jessica Savitch, news reporter

Putting together a social engineering report is by far and away the most tedious part of the whole social engineering process, but it has to be done. The report is the only tangible output from the social engineering process and, as such, is effectively what your client is paying for. It's especially hard to put together because it comes after you have had so much fun actually executing the test. Unfortunately, as a result, this chapter is probably the most boring one in this book, although I will try to make it as interesting as possible. On some very lucky occasions, your client may not want a report. By all means, skip ahead if you don't have to write one.

If a report is required, however, first check to see what format your client would like the results delivered in. Although it may be in the form of a traditional report, a debriefing or a presentation might suffice. For example, on occasion, instead of providing a traditional report, I've done physical walk-throughs, explaining how I social engineered an organization and pointing out the weaknesses I identified during the process, or I've simply held a debriefing directly after the test to talk through what I did and any weaknesses I identified. Most of the time, you will have to produce a report to explain what you have done and the outcome. A social engineering report is similar to a penetration testing report, in that you describe the methodology, point out weaknesses, and provide suggestions for how to fix them.

The intent of this chapter is not to tell you how to write a report. There are countless books and publications available on this topic by people far more qualified than me. Guidelines for penetration testing reports, such as those produced by the Penetration Testing Execution Standard group (http://pentest-standard.org) or the SANS Institute (www.sans.org) are equally applicable to social engineering reports. Rather, this chapter considers what should or should not be included in the final deliverable. Over the course of your social engineering test, you will collect vast amounts of information. You could probably write each report as a short 2-page document or a rather lengthier 200-page document, depending on how much detail you want to go into. This chapter will hopefully provide some advice on how to manage this and produce a report that is insightful and provides value to your client.

Continuous Feedback and Reporting

Ideally you should provide feedback to and communicate with your client throughout the entire social engineering process, from the planning stages to report delivery and follow up. More often than not, clients have never commissioned a social engineering test and may be a little nervous about doing it, so regular reporting and feedback can go a long way toward reassuring them that you are performing an ethical and worthwhile test in a professional manner.

As with penetration tests, you are usually required to report high-risk findings straightaway, so they can be fixed as soon as possible. Examples of such findings could include key physical security controls that don't appear to be working, such as a broken ID card reader or an important CCTV camera that is out of order. You may even come across high-risk issues during the information-gathering phase if you discover some particularly sensitive information such as internal configurations in the public domain. You should also report any unexpected or adverse events encountered during the test. For example, while you are executing the test, you might uncover some unsavory material or discover that an employee is leaking information to a competitor, both situations that my team and I have come across in our social engineering tests.

> **Tip** It's always easier to talk through the social engineering test results before committing them to paper or email.

As soon as possible after the test ends, I inform my client of the outcome, sometimes via a face-to-face meeting if I have obtained physical access to the building in which the organization is located; sometimes via a phone call; or, if there is no other way to contact my client, via email. Therefore, my client knows the outcome of the social engineering test and is aware of high-risk vulnerabilities in advance of receiving the report. As with penetration tests, if you have introduced any weaknesses or left anything behind, you should also report this as soon as possible. Here are some examples of issues you should report right away:

- You may have picked a lock on a drawer and were unable to lock it again. Arrange for the drawer to be locked again as soon as possible so unauthorized individuals cannot access the contents.
- You may have left calling cards inside a building as evidence that you got in. Give your client a list detailing precisely where you left these so they can be collected and used as evidence by your client.
- You may have planted a listening device or a wireless access point for the duration of the test. Ask your client to remove such devices as soon as possible so they cannot be abused by other parties.

As in penetration testing, some clients like to receive daily status reports throughout the execution phase of the social engineering test to update them on how testing has progressed and, in some cases, to discuss the plans for the next day. Check with your clients to see if they would like this. If it's your clients' first social engineering test, daily updates can keep them informed of your progress and reassure them that the test is proceeding as planned.

Recording Events During the Test

During the test, keep a log of exactly what activities you perform and at what time you perform them. If you can't write this down as you go along, write it up as soon as possible after the test, doing a brain dump of everything you can remember in as much detail as possible. Of course, you may be able to use recording devices (hidden cameras, audio recorders, and so on) during the test, depending on the legal situation and whether your client has authorized it. Making notes, taking photos, and even leaving yourself a voicemail on your cell phone is ideal, as mentioned in the previous chapter, as it timestamps each recorded entry, making it easier to recall what happened and when.

How Much Time Should You Allow for Report Writing?

Social engineering reports take a great deal of time and effort to prepare, even more so than penetration testing reports as there are very few overlaps between different organizations and few, if any, "standard" findings. Unlike penetration testing reports, there is also little "boilerplate" material that you can use from one report to the next, again adding to the work required to write the report. The only standard text you may wish to include are a few sentences on what social engineering is, an explanation of your risk ratings, and a comment or potentially a finding on the general lack of security awareness that affects nearly all organizations.

Unfortunately, the social engineering test is pointless, regardless of how well it has been carried out, unless you can give your findings to your client either verbally or, more commonly, via a written report. However, we often don't allow enough time to write a decent report, whether it's because we have used up all our time and budget on the test preparation and execution or because the client hasn't given us enough time to write a thorough one.

The amount of time you allow for report writing will probably be dictated by how much budget you have left over after the social engineering test. You may have to take a hit on the financials here so you can prepare a decent report. Based on my own experience, I suggest that for every five days spent on each stage of the process—from planning through execution—you need the best part of two days to prepare a worthwhile report. Also take into account that social engineering reports may require a lot of quality assurance time, as each report is so different from the next.

Ensure that you allow enough time to gather and analyze all the information you have, prepare a draft version of the report, review it, and rewrite it where necessary before issuing it to your client. Your client may wish to provide feedback on the report, and, in some cases, you may have to incorporate the feedback into the report. If you're creating an audit report, a client response is typically included along with agreed-on actions and a timeline. This will also affect your budget and how much time you have allowed for the report-writing process.

Planning the Report

The first phase of the report-writing process involves gathering all the necessary information (such as logs, evidence, information from the research phase), analyzing the results, deciding what information needs to be conveyed within the report, and planning what sections to include. Before you start writing, consider what the report should accomplish. What was the purpose of the test? Was the test done to provide a justification for increasing the security budget, to find specific vulnerabilities, to test adherence to the client's security policy? Should your report persuade or inform your readers? What are you persuading your readers of—to take certain actions or increase their security budget, perhaps? If your report is intended to inform, then who is your audience and what are you telling them? Maybe the report has been designed to identify certain weaknesses or show that staff are not sufficiently security aware. Whatever your objective is in writing the report, keep it in mind throughout the writing process.

Consider what kind of analysis your report will provide. For example, the report may compare the social engineering test results against current security policies your client has and may suggest improvements to the policy or highlight where the policy has not been adhered to. Maybe you want to provide an analysis of the current state of the assessed security controls and awareness levels within your target organization. Sometimes clients also like effective security controls to be identified. If this is the case, review your test notes for evidence that you can present in a positive manner.

You may wish to present your results in the context of other social engineering assessments you have performed. Was your client above or below average in terms of the security controls you observed during your test as compared to other similar-sized organizations in the same industry? Compare like with like. There is not much point in comparing the results for a small office that has a limited security budget to the results for a government organization that has the latest security controls. What controls would you recommend that your client implement based on your experience of other similar organizations?

Bear in mind the realistic threat the organization is facing and its available budget. I once waltzed into a financial organization at the height of the recession. I walked in through the garage door and forced open the glass door to the server room (with a little help as I wasn't strong enough to do it on my own); I accessed unlocked PCs, opened drawers, connected to the network, and collected ID cards. In short, the organization had dozens of failings but unfortunately a very limited budget with which to fix them. There was no point in pushing very expensive security controls as it just could not afford them. Therefore, as a joint exercise with the client, we created a road map that prioritized recommendations that would fix the most critical vulnerabilities followed by recommendations that were inexpensive or free to implement, such as requesting that staff lock their PCs when unattended. As a longer term plan, we recommended fixing medium- or low-risk issues.

Establish Who Your Target Readers Are

Identify your target readers and keep them in mind throughout the report-writing process. Your target audience will almost always be a combination of technical and nontechnical readers, so the report needs to cater to both. It is likely that different readers will focus on different sections of the report. For example, senior management will probably read the executive summary, whereas the technical and facilities or physical security staff will read the technical findings and recommendations. For each section, consider the target audience and take into account the audience's background, experience, and potential limitations. The report should convey information in an understandable manner.

Specific Client Requests

Before you begin writing, find out if your client has any particular requests with regards to the report. For example, a client may have a particular report format that she would like you to use. This is often the case if the test has been commissioned by an Internal Audit department. Your client may have certain requests in terms of sanitizing particularly sensitive data. For example, you may need to obfuscate any user credentials you have found. On a similar note, your client may require a certain level of classification, depending on the sensitivity of the information presented in the report. The organization may also have its own defined risk categories that it would like you to utilize in order to rate each identified vulnerability. Checking for specific requirements in advance of writing the report can save a lot of unnecessary rewriting later in the process.

Risk Ratings for Social Engineering Findings

Most security reports contain some kind of risk rating for each vulnerability identified. The risk rating scale is generally based on a combination of the likelihood of the vulnerability being exploited combined with the impact it would have on the organization if it were to be exploited. Findings in social engineering reports are generally classified as high, medium, or low risk, but can use any risk classification that you or your client consider appropriate. The National Institute of Standards and Technology (NIST, www.nist.gov) and the Open Web Application Security Project (OWASP, www.owasp.org) have great risk rating methodologies on their websites, including NIST's Common Misuse Scoring System (CMSS), a metric system for software feature misuse vulnerabilities that takes into account social engineering. Whatever risk-rating scale you use, ensure that you define it within your report. These ratings usually go in a table before the detailed findings and recommendations section.

Assigning a risk rating can be a little tricky for social engineering findings. For example, how would you rate the risk level of an employee lending you his ID card, supposedly so you can slip out to the bathroom? You could potentially clone his card. Once you have his card, you could also access many areas within the building, including critical areas such as the server room or the HR department, but this depends on what kind of access the employee in question has. On the other hand, once you are inside the building, you have probably already bypassed numerous controls that should have kept you out in the first place. If this is the case, consider if a real attacker would do this and risk drawing attention to herself. It is a brazen move for someone who does not want to be identified. So is it a real risk at all and how would you measure it on your risk scale?

NIST's Common Misuse Scoring System (CMSS)

NIST proposed the Common Misuse Scoring System (CMSS) for rating software feature misuse vulnerabilities in 2012. It follows from its well-known Common Vulnerability Scoring System (CVSS) for rating software flaw vulnerabilities, and its Common Configuration Scoring System (CCSS) for rating software security configuration issue vulnerabilities and can be used to complement both of these systems.

NIST defines a software feature misuse vulnerability as a vulnerability in which the feature also provides an avenue to compromise the security of the system...caused by the software designer making trust assumptions that permit the software to provide beneficial features, while also introducing the possibility of someone violating the trust assumptions to compromise security[1].

Software feature misuse vulnerabilities may be exploited by social engineers who violate the trust assumptions in place. Software misuse vulnerability examples include

- Users following a link to a spoofed website
- Malicious file transfer via instant messaging software

Like its other two vulnerability measurement and scoring systems, CMSS assigns vulnerability scores on a scale of 0 (lowest severity) to 10 (highest severity). Scores are calculated according to three metrics: base, temporal, and environmental. Base metrics describe the characteristics of the vulnerability in terms of exploitability and impact. Temporal metrics describe the characteristics that may change over time but remain constant across user environments, such as the frequency of attacks (attacks for which exploit code is publicly available will be more prevalent than attacks for which there is no publicly available exploit code, for example). Finally, environmental metrics are used to customize the base and temporal scores according to the environment in which the vulnerability is present.

For more information on NIST's proposed CMSS, please refer to the NIST Interagency Report 7864 at http://csrc.nist.gov/publications/nistir/ir7864/nistir-7864.pdf.

---

[1]http://csrc.nist.gov/publications/nistir/ir7864/nistir-7864.pdf

Standard Report Contents

Consider what to include in the report. What sections should it have? Typically, a report contains some or all of the following sections:

- Executive summary
- Technical details
  - Methodology used
  - Timeline
  - Findings
  - Recommendations
- Appendixes

Each section should be as self-contained as possible, so your target readers can separate out your report and only read the sections that are relevant to them.

Executive Summary

The executive summary is a condensed version of the rest of the report, designed to give readers a preview of its contents. From a business point of view, the executive summary is the most important part of the report because it is typically read by senior management and will often be the only part of the report that these stakeholders will read. Such readers are likely to be people who make budgetary or policy decisions and need information quickly and efficiently. Therefore, the executive summary should be a brief summary of the document, explained in a clear and concise manner, and free from technical terms. In some cases, you may have to explain briefly what "social engineering" is, as it is not a term that tends to be widely known by nontechnical management.

Throughout your report, and in the executive summary in particular, everything should be measured and aligned to business impact. A reader of the executive summary should know at a glance the outcome of your social engineering test and what actions are required as a result.

The executive summary should contain the following elements:

- Scope and objectives
- Summary of methodology
- Overview of key findings and recommendations

The scope and objectives should reflect those that have previously been agreed on and hopefully documented in your contract or statement of work. Explain the background of the test and what has driven the requirement to commission a security test, if known. Was your test particularly timely? Was it commissioned as a result of a social engineering breach at your client's or at a similar organization, which has put social engineering on the client's agenda? Remind the readers of the scope and objectives you previously agreed on.

This section is where you tell readers who weren't involved in planning the test (which will probably include senior management) what the test was about. Perhaps the objective of the test was to attempt to gain physical access to a particular office location or to attempt to elicit certain information over the phone or via email. The test may have been driven by requirements to determine the level of security awareness among staff or adherence to the security policy or to identify security weaknesses, for example. If there was anything that was explicitly out of scope (which you would have expected to be in scope), mention that here too. For example, maybe you weren't allowed to target a certain area within the building, or perhaps you weren't allowed to target a certain individual or group of people.

After the scope and objectives comes a short summary of the methodology you followed to perform the test, which focuses on the scenario used. For example, the methodology may simply be something along the lines of "the methodology involved phoning the helpdesk and attempting to convince a helpdesk worker to reset a password by using only publicly available information." Then you explain the outcome. Were you successful in resetting a password? If not, why not? Clients often like to have one or two effective controls highlighted.

Finally, you provide an overview of your key findings and recommendations. This should be just a brief preview of your social engineering results and the potential business impact associated with those results. If you were able to draw any statistics out of your results, you can mention them here. If 30 percent of your calls to the helpdesk resulted in a password reset, stating this can have great impact in the executive summary. If there are any more strategic recommendations or if the organization has requested some kind of road map for improving its overall security posture, this is the place to introduce them.

Although the executive summary is the first part of the report, I suggest writing it last as it is a summary of the main body of the document and will allow you to emphasize key findings and recommendations. The executive summary is usually proportional in length to the body of the report, typically 5 to 10 percent of the length of the rest of the report. Your aim in the executive summary is to condense the maximum amount of relevant information into the minimum amount of text.

Technical Details

The technical body of the report is where you present the details of your work, what you did (and when), and findings you have identified, along with proposed recommendations on how to improve your client's security posture. This section is the narrative body of the report and is likely to be read by more technical staff and physical security or facilities staff. I like to think of this part of the report as telling the story of what happened, followed by detailing specific weaknesses identified, and then giving recommendations for improvement. The technical body of the report contains three elements:

- Methodology used and timeline
- Detailed findings
- Recommendations

Methodology Used and Timeline

This section is the "what happened" part. Describe the methodology you used to perform the test and how and when it played out. Providing a timeline will give this section a narrative feel, with a step-by-step explanation of what happened and when. "We made a series of phone calls between 2 P.M. and 3 P.M. on 5th July where we purported to be employees of your organization requiring access to a particular helpdesk ticket." The social engineering test methodology described in your report should be repeatable. In other words, an independent party should be able to pick up your report and execute the test again following the same methodology.

> **Tip**   If a year down the line, your client requests a retest, would you or your colleagues be able to reproduce your test methodology using only the information provided in the report?

Detailed Findings

This section contains detailed information about each vulnerability identified along with recommendations on how to fix or improve them. Each finding should describe the vulnerability you identified, how you were able to exploit this during your social engineering test, and what the impact was. Remember to tie your findings back to

Including Evidence

Sometimes the social engineering results can be a hard pill to swallow for clients and very occasionally you may encounter a client who challenges the report. It is useful to have evidence of what you found. Evidence may include

- Photos
- Screenshots
- Voice recordings
- Video recordings

Such evidence also gives the report more impact. Evidence can be provided in the detailed findings section or the appendices.

On some occasions, you may wish to withhold or redact evidence. For example, if you discover passwords during the course of your test, discuss with your client if and how passwords should be presented within the report. Also remember that an employee's personal information doesn't belong in the report—and this includes information from his or her social networking pages. You can refer to information you have found about employees and even say where you found it, but if it's personal information, don't include it. I have found passports, driving licenses, utility bills, degree certificates, personal photos, office party photos (often the worst of the lot!), and more, during my social engineering career, not to mention pages and pages worth of social networking information. Although I listed this information in my reports, I didn't include copies of it.

the business; every vulnerability you describe needs to be measured against the engagement goals and the business impact to your client.

Present each finding in the simplest way possible, while also providing enough information so that a third party could, in theory, be able to retest it. The finding might be that a staff member handed his ID card to an unknown individual. Explain how you achieved this: "We asked a staff member to borrow his card so we could use the bathroom." If you have evidence of the vulnerability identified, then use it. In this example, maybe you took a photo of the ID card so you can include the photo in the report.

Recommendations

The recommendations section is the most valuable part of the report because the whole purpose of the report is to present a problem and provide suggestions about how to fix it. The recommendations you provide give you the opportunity to persuade your client to do something about the vulnerabilities you have identified and to improve the organization's security posture. Your recommendations must be appropriate for your client—in other words, it is important that they be achievable and results oriented and preferably suited to your client's budget. For example, I would

Naming Individuals

As a policy, I don't identify specific individuals in my reports, and I let the client know this in advance of the test. The point of the social engineering test is not to single out or embarrass individual employees. I usually try to blame the problem on poor processes and procedures or a lack of security awareness. However, I make a couple of exceptions to this rule, namely people who have failed the test before and senior people within the organization. If the same person repeatedly falls for a social engineering test and if she has been informed about previous tests and/or received security-awareness training that covers social engineering, she might be a weak link within the organization and a stronger action needs to be taken. This might include attending a training course, enforcing some kind of penalty, or, in extreme situations (such as a security guard repeatedly missing multiple social engineering attempts), managing them out of the company. I also find it hard to resist identifying individuals if they are very senior people within the organization.

If my clients insist on asking for a list of employees who fell victim to the social engineering test I try to understand their reasoning for this. If it is for the purposes of sending the named individuals on a security-awareness course, I will gladly hand over their names. If it's to reprimand certain employees or, worse still, to fire them, I try to help my clients understand the pros and cons of doing so, especially from an ethical or contractual point of view. To the best of my knowledge, none of my clients have let any of their staff go as a result of my social engineering tests.

never recommend that a security guard be fired from his position because he failed to spot the social engineering test. This is not results oriented as a new security guard may not spot the social engineering test either, and besides, the original security guard will hopefully be far more aware of social engineering threats once he finds out what has happened. Instead, I would recommend that security guards receive training in identifying and managing social engineering attacks. Of course, if the security guard repeatedly fails to spot the social engineering test, that is a different issue altogether.

There are one or two standard recommendations that generally apply across the board for social engineering tests. I have raised them in nearly every social engineering report I have ever written. These are

- Ensuring that staff are aware of the threat of social engineering, through security awareness programs and training.
- Ensuring that there is an escalation policy that describes the steps staff should take if they suspect they are being targeted by a social engineer.

More recommendations for defending against social engineering attacks are in Chapter 10.

Example Report

Here is a much abbreviated example of the technical body of a report where the objective was to gain physical access to a particular building.

Methodology Used and Timeline:

During our information-gathering phase, we discovered that Ben Smith, a marketing manager at XYZ Ltd, was on holiday for two weeks. At approximately 8.30 A.M. on 15th October, we arrived at reception claiming to be from ABC Ltd and said we had a meeting with Ben Smith, knowing he was out of the office. The receptionist gave us a visitor's pass and directed us up to the second floor, where Ben's desk was located.

Detailed Findings:

- We arrived in the office and claimed to have a meeting scheduled with a staff member. The receptionist issued a visitor's pass and sent us straight to the second floor without verifying that we were expected.
- Visitors are permitted inside the building without being escorted. We were directed through to the office but were not escorted at any point.

Recommendations:

Ensure that there are documented visitor control procedures. These procedures should mandate that visitors are collected from reception by a staff member, and that visitors must be escorted at all times. Staff should be made aware of these guidelines.

Appendixes

Sometimes social engineering reports can be overly detailed and far too long. If your report is edging toward this, consider putting parts of it in the appendixes. The appendixes can contain material that is too detailed to include in the technical body of the report, such as raw data. This supporting information is not essential to understanding the results of the test, but it supports your analysis. It may be useful for someone trying to gain a better understanding of the process followed and the results you obtained.

Often part of the data set included in the appendixes will be presented in the technical body of the report with the full data set included in the appendix. In the example described earlier, where we obtained physical access to a particular office, we noticed many seemingly sensitive documents lying on the desks. Our findings documented this and provided a couple of examples. It also made reference to the appendix that contained further photos of the types of documents we observed. Note that when you are taking photos during the social engineering test, you are probably using your cell phone or some kind of secretive recording device rather than a decent camera. Added to this, you are under time pressure and do not want to arouse suspicion, so you take the photo as quickly and as discreetly as possible. As a result, not all of the photos are necessarily of the quality you would hope for. Therefore, they don't all make it into the report.

Here is some other information that you might include in the report appendixes:

- Call transcripts
- Logs
- Information found during the information-gathering phase
- Figures/tables/charts/graphs
- Statistics
- Copies of phishing emails and responses
- Maps of buildings
- A glossary of technical terms
- Any kind of raw data

There is no limit to what can be included in the appendixes as long as it is relevant and referenced in the body of the report.

The Quality Assurance Process

Once you have prepared your report, ask a colleague to evaluate it according to whatever quality assurance (QA) processes you have in place within your organization. Have someone review your report who was not involved in the test and is, therefore, reading it from a completely blind perspective. See if they understand the test methodology from an outsider's point of view and agree with your findings. The QA process shouldn't take too long. It depends on the length of the report. As well as picking up on content and format issues and spelling or grammatical mistakes, the report reviewer may be able to spot issues that you missed. Ask the reviewer to also check for the following:

- Does the test meet the objectives agreed on with the client?
- Does the executive summary reflect the report's contents?
- Does the methodology accurately describe the test?
- Are all findings documented and is evidence provided?
- Are the proposed recommendations appropriate?
- Are assigned risk ratings reasonable?

 Potential customers sometimes ask for a sample report when they are selecting social engineering testers. Providing a meaningful social engineering report that has been appropriately sanitized is difficult without identifying the original target organization. If you do have to provide one, make sure the potential client can't identify the target.

Distributing the Report

It is important to control the distribution of the report to ensure that the right people within your client's organization receive it. In advance, consult with your client about who should receive the report, how it should be classified and the mechanism through which the report will be delivered. In my organization, we only issue the report to the person(s) who commissioned the test to ensure that it goes to the correct individual. It is common practice to put a distribution list on the front of the report, usually along with version control and classification information.

In terms of delivering the report, will you need to send your client both a hard copy and a soft (electronic) copy of the report? Decide how these will be distributed. Ideally, electronic copies would be distributed using public key cryptography but this is not always possible. Hard copies can be delivered in person or via a trustworthy and reliable courier. Come to an agreement in advance with your client about how the report should be delivered, reminding the client of any security implications if necessary.

Tip Remember that you are responsible for keeping the contents of the report confidential and for securely storing the report, your logs, and any information gathered along the way. Should this information fall into the wrong hands, it could potentially be used to compromise the target organization.

Final Thoughts

The report-writing process can be arduous. You have to plan the report, collect and analyze information, write a first draft, and have it reviewed before issuing it to your client. Even then, your client may want you to make changes or incorporate feedback into the report. It is a long process, and it is easy to put it off after the thrill of the actual test. From experience, I have learned to get the report out of the way as soon as possible after the test, while I can still remember what happened.

The past few chapters have presented a methodology that you can use to perform an ethical social engineering test. In the next chapter, I will suggest some tools that you can use throughout the various phases of the test.

9

Tools of the Trade

It's best to have your tools with you. If you don't you're apt to find something you didn't expect and get discouraged.
—Stephen King, *On Writing: A Memoir of the Craft*

You can use various tools throughout the social engineering test, from the planning to the reporting phase. This chapter describes the most common software and hardware tools that my team and I have used in our social engineering tests for research and reconnaissance, scenario creation, and test execution. These tools change all the time; new software may be released or a different hardware tool may be appropriate for your chosen test scenario.

You'll find certain tools are more relevant for different phases of the test. Tools can be particularly handy during the research and reconnaissance phase. There are mountains of information available about most organizations. It would take weeks if not years to gather and sort through it manually. Automated information-gathering tools can speed up this process, giving you access to potentially useful information about your target organization or individual at the click of a mouse. In this chapter, we'll look at the following tools for research and reconnaissance:

- Maltego
- Cree.py
- Spokeo
- The Wayback Machine
- Metadata collectors

For the scenario creation phase, you can use several tools, most often for creating props or costumes that add credibility to your scenario. In this chapter, we'll look at the typical contents of the social engineer's "fancy dress box" and see what other kinds of tools you can use to create realistic props.

Finally, for the test execution phase, you may require a suite of tools, depending on what kind of test you are executing. For a telephone test, you may need to spoof your caller ID, for example. On phishing tests, a phishing program can help you to run an effective phishing campaign by automating elements of the process. You can choose from a plethora of tools if your social engineering test involves a physical, or onsite, element, from recording devices to lock picks to RFID cloning kits. In this chapter, we'll examine the following test execution tools:

- Recording devices
- Bugging devices
- Keystroke loggers
- Storage devices
- Cell phones
- Phone tools and caller ID spoofing tools
- The Social-Engineer Toolkit

Whichever tools you choose to use, remember that you must use them responsibly and as part of an authorized test.

Research and Reconnaissance Tools

The proliferation of social networking and the sheer volumes of information that individuals publish online about themselves and others has led to the rise of automated information-gathering tools (alternatively called *data aggregator* tools) that can save you hours of research. Gathering information manually can be tedious and time consuming. Information-gathering tools make the social engineer's work easier by harvesting information from social networks and other online resources in a matter of seconds. In this section, I present a selection of the most commonly used information-gathering tools in social engineering.

Be aware that information-gathering tools also have limitations. It is quite easy to suffer from information overload. Filtering through the collected data to obtain useful information can also be quite time consuming, although tools such as Maltego allow you to write your own transforms (more on this in the next section) to provide meaningful data more rapidly. Furthermore, gathered information may contain false positives; information is only as good as its source. For example, if your target is called "John Smith," you will probably receive hundreds, if not thousands, of pages of information, not all of which will be relevant to your target.

If you are going to practice using any of these information-gathering tools, please pick an organization that you are authorized to research. Although the tools described here all collect publicly available information, running automated tools on an organization's domain may be construed as a hostile activity. Get permission first!

Maltego

Maltego is one of the most popular tools used by ethical social engineers. It is quite possibly the best and most comprehensive passive reconnaissance tool currently available. Maltego uses open source intelligence (OSINT) to determine the relationships and real-world links between various entities and then presents the results in a layout that makes spotting patterns easy. The various entities that Maltego can research include

- Individuals and groups
- Companies and organizations

- Websites
- Internet infrastructure including domains, DNS names, netblocks, and IP addresses
- Phrases
- Affiliations
- Documents and files

In today's world, we suffer from information overload. On a social engineering test, you can easily become overwhelmed with information about your target and finding links between seemingly random and unrelated data can be difficult. Maltego will come to your rescue! Maltego outputs links between entities using an accessible graphical representation (shown here), making it easier for us mere humans to identify patterns and previously unknown relationships quickly, even when these links are more obscure or three or four degrees removed.

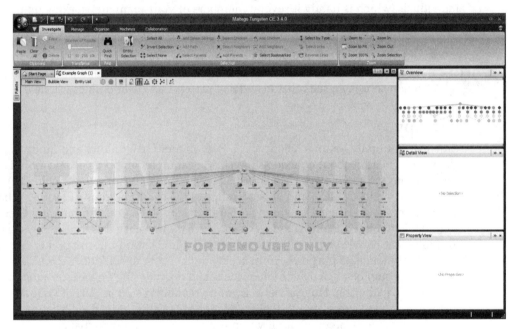

Maltego discovers these links between various entities via *transforms*. Transforms are pieces of code that take one type of information to another. Think of a transform as the question you might ask about two entities, for example, "How is John Smith related to ABC Corporation?" or "What email addresses are associated with this particular domain?" or "What other domains are associated with McGraw-Hill Education?" Maltego comes with a library of standard transforms, including a transform for returning the IP address for a specified domain, and finding the email address or social networking accounts associated with a named individual. New transforms are added frequently. In addition, you can write your own transforms to model relationships between almost anything.

Maltego runs on Windows, Mac, and Linux and is included in Kali Linux. There is a free community edition and a more powerful commercial version. The community edition has a number of limitations, including a maximum of 12 results per transform and the API key expires every couple of days. If you want to upgrade to the professional version, the cost is $760 for the first year and $320 per year thereafter, as of the time of publication.

Many good tutorials are available online to teach you how to use Maltego, particularly on Paterva's YouTube channel at www.youtube.com/user/PatervaMaltego. In brief, you start by opening a new graph and selecting the type of entity you would like to research (domains, locations, usernames, and so on). Right-click your new entity, and select the transform you want to run. You can drill down further, running additional transforms depending on the type of information you want to discover for each entity returned. Maltego can be used as a collaborative tool among multiple individuals, which is handy if several members of your team are working on the same social engineering job.

Tip   Unless you have the results slider set quite low, try to resist selecting the option to run all transforms. Doing so will use up a lot of your system's resources and can return so many results that identifying patterns and relationships will be difficult.

Cree.py

Cree.py, written by Ioannis Kakavas, is a Python tool for Windows and Linux that gleans information about a person's physical location by grabbing geolocation data from various social networking platforms (at the time of writing this included Twitter, Foursquare, and Gowalla[1]) and image hosting services (at the time of writing, Flickr, Twitpic, img.ly, and TwitrPix, among others). Kakavas's reasons for building Cree.py were twofold. First, he aimed to raise awareness of how easy it is for the physical locations that people share online to be abused. Geolocation information is useful for all kinds of malicious purposes, from social engineering to stalking. Second, Kakavas thought it would be a good addition to the social engineering toolbox, as a tool for information gathering. He was right. Even if you don't use it as part of your social engineering tests, it is a superb tool for awareness raising. As the tool's name suggests, people can get very creeped out if you present them with a map that shows their movements!

To use Cree.py, you simply provide a Twitter or Flickr username. Cree.py uses these websites' APIs to identify photos and tweets published by that username and analyzes them for geolocation data. The tool then plots all the locations identified on a map, as shown here, along with their associated timestamps. Seemingly random bits of information can be pieced together, for example, locations that show clusters are likely to be home addresses, places of work, or other areas the target frequently visits. Depending on the amount of geolocation data discovered, Cree.py can potentially

---

[1]For Foursquare and Gowalla, Cree.py only aggregates geolocation data from posted check-ins.

build a minute-by-minute timeline of a person's movements. Cree.py can make it easy to map out a person's routines: "John arrives at the office at 8:55 A.M. every day and leaves for the gym at 6 P.M. He arrives home at 7:30 P.M." It is, therefore, a great tool for helping social engineers (and unfortunately stalkers) track the physical location of their targets and it certainly lives up to its name. For example, if you find out using Cree.py or some other source that your target has a favorite lunchtime spot that he frequents several times a week, you could send him a discount voucher offering the next meal courtesy of the restaurant or for 50 percent off. All he has to do is download the voucher…

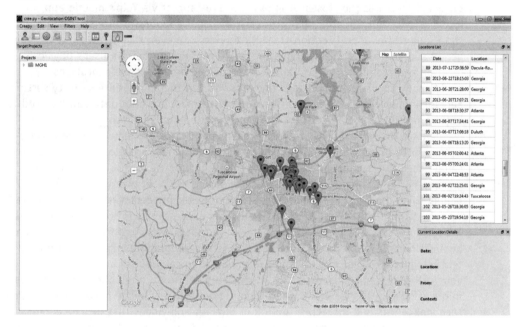

Cree.py is available at http://ilektrojohn.github.com/creepy/ and is also included in Kali Linux. Note that Twitter users can restrict who sees their location broadcasts. This means tools like Cree.py will not be able to aggregate geolocation data for these users.

Spokeo

Spokeo (www.spokeo.com) is an online information broker website that aggregates personal information from phone books, social networks, marketing surveys, real estate listings, business websites, and other public sources. The aggregated data may include photos, family trees, current address, social profiles, estimated income, and a lot more. Results are organized by location within the US (weak US privacy laws means that Spokeo works best for researching US citizens). Officially, Spokeo's raison d'être is, on a personal level, to enable friends and family to reunite; on a business

The Dangers of Geolocation Information

An increasing number of social networks and applications are using location-based information to figure out where their users are. This could be GPS information, location information that you provide yourself (maybe via a location-based check-in, for example), or information that is triangulated between two different points. Location-based services (LBS) can be really helpful. The rise of smartphones has really helped these services to take off. Being able to find what you're looking for nearby, such as the closest ATM or a good restaurant via Yelp's mobile app, for example, is useful. It can be hard to resist discount coupons or offers for nearby shops and restaurants. Location-tracking services can even save lives. However, the geolocation data that these services generate can also pinpoint a user's physical location and profile his or her habits. Many people broadcast their locations unwittingly, maybe by publishing check-ins without the appropriate security settings and sometimes even just through sharing photos. Geolocation data can be used to build a profile about a user's location, personal habits, and activities.

There are many other ways to gather geolocation data. The payments we make by card or by phone and the GPS devices we use all generate geolocation data that can be used to track our whereabouts. People regularly use location-based check-in services on Foursquare, Facebook, and other social media, or post geolocated tweets. Simply using the Web may generate geolocation data; the geolocation API is enabled, by default, in many browsers, including Firefox and Internet Explorer. Applications increasingly access this geolocation data. In fact, it is estimated that a third of the applications on Apple's App Store access a user's geographic location. Cellphone technology makes wide use of geolocation data. You can publish a photo taken on your cell phone virtually instantly. More often than not, that photo will include information such as where and when the photo was taken. Image hosting sites such as Facebook, Flickr, and Instagram are full of pictures and videos that include geolocation data. Just by sharing a photo online, you may be telling people where you are. A member of the hacking group CabinCr3w posted a provocative photo of his girlfriend holding a written taunt to the FBI ("PwNd by w0rmer & CabinCr3w <3 u BiTch's !"). The agency used the EXIF-encoded GPS coordinates in the image, which identified his girlfriend's house. The availability of this data brings with it a host of risks, from burglary to stalking and, of course, social engineering.

Even where data is supposedly anonymized, it can be dangerous. It turns out that location data is highly unique to each user. A study by scientists at MIT[2] examined 15 months' worth of anonymized cellphone records for 1.5 million individuals. They found that for 95 percent of people only four locations and times were sufficient to identify a particular user.

[2]Yves-Alexandre de Montjoye, Cesar A. Hidalgo, et. al, "Unique in the Crowd: The Privacy Bounds of Human Mobility," Scientific Reports 3 (2013).

The Phone Losers of America uses geolocation data for some of their pranks. In what they call "Foursquare stalking," they look up unsuspecting targets who have checked in to various locations on Foursquare. Then they call the locations and ask to speak to that individual. For example, if they see that someone has checked into a Starbucks café, they might call the café and have the store manager page the target. Some calls are downright funny—like the caller who tries to convince his target that the caller is a future version of the target, calling the target from the future, and there are some that are just scary or humiliating. For example, a Blockbuster customer entered a store only to receive a call supposedly from the Corporate Office explaining that she was no longer welcome there and asking her to leave. Of course, geolocation data can be used much more aggressively by malicious individuals—for cyberstalking, burglary, and more. The Waledac botnet in 2009 lured victims to a fake Reuters website with a news story about a terrorist attack. The news story was customized based on the victim's geolocation data to make it appear as though the attack was happening locally.

level, to find contact information for new leads and keep in touch with current or past customers; and on a nonprofit level, to expand the network of support. The site has plenty of success stories in each of these categories. It also has plenty of success stories in the social engineering space.

Many people have heard of Spokeo because of the various emails and Internet posts making scary claims about the kind of information that Spokeo reveals. Emails along the lines of "FYI EVERYONE – There's a site called spokeo.com and it's an online phone book that has a picture of your house..." have been circulated since Spokeo started. In fact, Spokeo results come with a warning that "this information is potentially shocking." The results verge on intrusive, although all the information provided is publicly available from its original sources. In 2012, the Federal Trade Commission served Spokeo with an $800,000 fine for the alleged deception and violation of the Fair Credit Reporting Act.[3] Spokeo paid the fine but did not admit any wrongdoing. Shortly after, Spokeo updated its website with the tag line "Not your grandma's phone book"!

You can search for people on Spokeo using five categories: name, email address, phone number, username, or physical address. The "basic profile" information returned includes details such as name, address, phone number, age, gender, some family tree information, home ownership status and even the estimated value of their home. There is a paid subscription available for a nominal fee that gives you access to

---

[3]Spokeo had marketed its services to human resources departments as an employment background company, encouraging HR professionals to "explore beyond the resumé." However, the Fair Credit Reporting Act places legal obligations on any company acting as a credit reporting agency, including providing consumers with a process to challenge incorrect information, which Spokeo had not done.

more complete information, such as information about the target's religion, political leanings, birthday, estimated income, investments, and mortgage value.

Spokeo does offer an option to remove personal data from its results. There is an opt-out form for this available at www.spokeo.com/optout. However, reports on how effective this is vary. If you have multiple listings, you must go through this process for each record. So each time your information changes (for example, you move house or subscribe to a new social network), you have to go through the process again. Bear in mind the opt-out feature does not remove the data from the original source, so it may be discovered by other information aggregator sites or search engines.

The Wayback Machine

I always find it useful to look up my target organization's website in the Wayback Machine at www.archive.org. People haven't always been as concerned about privacy or security as they are now and did not always realize the consequences of posting sensitive information online. I have found helpful information such as staff announcements, product launches, staff charity days, just by seeing what my target organization posted on its website in previous years. For example, the Wayback Machine has saved the McGraw-Hill Education website 588 times between December 6, 2000, and February 24, 2014, as shown in Figure 9-1. The first website snapshot saved on December 6, 2000, as shown in Figure 9-2, looks very different from the website the publishers display today.

In one test using the Wayback Machine, I found that my target organization previously published a monthly company newsletter. A previous newsletter mentioned that the CEO was celebrating his 40th birthday, so deducing his date of birth was pretty easy. When I presented this information in the report, the CEO's jaw dropped; he was shocked!

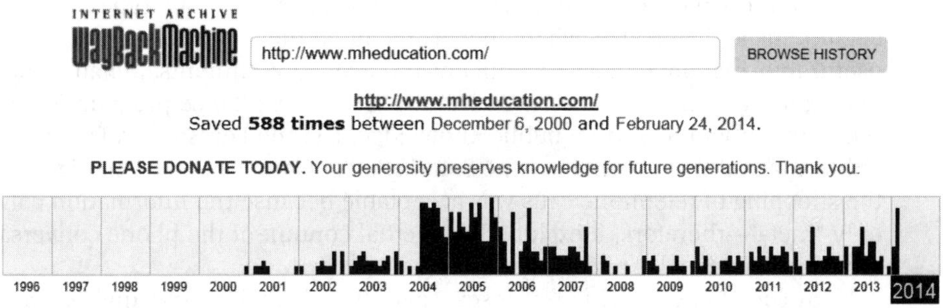

INTERNET ARCHIVE
WayBackMachine   http://www.mheducation.com/   BROWSE HISTORY

http://www.mheducation.com/
Saved **588 times** between December 6, 2000 and February 24, 2014.

PLEASE DONATE TODAY. Your generosity preserves knowledge for future generations. Thank you.

1996 1997 1998 1999 2000 2001 2002 2003 2004 2005 2006 2007 2008 2009 2010 2011 2012 2013 2014

FIGURE 9-1   The Wayback Machine has saved this website 588 times!

Metadata Collectors: FOCA and Metagoofil

Metadata is data about data; it is generated each time you use technology and it records transactional data about how you have used it. For example, metadata about your email does not include your email's contents, but it may include the location from which you accessed your email account, who you sent the email to, the time

FIGURE 9-2   The McGraw-Hill Education website in December 2000

you sent the email, and so on. Metadata can be found in many types of files, from documents and spreadsheets to photos and audio files. This data can reveal a lot of useful information for social engineers and even governments. Metadata has been a huge talking point since the NSA's secret PRISM surveillance program was revealed. When the program became public knowledge, Dianne Feinstein, a Democrat from California and the chairman of the Senate Select Committee on Intelligence, said that the snooping of telephone calls was acceptable because the information collected was only "meta"—therefore, it excluded the actual content of the phone conversations. But metadata can do a lot of damage.

For social engineering purposes, several tools collect and analyze metadata, including FOCA and MetaGoofil. Both of these tools identify and analyze various document files from the target domain that they are given. I have used these tools to find a range of potentially sensitive data, including internal IP addresses, staff names, project names, and more. If the organizations I had tested had used a metadata removal tool to clean the documents before publishing them, the social engineering test would have been much more difficult. Unfortunately, most users are unaware that metadata even exists, let alone understand the problems associated with it, so this rarely happens.

FOCA, or Fingerprinting and Organisation with Collected Archives, a tool developed by Informatica64, identifies various types of files on a target's website, including Microsoft Office documents, PDF files, Open Office files, WordPerfect files, EXIF, and more, downloads them, and then analyzes their metadata. You can either download the tool from http://informatica64.com/foca/ or use the online version. For a social engineering test for a third party, it is best to download the tool so the analysis is done locally on your machine, thus bypassing potential privacy issues. You can either provide FOCA with a target domain or add files to be analyzed manually.

Metagoofil, developed by Edge-Security, is another metadata collector. It uses the Google search engine to identify and download documents (.pdf, .doc, .xls, .ppt, .docx, .pptx, .xlsx) from the target domain and generates a report with useful information for social engineers, including usernames, software versions, and server or machine names.

Scenario Creation Tools

Based on the information found during the research and reconnaissance phase, you create the scenario you are going to use for your social engineering test. We have a selection of items in the office that we use for scenario creation—basically props and costumes or tools for making props and costumes. A team that performs social engineering will end up owning quite an extensive "dress-up box." Among the different items we have in our team's box are

- A selection of yellow jackets such as those that might be worn by facilities staff, maintenance workers or public work officials
- Pizza delivery T-shirts
- Courier costumes (bicycle gear)
- Cleaner's overalls

- A Royal Mail delivery jacket (we have never actually used this as impersonating a public official like a mail carrier is against the law)
- Various t-shirts collected from different organizations we have targeted (collected at conferences or even made by us)
- Clipboards
- Mouse and rat traps (for pretending to be pest control inspectors)
- Fake cigarettes (once I challenged a team member to use a fake cigarette that you puff flour out of to join some smokers and get into a building. He did it. I wouldn't necessarily recommend trying this though).

I would also include suits or general IT wear, but most of our guys bring their own clothes for this! We also have transfer sheets and an iron for creating T-shirts or jackets that look halfway official. There are plenty of websites where you can also get T-shirts made. In terms of ID cards, we have an ID card printer that allows us to make very official-looking cards. We use this quite regularly. Otherwise, I would probably get them made online. Many websites offer this service; they are actually aimed at small businesses that need ID cards printed for staff.

Test Execution Tools

Depending on the type of test you are performing, you can use a variety of tools to add credibility to or even automate parts of your social engineering test. For physical tests, we have a range of toolkits to choose from, containing everything from lock picks to bugging devices. For remote tests such as phishing, it's hard to beat the Social-Engineer Toolkit (SET). For tests that include the telephone, you may need to spoof your caller ID. You can really be imaginative with the tools you use to execute your test and how you disguise them.

What to Bring on Your Social Engineering Test

It may sound obvious, but the kit you choose to bring depends on the size of the bag you are carrying. I usually carry a lady's handbag, so fitting a lot of stuff in it is difficult. Sometimes I carry a backpack with a laptop in it, which affords me a bit more space. Again, it depends on the role I am playing. If I am wearing a suit, I usually have to go with the handbag. A briefcase would potentially match a suit also, although it may look a bit old school! If I am playing a more casual role, I might take the backpack. Of course, a backpack usually looks more suspicious than a handbag, unless you can conceal the backpack without looking suspicious. There are some slim-line backpacks on the market that you can easily wear underneath a jacket without anyone noticing, such as the BUILT laptop backpack. Various items I have brought with me in the past include the following:

- Lock picks (when permitted). I like to hide these in a manicure set, as shown in Figure 9-3.
- Recording devices, such as pinhole or button cameras, or bugging equipment

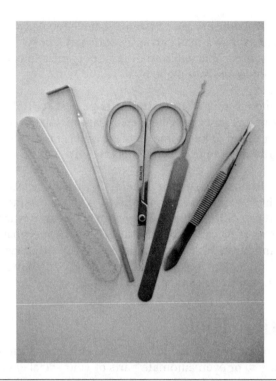

FIGURE 9-3   Lock picks can be easily concealed in a manicure kit!

- Binoculars—old school but sometimes useful.
- Keystroke loggers (which you will read more about later in the chapter).
- Wireless access points. You can use these to trick unsuspecting users into connecting to your bogus network (try giving your WAP a similar name to the target organization). Alternatively, once you connect a WAP to an open Ethernet port in your target organization, you can connect to the target's network from outside the building and use penetration testing techniques to explore or even take over the target network.
- Laptops and devices for penetration testing. Several penetration testing drop boxes are on the market. One of the most impressive ones is the ACE r00tabaga MultiPwner, which combines a penetration testing drop box with the WiFi Pineapple. You plug it into the target network, and it provides you with remote access to that network along with a selection of tools you can use for penetration testing. The Pineapple mode is a "hot-spot honeypot" which intercepts WiFi probe requests from nearby devices and automatically intercepts and reroutes their traffic. The device is tiny, less than half the size of an iPhone.
- Several cell phones (in case you have to hand one in).
- Storage devices for saving information or running programs from.

- Walkie-talkies. In some areas, the cellphone signal may be poor quality, so if I can fit them in, I bring walkie-talkies to stay in touch with my team.
- Radio scanners. If you are authorized to use these, they can be used to tune in to frequencies used by security guards, and you can listen in to see if they have spotted any suspicious behavior.

Dumpster diving requires its own set of tools, as described in Chapter 5. Whatever tools you choose to bring with you on your physical social engineering test, be careful of any legal implications such as "going equipped."

> **Tip**   If ever you leave a device onsite as part of your social engineering test, for instance, a wireless access point, drop box, or bugging or recording equipment, you may need to extract it afterward. You can do this with your client or you can do this as part of your social engineering test, in which case you need to take this into account during the scenario creation phase.

Recording Devices

There are a number of physical tools that you may wish to consider using as part of the social engineering test. Most of these fall into the recording device category. Many James Bond–style recording devices are easily and cheaply available. The quality of these tools varies widely. On my team, we have a handbag with a secret hidden camera (mostly used by me), as shown in Figure 9-4, various pinhole or button cameras, and a pen that records audio.

Very occasionally, you may want to leave a hidden camera onsite. Pinhole cameras are so tiny now that they are incredibly easy to hide. Hidden video cameras like the Sleuthgear Xtreme Life have a battery life of an entire year based on one charge and are available in the form of electrical boxes, mantle clocks, smoke detectors, and even a rock, as shown in Figure 9-5!

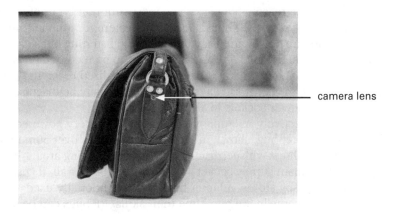

camera lens

FIGURE 9-4   Spy handbag with hidden camera

Source: www.kjbsecurity.com/products/detail/xtreme-life-landscape-stone/495/

FIGURE 9-5 The Sleuthgear Xtreme Life camera is concealed in a rock.

If you are going to use a recording device, remember to get permission and make sure that it is legal. Also try to practice a bit before taking the device on a test. I've had to go through a learning process for each of the devices that I use. For the handbag camera, I had to learn to point it in the right direction and at the right height. If I am at a meeting, I tend to put it on the table and try to point it toward the person I am meeting with. For pinhole or button cameras, I learned that it is most effective to hide them in a tie because then they record more or less what you are seeing, nearly at eye level. However, for me, the pen that records sound was the trickiest to learn. I have a tendency to chew my pens when I am concentrating, so sometimes the audio was atrocious, not to mention rather chewy and disgusting!

Bugging Devices

Audio bugging devices are becoming smaller (read: easier to hide) and less expensive to procure. There are some terrific audio listening/bugging devices that you can buy from spy shops for a reasonable price. The most common types of audio listening bugs are radio frequency (RF) bugs and Global System for Mobile Communications (GSM) bugs. Both are cheap and easy to use. Audio listening bugs either record directly to an internal device or transmit a signal to be recorded off premises. You can get both RF and GSM bugs that do not require specialized receiving equipment for the latter. Bugs are so tiny these days that they can easily be disguised in everyday equipment, from power sockets to air fresheners.

RF bugs are effectively microphones with a small battery-powered radio transmitter. The RF power adapter bug, shown in Figure 9-6, transmits over 50m in open areas and can pick up the slightest whisper from within its surrounding area. All you need to do is to plug it into a main supply socket and off you go. Best of all, it costs less than $100 from many online spy stores. Adapter bugs were traditionally used as training devices for bug-sweeping teams looking to hone their skills. RF bugs can be detected by bug sweeps and RF detection products when they are transmitting, but they are usually

Source: www.spy-equipment.co.uk

FIGURE 9-6   A power adapter bug

more than enough to prove the point when it comes to an ethical social engineering test—and besides, they are rarely ever detected in a standard office environment.

A *GSM bug*—also referred to in various configurations as an *infinity bug* (so called because it uses a telephone line to transmit, so it can work at an infinite distance) or a *harmonica bug* (so called because it was originally activated using the tone produced by a harmonica)—uses the GSM mobile telephone system to transmit the audio in the bugging area to any telephone in the world. The air freshener bug shown in Figure 9-7 is voice activated and can be programmed by SMS commands to dial a number of your choosing once activated. It has a battery life of four weeks and costs around $150.

If you don't fancy forking out a few dollars for a bugging device, you can improvise your own using a cell phone. You can easily turn a cell phone into a bugging device by

Source: www.eyetek.co.uk/gsm-air-freshener

FIGURE 9-7   A GSM air freshener bug.

using specialist spying software such as StealthGenie (www.stealthgenie.com) on the phone. This software monitors all phone activity, not just bugging calls, such as spying on SMS messages, viewing the user's GPS location, reading emails, viewing multimedia files, accessing the web browser history, and more. Technically, you don't even really need the spy software to use a cell phone as an audio listening bug. If you disable the ringing feature and enable auto answering, you can call the phone and listen in from anywhere.

> **Tip** Baby monitors can make useful bugs. They usually have a range of about three blocks. Consider this before you use one at home!

As always, check in advance with your client if you are permitted to bug the facilities. This one action can really rub clients the wrong way if you don't have authorization.

Keystroke Loggers

A *keystroke logger* is a recording device that creates a log of all keystrokes typed and sometimes the screen activity on the device on which it is installed. Keystroke loggers can be hardware or software.

If you are going to leave a hardware keystroke logger in the organization, consider how you are going to retrieve the information it collects. You may have to re-enter the organization to collect it, in which case you have to build this into your social engineering scenario. Alternatively, depending on the technical controls in place, you may be able to set up the keystroke logger to send the information to you electronically or even over a mobile network via SMS. In September 2013, four men were charged with the theft of £1.3 million (approximately US$2.2 million) from Barclays Bank using this method. A member of the gang allegedly posed as an IT engineer to gain access to a local Barclays branch in north London. While onsite, he connected a device to a computer. The device combined a KVM switch with a 3G router. It logged keystrokes and screen images and transmitted this information back to the gang, who used it to transfer money remotely to bank accounts under their control. They were charged with a selection of offenses, including conspiracy to steal and conspiracy to commit fraud by false representation.

Hardware keystroke loggers are typically attached between the keyboard and the computer or to a USB port. Most, including the keystroke logger pictured in Figure 9-8, are about the size of an AA battery, but there are some really stealthy ones that are barely visible at all. Hardware keystroke loggers can be installed in seconds, without even having to log into the target computer. The advantage of hardware keystroke loggers is that they do not depend on being installed on the target computer's operating system and, therefore, will not interfere with any program running on the target machine or be detected by any software. The disadvantage is that you have to get physical access to install them in the first place. You may also need to go in and collect them, if they do not transmit. You could always try mailing a UBS key with a keystroke logger on it to someone within your target organization and see if she'll plug it in to her computer.

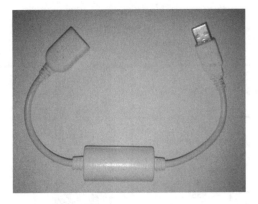

FIGURE 9-8 This keystroke logger is about the size of an AA battery.

If it is not in scope to get physical access to a building, you may want to consider using a software keystroke logger. If you can social engineer your target into installing a software keystroke logger, then you don't need to get physical access to the office. Unlike hardware keystroke loggers, software keystroke loggers may be detected and removed by antispyware or antivirus programs.

Disguised Storage Devices

In some more security-focused organizations, you are not allowed to bring any kind of electronics or storage devices on to the premises. As part of your test, however, you may want to bring some kind of storage media with tools you can run or even just to save data to. There are some great examples of disguised storage devices. I have a particularly blinging Swarovski crystal–studded necklace that has a hidden USB key in it, shown in Figure 9-9. You can even get flash drives disguised as tampons, which

FIGURE 9-9 A jewel-encrusted necklace with a concealed USB drive

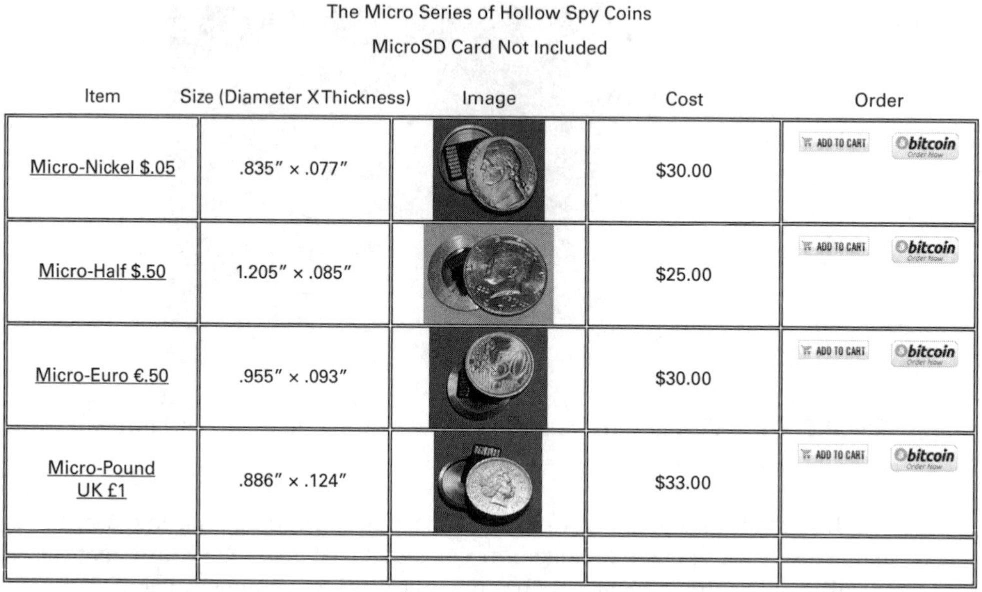

The Micro Series of Hollow Spy Coins
MicroSD Card Not Included

Item	Size (Diameter X Thickness)	Image	Cost	Order
Micro-Nickel $.05	.835″ × .077″		$30.00	ADD TO CART bitcoin
Micro-Half $.50	1.205″ × .085″		$25.00	ADD TO CART bitcoin
Micro-Euro €.50	.955″ × .093″		$30.00	ADD TO CART bitcoin
Micro-Pound UK £1	.886″ × .124″		$33.00	ADD TO CART bitcoin

Source: www.spy-coins.com/products.html

FIGURE 9-10 Spy coins are available in many different currencies.

I would be amazed if anyone detected ($29.90 for a 2GB drive from www.meninos.us). Another favorite of mine is the 50c Euro coin, which encapsulates a Micro SD memory card. No one would think to check all the small change in your pockets. You just have to be careful not to spend it! As shown in Figure 9-10, these hollowed out storage coins are available in several different currencies from spy shops online, such as www.spy-coins.com. Note that it may be illegal in your country to possess a hollow coin!

The Cell Phone

The cell phone is the single most useful item you can bring with you on a social engineering test. It has a myriad of uses, including

- Discouraging challengers. People appear to be less likely to challenge another person when that person is busy speaking on her cell phone. I have used this on multiple occasions to walk into a building without being challenged or to tailgate individuals inside a building. If I suspect someone is going to challenge me, I whip out my cell phone and start talking, or derail them by walking straight toward them and asking for directions. Asking the location of the bathroom seems to work well.
- Faking telephone calls to the person you are supposedly there to see or to anyone who can authorize your visit. Call a colleague instead, so anyone observing you will hear another person on the line.

- Using the camera to take photos for evidence. Sometimes I pretend I am sending a text message when I am really taking a photo. Just remember to turn off the clicking sound that most cameras make by default when you are taking a picture...
- Timestamping the test. I take notes on my phone and sometimes even leave voicemails for myself describing what I have done. The timestamps on these and on photos I have taken give me an accurate log of what happened during the test.
- Bugging, as described earlier.
- "Accidentally" leaving the phone behind, so you have to go in to retrieve it later.
- Communicating. If I am inside for an extended period of time, I use my phone to notify colleagues that either I am okay or I need help. It may be that I am stuck for what to do next. Being able to call colleagues and ask them for ideas can be helpful.
- Last but not least, playing games when you are hiding out in an office waiting to make your next move.

Remember, if you are going to fake a telephone call to avoid a challenge, to pretend to talk to someone, or for whatever reason—turn the ringer off. There is nothing worse than holding a fake conversation and having the phone ring in the middle of it! It's mostly easier and more natural to call a real person. I have colleagues who know what I am doing and are available to take my calls, so I can hold a real conversation with someone, which sounds more natural.

In some security-conscious organizations, particularly government and research organizations, you may be required to hand over your cell phone on the way in. This is one of the reasons I always carry two or three cell phones. They may ask you to hand in your phone, but they rarely ask you to hand in all your phones. When it was unusual for people to have more than one phone, I would always carry two phones. Now that it is perfectly normal for people to carry two phones (usually one for personal use and one for work use), I have to carry three. I always make sure that one of my phones is a cheap phone that I don't mind losing. If I "accidentally" leave my phone inside and cannot get back in, then I am not so concerned about retrieving it. Of course, if the organization uses a body scanner, then carrying extra phones will not work.

Phone Tools and Caller ID Spoofing

For many of us, the first thing we do when the phone rings is to check the display to see if we recognize the caller ID. If we recognize it, we can make an informed decision on whether to answer the call or to decline it. Caller ID is pretty standard nowadays in most businesses and many homes, as well as on cellphone technology. On a social engineering test, the wrong caller display could very quickly give the game away. If you are performing a telephone-based social engineering test, sometimes it's enough to hide the number you are calling from, but on other occasions you may want to spoof this number so a different number appears on the caller ID display. The caller ID can be very misleading.

There are some legitimate reasons for spoofing your caller ID, apart from an ethical social engineering test. Certain individuals may wish to keep their numbers private, for example, such as doctors returning a call on their personal phones or maybe an employee working from home who wants to appear to be working from the office. However, caller ID spoofing is often used by pranksters and troublemakers for malicious purposes. The IRS issued a scam warning in October 2013, in which fraudsters spoofed their caller ID to make it look like they were the IRS. They told their targets that they owed money to the IRS and demanded payment via a preloaded debit card or wire transfer, threatening police arrest or even deportation if the amount was not paid.

Another increasingly popular and particularly nasty use of caller ID is for *swatting*, which involves faking an emergency that results in the deployment of an emergency response team (such as an ambulance, police, SWAT team, or even bomb squad) to the home of the unsuspecting victim whose number has been spoofed. The callers may claim that a bomb is about to go off or that they are being held hostage. In one case, authorities charged a 19-year-old man who pretended to be calling from a family home in California in the middle of the night, saying he had just shot and murdered someone. The family was fast asleep when the local SWAT team arrived. The father heard something going on outside, so he picked up a knife from the kitchen and went out to investigate. He was met by a group of SWAT assault rifles aimed directly at him. Luckily, no one was hurt. Of course, it turned out the family's number had been spoofed. A number of celebrities have also fallen victim to swatting, including Tom Cruise, Clint Eastwood, Miley Cyrus, Ashton Kutcher, and Justin Bieber. A 12-year-old was arrested for the swatting incidents against the latter two in December 2012. He allegedly placed a call from their numbers to report an armed intruder on the properties. To prevent swatting and criminal behavior and fraud, some caller ID spoofing services will not allow users to spoof emergency numbers, law enforcement agencies, and some financial institutions.

In a social engineering situation, there are many reasons to spoof your caller ID. You may want to make it look like your call is originating from inside the organization or from another office (maybe you want to call the helpdesk as an "employee" and ask to have your password reset), or you may want it to appear as if your call is coming in from a third party such as a client or supplier. Don't forget to check with a lawyer regarding the legalities of using caller ID spoofing as part of your social engineering test. Caller ID spoofing is legal in the United States as long as it is not done with "the intent to defraud, cause harm, or wrongfully obtain anything of value." However, some states have challenged this. In the UK, you can only spoof a number if you have the permission of the owner of the number you are spoofing.

Caller ID spoofing used to be relatively difficult to set up—the spoofer had to own and operate a telephone switch for a start, which could cost thousands of dollars—but now it is incredibly easy. There are plenty of ways to spoof your caller ID—in fact, there's an app for that, dozens of them! Even Paris Hilton has allegedly given caller

ID spoofing a go. In August 2006, she was accused of spoofing her caller ID to hack into a voicemail system rumored to be that of her rival, Lindsay Lohan, with whom she had a long-term feud. The voicemail system in question allowed users to retrieve their voicemail without entering a PIN if they appeared to be calling from their own phone. To bypass this authentication, you simply spoofed the number belonging to the voicemail user; Hilton apparently availed herself of SpoofCard's services to do this. SpoofCard subsequently terminated Hilton's account.

> **Tip** Landline users can dial ***67** in the US or **141** in the UK before dialing their destination number to hide their phone numbers.
> Cellphone users can dial **#31#** or **141** in the UK to do the same. These numbers are not permanent solutions. You will need to enter them each time you want to hide your telephone number.

Most cell phones provide the option to keep your number hidden on a more permanent basis. On Blackberries, set the Restrict My Identity field to Always. On iPhones, you can permanently hide your number by setting the Show My Caller ID option to Off.

Note that different carriers may have different combinations for hiding your telephone number, so always do a test run to check that it is working.

Spoofcard

The easiest way to spoof your caller ID is by using a caller ID spoofing service such as www.SpoofCard.com.[4] These services allow you to substitute a number of your choosing as your caller ID. SpoofCard works like a prepaid calling card; you purchase a set number of minutes. You then dial the toll-free SpoofCard number and enter your access code or PIN, followed by the destination number and the number you want to spoof. The recipient will see the spoofed number instead of your real number on his caller ID.

SpoofCard also offers a selection of other useful features for the social engineer:

- The caller can change his or her voice to male or female. This option is helpful for tests in which you have to make repeated phone calls to the same organization but do not want your voice to be recognized. I wouldn't rely on it too much, but it is good for when you have to call reception and ask to be put through to various staff members.
- Conversations can be recorded, so you can listen to them afterward and transcribe the conversation or keys parts of it. You can also provide it as evidence to your client. Remember, don't record the conversation unless you have permission to do so from your client.

---

[4]There are dozens of providers in this space. SpoofCard is one of the biggest and oldest. Other caller ID spoofing services of note including Bluff My Call, SpoofTel, Stealth Card, and CrazyCall.net. Many of these services offer free trials so you can find the one you like best.

- It offers a selection of background noises (as shown here) that can add credibility to your call. For example, you might want to sound like you are near traffic, in an airport, are experiencing cellphone interference, or even being chased by police sirens!

SpoofCard works on most phones. It even has an extremely convenient mobile application for caller ID spoofing available through the respective app stores for both iPhones and Androids. Don't forget to make sure you have enough minutes left before you make your social engineering call!

Caller ID Spoofing over VoIP

Spoofing caller ID over landlines and cellphone technology was traditionally rather difficult, as there was no interface where you could alter the caller ID number. However, Voice over IP (VoIP) technology makes spoofing your caller ID easy if you have time to configure some private branch exchange (PBX) software and connect to a VoIP carrier.

Even easier, most VoIP providers allow you to configure your caller ID number. For example, with Skype, you can spoof your caller ID as long as you have credit in your account. Once you add some credit to your account, you can enter your preferred caller ID number on the Caller ID page, as shown in Figure 9-11. Your chosen number does need to be verified via a text message, so you can't spoof any old number, although you can be creative. The Phone Losers of America have some interesting ideas on how to get various phone numbers authorized in an article entitled "How to Change Your Skype Caller ID" available on their website, www .phonelosers.org. One of their sneakier ideas is to use the phone number from a display phone in a phone store.

You may also wish to set up your own telephone switch to allow you to spoof your caller ID for free, without as many restrictions as the previous methods described.

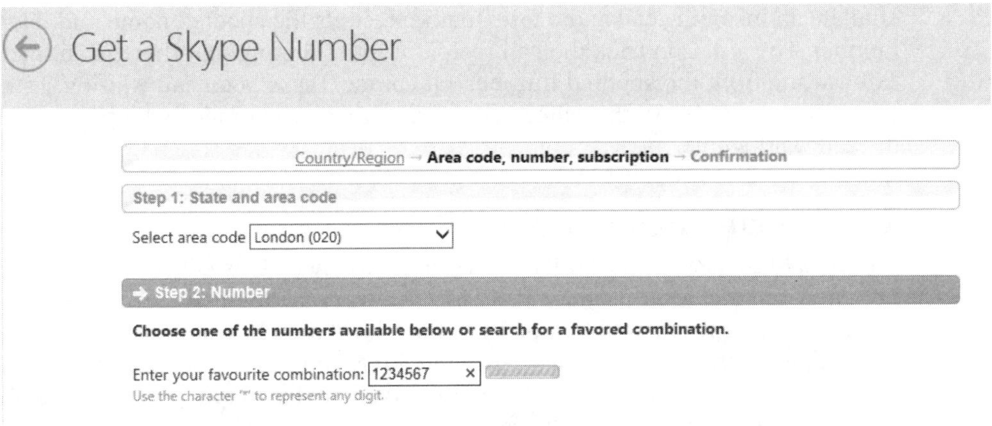

FIGURE 9-11   Skype allows you to enter your preferred caller ID.

You have to install some PBX software such as Asterisk or FreeSWITCH, both of which are open source. Asterisk, one of the first software-based PBX solutions, is Linux-based PBX software available from www.asterisk.org. FreeSWITCH was created by a group of former contributing Asterisk developers and is cross-platform PBX software available from www.freeswitch.org. Once installed, you then connect to a VoIP service that supports caller ID forwarding, such as Nu-Fone or VoicePulse, by editing a few lines in the PBX configuration file. Once you have set your caller ID, when you place a phone call, the source device (such as a VoIP soft phone) sends the caller ID number to the destination as part of the data packet. Caller ID spoofing does not cost anything using this method (apart from the cost of the call over VoIP, of course) and has fewer restrictions than using a caller ID spoofing service or changing your number on a VoIP carrier, although it is much more time consuming to set up than just purchasing a call card from SpoofCard.

Caller ID spoofing using VoIP is frequently used for vishing attacks—voice phishing—or social engineering over the telephone. In a vishing call, the victim receives a call that appears to be from his or her bank or some other related financial institution. The call may be an automated recording that asks the victim to call a certain number or from a human operator who tries to convince the victim to hand over personal information or financial details. A press release issued by Financial Fraud Action UK in August 2013 suggests that 1 in 25 adults in the UK may have been a victim of vishing.[5]

Orange Box

Another method of caller ID spoofing involves using an orange box, which is a piece of hardware or software that spoofs the call waiting caller ID. The person who is making the call places the call as usual and, once the call is established, uses the orange box to

---

[5]www.financialfraudaction.org.uk/cms/assets/1/22082013%20ffa%20uk%20vishing%20press%20 release%20final.pdf

emulate an incoming call audio tone that represents the spoofed name and telephone number. The aim is to trick the call recipient into thinking that there is an incoming call waiting from the spoofed number. Of course, there is no call waiting. In more sophisticated scenarios, the caller may work with an accomplice who pretends to be on the call-waiting line.

The Social-Engineer Toolkit

The Social-Engineer Toolkit (SET) by Dave Kennedy of TrustedSec is an open source Python-based tool written specifically for use by social engineers. It is the ultimate social engineering tool and a must-have for ethical social engineers. It offers a full suite of attacks from generating realistic-looking web pages with hidden exploits to crafting phishing emails or even creating road apples in one package. It is often referred to as the "Swiss army knife" of the social engineer's toolkit.

For the various attack options offered, you can opt to create your own templates or use the predefined templates included. Although SET provides default templates, you are probably going to get a higher hit rate by creating a customized template for each specific test, based on your research and reconnaissance. Similarly, you can use the payloads included (SET is integrated with Metasploit for both the exploit repository for client-side attacks and payloads) or create your own. Most of the attacks can be directed at an individual or sent to a group of people. The beauty of SET is that it allows you to be creative with your attacks without binding you to a particular set of options.

Many good tutorials teach you how to use SET including

- https://www.trustedsec.com/downloads/social-engineer-toolkit/
- www.social-engineer.org/framework/se-tools/computer-based/social-engineer-toolkit-set/

SET is easy to use and has a straightforward menu-based user interface. You can customize and tweak SET to fit your assignment perfectly, depending on what attack vector you want to use and how you would like to deliver it. To date, SET offers the following attack vectors:

- **Spear phishing**   Allows you to craft phishing emails and send them to target recipients (groups or individuals) with attached file format malicious payloads.
- **Website attack**   Creates a phishing attack designed to lure the recipient(s) into clicking a link within the email.
- **Infectious media generator**   Allows you to create road apples in the form of a USB key that, when inserted into a machine, will trigger an autorun feature that attempts to compromise the system.
- **Create a payload and listener**   Allows you to create a Metasploit payload, for which it will export and generate a listener. If your victim downloads and executes the .exe file, you will hopefully get a command shell.
- **Mass mailers attack**   Allows you to perform a mass phishing attack.
- **Arduino-based attack**   Allows you to load an attack on an Arduino-based device, such as a Teensy USB device. If you have physical access, you can plug

in your Arduino device to your target system and it should bypass any autorun disabled or endpoint protection features.

- **SMS spoofing attack**   Allows you to send a specially crafted SMS message to the recipient(s), spoofing the number the SMS is coming from. The aim of this message is to get the recipient(s) to visit a link, included in the SMS, on their browser and then steal their credentials or perform another attack.
- **Wireless access point attack**   Creates a fake wireless access point and DHCP server and spoofs DNS to redirect traffic to the social engineer's machine. All DNS queries will be redirected to the social engineer's machine.
- **QR code attack**   Creates a QR code that redirects to a URL of your choosing.
- **PowerShell attack**   Allows you to create PowerShell-specific attacks such as dumping the SAM database or injecting shellcode. PowerShell is available by default on all Windows operating systems from Vista onward.

Updates to SET are frequent; as new attack vectors are discovered, they are quickly implemented. I am sure that by the time you read this book a whole host of new attack vectors will be available on SET.

You'll find it's easiest to run SET from Kali Linux. It can also be downloaded through github using the following command:

```
git clone https://github.com/trustedsec/social-engineer-toolkit/ set
```

Social Engineering Tools on Kali Linux

Many of the tools mentioned in this chapter are available on Kali Linux, the popular Linux security distribution. In addition to the suite of penetration testing tools that Kali Linux provides, the distribution also has an arsenal of tools that can be used in social engineering, including but not limited to

- SET
- Maltego
- Cree.py
- Metagoofil
- Jigsaw, for information gathering
- Uberharvest, an email and domain harvesting tool
- BeEF, a browser exploitation framework
- CaseFile, from Paterva, creators of Maltego, billed as "the little brother to Maltego" or "Maltego light." It is more focused on intelligence analysts who work with internal data.
- KeepNote and MagicTree, note-taking and reporting tools
- Honeyd, honeydctl, and spamhole, tools for creating honeypots
- VideoJak, a physical exploitation tool that simulates a proof-of-concept denial-of-service attack against a targeted user-selected video session and IP video phone, and tools for exploiting Arduino and Kautilya toolkits
- SIPSAK and VoIP Hopper, VoIP spoofing tools
- Various RFID tools, some of which allow for cloning of RFID tags

Final Thoughts

There are dozens of tools you can use throughout the social engineering test to make the process quicker and more professional. However, tools don't make a social engineer. You still need to create a believable scenario. You won't get to use your keystroke logger or hidden camera if you can't even get in the door! Some tools can help you to discover information that can inspire and lend credence to your scenario or pretext. Others help you to look more convincing during the test or to further the test itself.

Many of the tools available to social engineers are very powerful. As Peter Parker's uncle tells him in Spiderman, "With great power comes great responsibility." Use these tools wisely.

With social engineering becoming more sophisticated—thanks in part to the tools that attackers can use to improve their attacks—it is becoming more difficult to defend against. In the next chapter, I will propose some measures you can take to help prevent social engineering attacks from being successful.

10 Defense Against the Dark Arts

Security is mostly a superstition. It does not exist in nature, nor do the children of men as a whole experience it. Avoiding danger is no safer in the long run than outright exposure. Life is either a daring adventure, or nothing.
—Helen Keller

There is no 100 percent defense against social engineering.

However, there are one or two things you can do.

It is notoriously difficult to defend against social engineering because it targets the weakest link in the security chain: the users. Con artists and fraudsters have been ripping us off for time immemorial, and yet we still fall for their scams. Once we wise up to certain attacks, social engineers devise new ways to exploit us. We are not machines, and we cannot be configured to prevent every attack. You can't just roll out a patch and immunize your staff against the latest social engineering attack. We each come with our own set of vulnerabilities ripe for exploitation. Social engineering attacks don't need to work against everyone. If even one person within an organization falls for the attack, then it is successful. A single point of weakness can lead to the compromise of the entire organization.

Different types of organizations are vulnerable to different types of social engineering attacks. Organizations with call centers are obviously more vulnerable to telephone-based attacks than other organizations. Data centers and organizations with high-value physical assets or assets that store confidential information may be more at risk from physical social engineering attacks. I can't think of an organization that wouldn't be susceptible to a phishing attack.

Define the types of attack that your organization may face and analyze the level of risk that you are exposed to. Then, for each of these attacks, implement an appropriate defense. A social engineering attack could lead to the compromise of confidential information and loss of business credibility; it could affect business availability and cost time and money to remedy. Be realistic about your level of risk and plan your defense accordingly. If your organization receives only a handful of visitors a week, for example, you may not be able to justify spending a lot of money on rolling out complicated visitor procedures. A sign-in book and receptionist may suffice.

In a way, this whole book has been all about defending against social engineering. By understanding the tools and techniques that malicious social engineers use, you stand a better chance of defending against them. Awareness and constant vigilance are key to your defense. Your employees need to be aware that social engineering is a problem and that it could happen to them. They need to be able to recognize social engineering attacks (both during an attack and, failing this, after the attack has happened) and know what to do if they suspect they are being, or have been, social engineered. Nevertheless, a social engineer may still be convincing enough to bypass your staff or successfully mislead them. In this case, appropriate technical and physical security controls should be in place to minimize the damage and help mitigate human error.

You cannot rely on technical or physical security controls alone. Neither can you rely solely on education and awareness. A suitable social engineering defense program combines all of these elements: awareness and education and physical and technical security controls.

In this chapter, we'll look at how to defend against social engineering on an organizational level. In particular, we will look at

- The indicators of a social engineering attack
- Responding to social engineering attacks both during and after the incident has occurred
- Security policies
- Education and awareness
- Technical and physical controls
- Social engineering tests

Indicators That You May Be Experiencing a Social Engineering Attack

By identifying social engineering techniques from both successful and failed attacks against your organization, you can identify the "indicators of compromise" that are relevant to your organization. These indicators can help you to recognize future social engineering attempts and inform post-incident detection, helping you to determine whether an event is part of an actual attack. If a staff member thinks that he or she may have fallen victim to a social engineering attack, having this list of indicators of compromise will be helpful.

Social engineering attacks that may appear obvious to some people will fool others. It's amazing what people will fall for. In the UK, there is a comedy show on TV called *Fonejacker*. It involves a prankster making a series of prank phone calls to unsuspecting members of the public using a number of different characters. One of the characters is George Agdgdgwngo, a bank manager from Uganda. He calls various people under this guise and asks them for their bank information. He uses quite ridiculous reasons to explain to his targets why he needs their information, and he is rarely successful, although very entertaining nevertheless. However, in one case, he called an elderly gentleman, explaining that he was the man's bank manager and needed to access his bank account as there was a pigeon trapped in the bank vault! The man gave him his bank account number and answered the security question. Luckily, the TV station bleeped out the numbers.

Most serious social engineering attacks won't be quite as easy as this to identify! Defending against social engineering is all about context and deciding whether certain requests or actions are suspicious or out of context. However, each organization has a different context. What is a normal and acceptable request in one organization may raise an alert in another. Broadly speaking, unusual behavior or situations in each of the following six categories may indicate that you are dealing with a social engineer:

- The person's attitude
- Establishing a connection
- The nature of the request
- Pressure/urgency of the request
- Small mistakes
- Difficulty of independent validation

For each of these categories, consider what is "normal" behavior in your organization and what might be identified as a social engineering attack. Take pressure/urgency for example. When might it be "normal" to receive an urgent request? When would an urgent request seem unusual? How might a social engineer use urgency or pressure to further his attack? How might you identify this? Once you have determined this, include the information in your security policy so staff are aware of what kind of indicators to look for.

Also consider previous social engineering attempts that have occurred in your organization or industry. What were the indicators that it was a social engineering attack? Are they covered within the categories outlined here, or should you add another category to the list that is specific to your own organization?

This list of categories is not exhaustive—every social engineering attack is different and these indicators do not necessarily mean you are being targeted by a social engineer. Obviously, real requests from genuine individuals may also raise one or two of these flags. However, it is better to be aware and flag them just in case.

The Person's Attitude

Social engineers may favor certain attitudes during their attacks, in particular:

- Acting overly social (very chatty, flirtatious, or unusually grateful, for example).
- Making an effort to convey authority.
- Acting in an aggressive or potentially even threatening manner (*I will report you if you do not do this*). I have heard several Microsoft Support scam phone calls where the intended victim has questioned the caller and the calls have quickly turned quite nasty.
- Being particularly emotional, maybe even crying or becoming upset.
- Sounding unnatural or uncomfortable.

Think about how your suspected social engineer sounds during the conversation. In many social engineering calls that I have listened to (mostly recorded from call centers), the social engineers sounded nervous, unnatural, or stilted. How does your suspected social engineer react when questioned? Does he show discomfort? Are his answers a bit vague? If you are confident enough, you could even consider using the Conundrum Technique, described in a sidebar later in the chapter, to try to catch out the suspected social engineer.

Establishing a Connection

Social engineers often make a point of establishing a connection with their target. They do this via a variety of means, such as

- Name dropping ("I was speaking to John Doe from the IT department the other day.")
- Acting particularly friendly to build rapport quickly
- Using company terminology (staff names, project names, or other internal jargon) or even office gossip to establish insider status
- Using personal information about you (asking about recent holidays, using details about hobbies, work, or other activities that could be obtained via online research)

The Nature of the Request

The person's request might somehow be suspicious or unusual. Consider these questions in particular:

- Is the person authorized to access the information she has requested?
- Are you authorized to access the information the person has requested?
- Are you usually asked this kind of request?
- How did the individual contact you? Was it via the usual means?
- Did the request come in at an unusual time? For example, maybe the individual called you earlier than most of your clients or emailed you over the weekend.

Pressure/Urgency of the Request

Social engineers sometimes make their requests urgent, or they apply some other kind of pressure to force their victims to comply. They make some excuse to explain why they need the information they have asked for immediately—perhaps they are just about to go into a meeting where they need to discuss this information or their boss desperately needs the information.

Social engineers may play the authority card, threaten negative consequences, or even use emotional pressure to try to convince the intended victims to comply with their request.

Small Mistakes

Social engineers may make small mistakes in what they say or do. Maybe they are unfamiliar with the usual processes. Maybe their use of language is not quite right—they do not use company jargon where it would be appropriate to do so, or they overuse it to the point of seeming suspicious.

Difficulty of Independent Validation

How easy is it to independently verify the person's identity and the legitimacy of their request? Social engineers may use various tricks and excuses to refuse to give their contact details, or they may be a bit hazy on why they need certain information. Maybe you can't call them back because their cell phone is about to die, or they might be just about to board a flight.

> **Tip** Social engineers are full of excuses: excuses for why they need the information they have requested, why they couldn't get the information in the usual manner, why they weren't up to date on certain processes or procedures, why they can't provide contact details. If you hear an excuse, you may be dealing with a social engineer and it may warrant further examination.

Have You Been Social Engineered?

Many times you won't even realize you have been social engineered until it is too late—an unexpected charge appears on your credit card or information has been leaked from within your organization. Social engineering might have played a role in a wider technical attack, in which case you are far more likely to spot the technical breach and may not realize that social engineering was a factor. But sometimes you will know that something is wrong—maybe someone is acting suspiciously in the office or you have a vague sense of unease after a telephone call.

In this case, you could use a checklist based on the categories described earlier to establish the likelihood of you having been targeted by a social engineer. Take the scenario where, for one reason or another, an employee realizes after the event that he may have been targeted by a social engineer. You could go through the checklist with him to discover what flags were raised beyond a sense of unease after the supposed attack.

The following is an example of one such checklist I have used on many occasions to investigate suspected social engineering breaches. The aim of the checklist is to find out what, if any, indicators of compromise were present, what kind of scenario the potential attacker used, and how successful she was.

Social Engineering Checklist: Have You Been Social Engineered?

- Who did the person in question claim to be?
- Did the person provide contact details?
- Did you verify those details? How?
- How did the person get your contact details?
- Have you had any previous contact with this person and was it via the same channel?
- If you met/saw the person, can you provide a physical description?

- Did the person know personal information about you, such as anything about your background, hobbies, work, or holidays?
- Did the person use insider knowledge or jargon, such as staff names, project names, or office gossip?
- When and where did the suspected attack take place?
- What information did the person in question want or what request did they make?
- Did the request involve sensitive information or access to IT systems?
- Are you the owner of the information requested?
- Did you give the person access?
- Was the request urgent?
- Did the person act in an unusual manner, for example, emotional/crying, threatening, incorrectly using jargon or project/staff names?
- Was the person particularly friendly or chatty?

The Conundrum Technique

The conundrum technique can help you to spot a liar by asking a single question. In this question, you introduce a piece of evidence that only a legitimate person should know and see how the suspected liar handles it. Make sure the evidence is something that your subject would know about if his story turns out to be true. The evidence should be untrue, but plausible, so it doesn't give the game away. Watch out for how the suspected liar reacts, in particular with regards to hesitation, evasion, and, of course, incorrect responses. This technique can take a bit of practice. Many people are socially incapable of lying or challenging others, even if it just involves making up a bit of evidence to check if the person they are speaking to is lying. Pulling off the conundrum technique gets easier with practice.

There is a really good example of this in the social engineer's favorite movie, *Catch Me If You Can*, although it doesn't quite work out as planned. Abagnale is having dinner with his girlfriend and her parents. At this stage, he is claiming to be a doctor but explains that he is looking to get back into law. He tells the family that he passed the bar in California, having studied at Berkeley. It turns out that his girlfriend's father also went to Berkeley. The father appears to be quite suspicious of Frank, so he asks him a question, introducing the first piece of evidence. "Was that snake Hollingsworth still there when you were at Berkeley?" Frank reads into his question. He called Hollingsworth a snake, so he clearly didn't like him. Frank responds, "Hollingsworth? Yeah...Grumpy old Hollingsworth." But the father, still not convinced, continues with his questioning and introduces a second piece of evidence. "And that dog of his. Tell me, Frank. What was the name of his little dog?" There is an awkward silence at the dinner table. Eventually Frank answers. "I'm sorry. The dog was dead." What quick thinking! Most people would have stumbled at one of these hurdles.

- Did the person offer you anything, such as entry to a competition or goods or services?
- Did you download anything, click an attachment, or visit a website at the person's request?
- Did the person give any reasons for why he or she needed the information, or couldn't get the information in the usual manner? Did the person indicate why he or she wasn't up to date, or why he or she couldn't provide contact details?

Responding to Social Engineering Attacks

Should a social engineering attack occur, simple procedures need to be in place that your staff can follow. The more complicated the procedures are, the less likely staff are to follow them. If staff suspect they are being targeted, they should be able to refer to the security policy to tell them what to do. The policy should include procedures for reporting the social engineering attempt, informing colleagues of the attack, and checking with the data owner or more senior staff members about whether they can comply with the suspected social engineer's request.

Consider how suspicious behavior should be reported in your organization. Your staff needs to know who to report suspected attacks to. Centralize reporting to a certain individual or small group of people, for example, the security team or IT department. Then those people can be alert to unusual activity and spot patterns or trends that may indicate the organization is being social engineered (or targeted by recruitment agents!). The incident reporting process should log the following information:

- Who was targeted (name, role, and department)
- The date and time of the attack
- A description of the attack
- How the attack was handled
  - Was it successful?
  - Was any information disclosed? If not, how did the staff member respond?
- Recommendations for preventing similar attacks in future, including any controls implemented or recommended as a result of the suspected attack
- Whether the attack needs to be reported to other bodies, such as the audit committee, law enforcement, or other external organizations such as the Federal Trade Commission (FTC) in the US or Action Fraud in the UK.

Finally, encourage staff to report suspicious behavior or events. Many people are reluctant to report suspected social engineering attempts in case they come across as overly paranoid; some may even feel their job may be in jeopardy if they report suspicious behavior and it turns out not to be an attack. As security professionals, we must ensure that staff realize we appreciate the information they have provided, regardless of whether it turns out to be a malicious attack, and reassure them they will not get into trouble for reporting it.

The ENISA LIST

The European Network and Information Security Agency (ENISA) proposes the LIST anagram for individuals who suspect they are being targeted by a social engineer:

- **Legitimacy** Does the request seem legitimate and usual? For example, should you be asked for this information, and is this how you should normally provide it?
- **Information** What is the value of the information you are being asked to provide or the task that you are being asked to perform, and how might it be misused?
- **Source** Are you confident the source of the request is genuine? Can you find a way to check?
- **Timing** Do you have to respond now? If you still have doubts, take time to make further checks or ask for help.

Security Policies and Procedures

Security policies are a must have for organizations of every shape and size. Your security policies and procedures should take social engineering into account and implement defenses against social engineering attacks. A known documented process is harder to exploit than an ad hoc process.

The documented policies and procedures should be readily available to all staff members, often by way of the organization's intranet. The staff needs to understand and adopt these policies and procedures. These documents should be written with the target audience in mind, so they are easy to understand. Many example policies and procedures are available online, on which you can base your own set; for example, SANS offers a number of information security policy templates on its website at www.sans.org/security-resources/policies/.

If you don't already have a security policy, start with a pilot strategy. Then talk to staff to assess whether it is working and if it is easy to implement. Your policies should include sanctions for non-compliance, such as suspensions, disciplinary action, termination of employment, or even civil or criminal penalties, depending on the extent of the breach. Policies should be reviewed periodically to ensure they are still relevant and take into account new and emerging threats. A good rule of thumb is to review policies on a rolling basis, with each policy being reviewed at least once every five years.

The following are some of the key policies that are relevant to social engineering:

- **Data classification policy** This should describe what information is considered to be sensitive or confidential, how it should be marked, how it should be handled, and who it can be released to, as well as how to dispose of it.
- **Waste management** This should include secure disposal of documents, electronic media, and so on, and should cover external as well as internal waste. In one organization I was in, I was able to lift documents out of the secure disposal bins because they were so full. Take action to make sure this doesn't happen to you.

- **Acceptable use policy**   This should describe what is considered acceptable use of computer systems and equipment within the organization. It should cover system accounts, network use, electronic communications, use of noncompany hardware or software, as well as monitoring of the same.
- **Network access policy**   This should cover wired and wireless network access, including IP telephony and mobile devices; it should describe who can access the network, how and from where, public access, guest access, and what is and is not permitted on the corporate network.
- **Remote access policy**   This should document remote access requirements, who can connect, requirements for connecting, termination of access, and so on.
- **Physical security policy**   This should cover the various aspects of physical security, including visitor procedures and physical access logs.
- **Password policy**   This should include password-strength guidelines, including how often the password should be changed. The policy should explicitly state that employees should not disclose their password to anyone, even if they claim to be from the IT department. It should also forbid employees from recording their passwords. I've lost count of the number of times I have seen passwords written on sticky notes and attached to a monitor or stuck underneath a keyboard.
- **Electronic communication policy**   This should describe how to handle email attachments, hyperlinks in documents, requests for information from both within and outside the organization, what instant messaging services staff are permitted to use, if any. Some policies may include examples of phishing attacks to help users to identify phishing attacks that they themselves receive.

Your security policies should fit your corporate culture and respond to the realistic challenges your organization faces or has faced in the past. Ideally, your security policies should include examples to help make them relevant to your staff. Using examples of attacks that your organization has actually been exposed to, either from malicious social engineers or as part of an ethical social engineering test, is a powerful motivator for staff. It makes the topic more believable and relevant for people.

Consider the resources you have available to accomplish your goals and don't overstretch yourself. A simple and achievable policy is best. There is no point in having a bells-and-whistles policy if nobody complies with it. Compliance with the security policy should be subject to audit to ensure that staff are adhering to it, which could include social engineering testing, where appropriate.

Two key policies in the defense against social engineering that I will discuss in more depth are

- The data classification policy
- The physical security policy, specifically in relation to visitors

Data Classification Policy

A data classification policy is one of the key policies in the defense against social engineering attacks. Data classification policies dictate how information is prepared, managed, used, accessed, or retained within an organization. It ensures that the right people have access to the right information at the right time. Having a data classification policy can help protect against social engineering for two reasons: first, it ensures staff can only access information that they are supposed to access; and second, staff will know from the protective marker on each piece of information whether and to whom they can release it.

Data can be classified according to various categories, such as financial, business, regulatory, legal, or privacy. Most data classification policies have three or four levels of classification. Any more levels can be confusing, not to mention potentially expensive to implement and more difficult for employees to remember. The data classification policy should define each level and give examples of the types of information that each category contains. Each set of data within the organization should be defined and assigned to one of these categories, according to its value, which risks it is vulnerable to, and who can access it. Example data classification levels might include the following:

- **Confidential** Data in this category may require certain levels of protection by law,[1] for example, personally identifiable information, health information, certain employee data, certain business and financial data.
- **Restricted** Data in this category should only be accessible to certain roles or functions. For instance, it may be restricted to certain departments, such as employee information being restricted to the HR department or systems data being restricted to the IT department.
- **Public** There is no expectation of privacy or confidentiality for data in this category. It could include public website information, press releases, and so on.

Each category should include requirements for protection, describe how the data should be stored, who can access the data, and how it should be disposed of. Take every type of data that your organization processes, including customer data, user data, and supplier data, and assign it to one of your defined categories. All staff should know how to handle and protect each category of information.

Physical Security Policy: Visitors

Your physical security policy should, at a minimum, consider the following areas regarding visitors:

- **Checking in and checking out** Visitors should be required to check in and check out in a dedicated area, usually the reception area. The process typically involves signing a visitors/contractors book and contacting the person that the visitor is meeting so he or she can escort them into the building.
- **Identifying visitors** Visitors should be required to present some kind of identification.

---

[1]In the UK, for example, the Information Commissioner's Office (ICO) is responsible for upholding information rights in the public interest, including enforcing data protection requirements. It has the power to carry out spot checks and fine offenders who break the data protection principles. Data classification policies have become very popular in the UK as a result.

- **Escorting visitors**   Visitors should always be escorted by an existing staff member (not by another visitor or contractor) into the organization. I have often gained physical access to an organization and then let my colleagues into the building once I am inside. Consider what level of escorting that visitors need once inside the building. Do they need to be escorted on the office floor, in production areas, in the kitchen or break room?
- **Visitor passes**   Are visitors required to wear visitor passes? If so, they should be required to return their visitor passes upon checking out. I have often used a visitor's pass from one branch of an organization to get into another branch of the same organization. Some more security-focused organizations use different colored passes for different areas or different days of the week. Visitor passes should, at least, be dated. Employees should be encouraged to challenge anyone not wearing an ID badge or a visitor pass. Visitor passes should be returned on leaving the building. Follow up on passes that have not been returned.
- **Accessing the network**   Can visitors access the computer network, and, if so, where from and how? Can they connect their own devices to the network?

 Employees should be encouraged to report any visitors, including repair people, who show up unexpectedly and to not grant access to offices or equipment until their identities can be verified.

Social Engineering Education and Awareness

Defending against social engineering attacks requires a combination of physical and technical controls and staff awareness. No matter how well considered your security policy, a good social engineer may still be able to bypass it if awareness is low among your staff. You can have the best technical controls in the world, the latest firewall, the most expensive intrusion detection system, but an attacker may still be able to circumvent these by social engineering your staff. An ongoing security education and awareness program is a key factor in preventing social engineering attacks from being successful. Staff need to understand what social engineering is, that it really does exist, and that they are at risk of falling victim to it. They also need to know what to do if they suspect they are being targeted by social engineers. Why spend time and money protecting your network and systems if you aren't educating your users?

Organizations need to create and maintain a security-aware culture. This culture has to be driven from the top down, with clear endorsement of security policies. Executive buy-in is crucial to this. A comprehensive security-awareness campaign can help to achieve a security-aware culture. Your campaign could include some of the following initiatives:

- Training courses, awareness workshops, and new employee security-awareness induction training
- Newsletters or other internal communications, such as circulars or intranet websites

- Security-awareness events and activities, such as talks, awareness weeks, presentations, seminars, quizzes, and competitions
- Videos
- Ongoing social engineering testing programs
- Promotional items (pens, stickers, mouse pads)
- Posters

An education program designed to inform staff about the dangers of social engineering can go a long way toward creating a more security-aware culture. The education program should train your staff on required security policies and procedures, and why they need to adhere to them. War stories, especially local ones, can help people to understand that social engineering really is a threat. I always start any course or workshop by asking people if they have ever been conned, either by a social engineer or a confidence man; if they have fallen prey to a phishing attack; or even if they have had their credit card number stolen. Almost everyone has a story to tell about how they or a friend or family member has been conned in the past. Having participants tell these stories to each other raises awareness and helps participants to understand the threat they are facing.

Security-awareness sessions and workshops do not need to be boring. My favorite type of workshop or training session involves asking staff how they would go about social engineering their own organization. I often run this workshop with frontline staff, such as receptionists and helpdesk personnel, or other groups that are at high risk of being targeted by social engineers. It's fun and can produce some useful insights and ideas about how to improve security within the organization. I have identified loads of unexpected vulnerabilities this way. Staff are more familiar with the organization and often think of creative ways to get into the building, or sometimes obvious ways that an external person might not think of. If nothing else, it alerts staff to the dangers of social engineering and encourages them to think about information security. Security is a way of thinking.

Training should apply to everyday life, at home as well as in the workplace. Take tailgating, for example. You would never hold the door open or allow someone to follow you through your front door at home, so why would you do it in the workplace? Ideally, participants should be able to apply what they have learned on the training course to all areas of life. By understanding the personal risk they are facing, participants will better understand the impact of social engineering attacks on their places of work. For example, people generally get freaked out when I tell them I have been employed to listen to what people are talking about at the pub, or to remove laptops that they have left unguarded as they have a pint in the pub after work. These examples make them more security aware, at least for a while.

Scaring the participants is not the intention of a social engineering awareness course, but can sometime be the outcome. At one training course I gave in Switzerland, a very concerned lady put up her hand at the end to ask if this was what the world was coming to! We want staff to maintain a healthy suspicion without being overly paranoid or unhelpful to clients and colleagues.

Any training and awareness program that you implement needs to be evaluated and adjusted as appropriate, to keep it up to date and meaningful to the target audience. There is a lot of denial when it comes to social engineering, and this can make it challenging to design or deliver a social engineering training and awareness program. Many people just don't think social engineering attacks happen or that they would be targets for social engineers. *That wouldn't happen to me. It only happens on TV. What would they want with me? I haven't got anything worth stealing.* There is a lot of denial of responsibility, too. *It's not my job. What's it got to do with me? The IT/Security department should be able to block those attacks.*

A thorough security-awareness and training program should help staff to recognize and respond appropriately to social engineering attempts, both during and after the suspected attack. Guidelines should be in place not only to help employees block social engineering attempts, but also to aid in detecting attempts during or after they occur. Although awareness and training can "harden" your staff, it may not prevent all social engineering attacks from being successful. Convincing social engineers may still be able to mislead your staff; therefore, you need to implement physical and technical controls to minimize the damage done.

Tip   It is important to understand what type of information is available about you, personally, and to consider how it could be used against you as part of a social engineering attack. Do an ego search! Put your name in a search engine and see what it turns up. Try researching yourself using some of the tools listed in Chapter 5.

Positive vs. Negative Reinforcement in Security Awareness

Should staff be rewarded for complying with the security policy or penalized for breaching it? It depends on your organization's culture. For some organizations, such as banks or other financial institutions, it may be appropriate to use negative reinforcement as that is the prevalent culture and that is what usually works within this type of organization. I know of one security-focused organization where if you breach the security policy three times, you get fired. It sounds severe but it works!

On the flip side, in another organization I work with, they use positive reinforcement to encourage compliance with the security policy. From time to time, they leave a chocolate on desks where the clear desk policy has been adhered to.

Each approach has pros and cons. If you use positive reinforcement, people come to expect rewards; therefore, they value them less because it is human nature to value free stuff less. On the other hand, staff may resent the use of negative reinforcement. To mitigate this, you could reward randomly, although this is what drives compulsive behavior such as gambling!

Physical and Technical Controls

Inevitably, social engineers will get past your employees and the awareness program will fail. Most employees know that they should not visit malicious websites, but a well-practiced social engineer may be able to convince them, for one reason or another, to visit a website under his control. In this case, your physical and technical controls had better work! Physical and technical controls can be implemented to respond to specific types of attacks, for example, you can have specific controls in place to prevent dumpster diving, as described in the following sidebar. Some of the key technical controls that can help stop social engineering attacks include

- Keeping your software up to date. Ensure you have a patch management process.
- Using antivirus at each relevant layer, including mail gateways and end-user desktops.
- Monitoring systems constantly. If a malicious individual gains access to your network, you want to know about it as soon as possible so you can block his or her access. In the Terremark Company Picnic example described in Chapter 2, attackers reportedly had access to the network for two weeks before they were detected. You don't want this to happen to you!
- Using audit logging everywhere.
- Limiting privileges to a need-to-know basis, only allowing staff access to the information they need to perform their roles. Try to limit the damage that a single user can do. People can only give out information to which they have access!
- Implementing a content filtering system to block employees' access to malicious websites and reduce exposure to system compromise.
- Requiring multifactor authentication to access critical systems and areas such as the server room.

Some of the physical security controls that can help to prevent social engineering attacks from being successful include

- Staff wearing visible ID badges and visitors wearing visible visitor passes. Staff should be encouraged to challenge any individuals not wearing a visible badge.
- ID cards should be presented whenever a staff member enters the building.
- Consider implementing physical barriers for entry into your organization, for example, turnstiles or swipe-card access.
- Sensitive documents and equipment should be kept in secure locations with restricted access.
- Keep an inventory of your computer equipment and check for missing equipment and even extra equipment (such as rogue wireless access points) periodically.
- Enforce a clear desk policy so social engineers can't physically pick up useful information from staff desks.

Try to implement controls sensibly. On one physical social engineering test I did, the organization had no physical barriers in place so we were able to walk past

Ideas for Preventing Dumpster Diving

To prevent social engineers and other dumpster divers from learning anything from your trash, consider implementing some of the following ideas:

- Use a cross-cut paper shredder (or even burn) documents that contain sensitive information, including client information, emails, phone lists, and calendars. This should be in your policy on waste disposal.
- Consider using a waste collection company that specializes in secure waste collection (they usually supply their own secure dumpsters).
- All media, including computers, smartphones and magnetic media, should be securely wiped prior to disposal.
- Keep the dumpster in a secure area that is inaccessible to the public, and keep the dumpsters under surveillance.
- Put a lock on the dumpster.
- Ensure that magnetic media is erased properly.
- Put a sign up saying "Danger, Radiation!"

reception without checking in. Of course, we recommended that the company install some kind of barrier to force people to check in at reception before getting into the office. The company complied and installed some turnstiles. Unfortunately, there was a pillar in between the reception desk and the turnstiles, which was right in the line of sight of any receptionist and blocked the view of the turnstiles. The next time we did the test, we jumped the turnstiles and no one noticed!

Social Engineering Tests as Defense

Having well-documented policies and procedures, sophisticated education and awareness programs, and a fine set of physical and technical controls in place is all well and good. How do you know if all these are helping to stop social engineering attacks? How about performing a social engineering test? Performing a social engineering test helps to assess an organization's current level of defense against social engineering attacks. It can give you a good indication of the level of security awareness in the organization and whether training and awareness programs have been effective. Best of all, social engineering tests give staff practice at identifying the types of tools and techniques used by social engineers. Through these tests, staff will learn to better recognize social engineering attempts. Either staff will block the test attack, which is great, or they will fall for the test attack, in which case, they get "burned" in a safe and controlled environment. Staff who have been taken in by an ethical social engineering test are going to be far more aware and alert to social engineering attempts in future.

Staff members who have fallen victim to social engineering tests or, indeed, to malicious social engineering attacks should be provided with additional training in social engineering awareness and prevention to make them less likely to fall for future social engineering attempts. They need to understand how and why they were targeted, and what they did or didn't do that enabled the social engineering test or attack to progress.

Final Thoughts

An organization can never be 100 percent secure from social engineering attacks. By teaching your staff how to recognize the signs of a social engineering attack and how to respond to it appropriately and by implementing physical and technical security controls, you can make it much more difficult for social engineers to succeed.

Defending against social engineers is a way of thinking. You have to think like a social engineer to design and test your defenses. You can never be too careful.

The next chapter explores what the future may hold for social engineering. With technology changing so rapidly, some of my predictions may not be as far-fetched as you might first imagine!

11 Social Engineering: Past, Present, and Future

The principles of successful stock speculation are based on the supposition that people will continue in the future to make the same mistakes that they have made in the past.
—Edwin Lefèvre, *Reminiscences of a Stock Operator*

As computers continue to become more secure, it is becoming more difficult, in many cases, to bypass security using purely technical means. Because of this more effective security and because users (at least some of them) are becoming more security conscious, social engineering attacks have had to become more sophisticated and more believable to succeed. Gone are the days when users could frequently be taken in by a dodgy-looking email with bad spelling and a glaringly obvious unauthorized email address (well, mostly gone). Now social engineering is a big business and can make some serious profit for the individuals or groups involved. Just look at the CryptoLocker ransomware attack that hit in the tail end of 2013. Victims were lured in by a social engineering–style email and were required to pay a ransom to regain access to their files. ZDNet reported that the attack netted the perpetrators about 41,928 bitcoins in two months—over $27,000,000 at the exchange rate at the time of the attack.

Nowadays finding potential targets for a social engineering attack is a cinch, and obtaining the tools required to execute the attack is easier and cheaper than ever before, whether you're using software (such as a mass emailing program that can send phishing emails to thousands of people at the click of a button) or James Bond–style physical tools. When I bought my spy handbag in the early 2000s, I went to a specialist spyware shop and paid nearly £1,000 (approximately US$1,689) for it. I had no choice of design, and frankly, my handbag looks like something my granny might carry. Nowadays spy handbags are widely available online for a fraction of the cost, and you can choose from all kinds of designs—all the better for blending in during the social engineering engagement.

On the plus side, organizations are beginning to understand the threat of social engineering. More and more companies are providing security-awareness training for their staff and performing ethical social engineering tests. Barely a security conference goes by nowadays without a presentation on social engineering. Attacks are becoming more sophisticated, but people are slowly becoming more aware. As a community, IT security professionals have started taking social engineering seriously. Now we just have to convince the masses—often easier said than done!

So what does the future hold for social engineering? It's likely to be more of the same, although it may be delivered via new and innovative means. For as long as humankind has been around, we've consistently fallen for scams—why stop now? The abundance of information available for social engineers to base their scenarios on allows for attacks that are more believable and harder to detect. In this chapter, we explore some ideas regarding the future of social engineering, in particular:

- How the same scams have been repeated throughout history and will be repeated in the future using new technology.
- How new technology gives social engineers more targets as well as provides new ways to deliver attacks.
- How the volumes of information available on the Internet and various emerging technologies can make for better profiling and more believable social engineering attacks.

CryptoLocker

CryptoLocker is a ransomware Trojan that first appeared in late 2013 and targets computers running Microsoft Windows. The primary means of infection is via phishing emails with malicious attachments. Here are some of the email subject lines designed to lure the victims into opening the attachment:

- Payroll Received by Intuit
- ADP RUN: Payroll Processed Alert
- Payroll Processed Alert Annual form ACH Notification
- DNB Complaint
- Voice Message from Unknown Caller
- We have received your secure message
- Annual Form—Authorization to Use Privately Owned Vehicle on State Business
- Administrator@<companydomain>
- Outlook Settings .zip file attachment
- Company Report .zip file attachment

The ransomware encrypts the user's files on the infected machine and on the local network it is attached to, as well as cloud-based storage in some instances. Infected users are asked to pay a ransom (an average of $300 in bitcoins) within 72 hours to decrypt their files. An ominous-looking count-down timer appears demanding the ransom in return for the decryption key. Social engineering skills are required in the initial phishing bait as well as in convincing the victims to pay and walking them through the use of Bitcoin.

Same Tricks, New Technology

To know where social engineering is going, you need to understand where it has come from. People have fallen for the same tricks throughout history. We want to make a quick buck, take a shortcut, fall in love with a beautiful person, or win a prize. We have seen the same scams repeated again and again, and we will continue to see them repeated in future. These scams take advantage of human nature, and someone is always going to fall for them. Sometimes we become wise to a particular scam, but when we do, fraudsters find new takes on tried-and-tested techniques.

Take the classic Nigerian 419 scam (advance fee fraud), for example, named after the article of the Nigerian penal code under which the perpetrator can be prosecuted. The fraudster poses as or represents a distressed but reputable person who, for one reason or another, needs some money to help him out of a jam; of course, the victim will supposedly be rewarded many times over for her generosity, although the reward never quite arrives owing to one complication or another, which usually requires more money to solve. The scam combines emotion (feeling sorry for the person who has made the request because, for example, his family has died, they have been wrongfully imprisoned, or they are being persecuted) with the potential to make a quick and hefty profit while feeling good for helping somebody, appealing to good Samaritans and business people alike. The scammer tries to convince the intended victim to advance him some money in return for sharing in the profit later.

This social engineering scam has been around in various guises for hundreds of years and yet we still fall for it. In spite of its name, the scam did not originate in Nigeria. Early records show that it dates back as far as the 16th century, when it was called the Spanish Prisoner scam, and then reappeared regularly throughout history, taking advantage of current events and new technology to deliver the scam in new formats. Today hardly a day goes by without each of us receiving some kind of advance fee fraud scam in our inboxes. Although many successful 419 scams go unreported, a 2006 US government report indicated that the average take is $5,100 per American victim[1]. It's £31,000 in the UK (US$52,346)[2]. Some lose a lot more. A US businessman, James Adler, lost over $5 million. Some victims have committed suicide as a result of falling for the scam.

The Spanish Prisoner, 16th Century

The Spanish Prisoner scam dates back to the time of the Spanish Armada and the Anglo-Spanish war. The scam specifically targeted aristocrats in England. The con artist would approach an English aristocrat with the story that he was representing a fellow aristocrat who had been imprisoned in Spain under a false identity. The aristocratic prisoner could not reveal his identity without putting himself in danger and had asked his friend, the con artist, to raise the necessary funds to release him. The con artist offered to let the victim contribute toward the prisoner's release, with the promise that he would be handsomely reimbursed by the prisoner, not

---

[1] www.ic3.gov/media/annualreport/2006_IC3Report.pdf

[2] www.chathamhouse.org/sites/default/files/public/Research/Africa/nigeria1106.pdf

only financially but also by way of marriage to the prisoner's beautiful daughter. An irresistible offer! On advancing the money, the victim would find out that some difficulties had arisen and further money was required to smooth things along. Of course, at this stage, the victim was hooked, both financially and emotionally. The scam continued until the victim had no funds left or refused to hand over any more money. The Spanish Prisoner was possibly one of the earliest examples of whale phishing, where attackers specifically targeted rich and powerful people with their scams.

The Letter from Jerusalem, 19th Century

Skip forward to France in the 1800s and a common criminal named Eugène François Vidocq (1775–1857). From his origins as a petty crook, Vidocq became a grifter, a smuggler, a master of disguise, and a deserter from both the army and the navy. He served several prison sentences although he seemed to be able to escape with consummate ease. In quite a staggering turn around, Vidocq cleaned up his act and went on to become a police spy and then a police agent. He finally worked his way up to chief of the Sûreté Nationale, which was the precursor to the French National Police! Vidocq is considered by historians to be the father of modern criminology. Among other achievements, he compiled the first database of criminals; he invented indelible ink and unalterable bond paper; and he took the first shoe impression using a plaster cast in the indentation left on the ground. Vidocq's life story inspired a number of classic authors, including Victor Hugo (who based two characters from *Les Misérables* on Vidocq), Honoré de Balzac, and Edgar Allan Poe. His exploits are well documented in several volumes of ghost-written memoirs, *Memoirs of Vidocq*, which are still available today and make for a very entertaining read.

In his memoirs, Vidocq describes a scam called "The Letter from Jerusalem," a scam plotted by prisoners while they were behind bars. The plotters obtained the names and addresses of wealthy individuals from new prisoners. They proceeded to write letters to these wealthy individuals with various stories to convince them to part with their money, an example of which is shown in Figure 11-1.

In the letter, the sender would purport to be a *valet-de-chambre* to a marquis who, on his travels, had lost or hidden a casket containing a large amount of money. The sender would request an advance toward recovering the casket and would, naturally, promise the recipient that they would be rewarded many times over. The plotters had quite a hit rate with their letters. Vidocq claims that 20 out of 100 letters were always answered. Even Parisians would fall for the scam:

...The Parisians themselves sometimes fell into the snare: and some persons may still remember the adventure of the clothseller of the Rue des Prouvaires, who was caught undermining an arch of the Pont Neuf, where he expected to find the diamonds of the duchess de Bouillon...[3]

It's essentially the same scam once again: a person of repute is in need of funds and will generously reimburse whoever provides the funds.

---

[3]*Memoirs of Vidocq: Principal Agent of the French Police until 1827*, Volume 1, Eugène François Vidocq

" Sir.—You will doubtlessly be astonished at receiving a letter from a person unknown to you, who is about to ask a favour from you; but from the sad condition in which I am placed, I am lost if some honourable person will not lend me succour: that is the reason of my addressing you, of whom I have heard so much that I cannot for a moment hesitate to confide all my affairs to your kindness.   As valet-de-chambre to the marquis de ———, I emigrated with my master, and that we might avoid suspicion we travelled on foot and I carried the luggage, consisting of a casket containing 16,000 francs in gold, and the diamonds of the late marchioness.   We were on the point of joining the army at ———, when we were marked out and pursued by a detachment of volunteers.   The marquis, seeing how closely we were pressed, desired me to throw the casket into a deep ditch near us, so that it might not implicate us in case we were apprehended.   I relied on recovering it the following night; but the country people, aroused by the tocsin which the commandant of the detachment ordered to be rung, began to beat the wood in which we were concealed, with so much vigour, that it was necessary to think only of escape.   On reaching a foreign province, the marquis received some advances from the prince of ———; but these resources soon failing, he resolved on sending me back for the casket thrown into the ditch. I was the more certain of finding it, as on the day after I had thrown it from me, we had made a written memorandum of the localities, in case we should be for any length of time without being able to return for it.   I set out, and entering France, reached the village of ——— without accident, near the spot where we had been pursued.   You must know the village perfectly, as it is not three quarters of a league from your residence.   I prepared to fulfil my mission, when the landlord of the auberge where I had lodged, a bitter jacobin and collector of national property, remarking my embarrassment when he proposed to drink to the health of the republic, had me apprehended as a suspected person : and as I had no passport, and unfortunately resembled an individual pursued for stopping the diligences, I was taken from prison to prison to be confronted with my pretended accomplices, until on reaching Bicêtre I was obliged to go to the infirmary, where I have been for two months.

· " In this cruel situation, having heard mention of you by a relation of my master's, who had property in your district, I beg to know if I cannot, through your aid, obtain the casket in question and get a portion of the money which it contains.   I could then supply my immediate necessities and pay my counsel, who dictates this, and assures me that by some presents, I could extricate myself from this affair.

" Receive, sir, &c.

(Signed)   " N———."

FIGURE 11-1   Vidocq's Letter from Jerusalem

Advance Fee Fraud Revival, Early 20th Century

The advance fee fraud scam experienced a revival in the early 20th century for two main reasons: easier cross-border communication and current events. The first scheduled airmail postal service was introduced in 1911, making it easier and quicker to correspond by writing internationally. Fraudsters began using current events to make their scams appear more believable. First, the Spanish-American war saw a surge in the Spanish Prisoner scam once again. Then the First World War inspired a series of scams, such as the scam where the fraudster claimed to be a Belgian who fled to Spain after the siege of Liège with £20,000 worth of Bank of England notes (US$33,772). The scam was updated yet again in the 1930s and 1940s when many people were trying to get their money out of Nazi clutches.

The Metropolitan Police have a collection of advance fee fraud letters targeting prominent Britons. The collection includes a series of typewritten letters from "Vincente Olivier" of Mexico City, written in the 1930s and 1940s. In a typical example, he claims to be imprisoned for bankruptcy but has a secret stash of dollars hidden away in a specially made double-bottomed trunk in a custom house in America! If only the recipient could forward him some money to help retrieve it...

In both the Spanish Prisoner scam and the Letters from Jerusalem, the perpetrators had to write their letters by hand, so they were limited in how many they could send out as it took more time and effort to pen each letter individually. Olivier, on the other hand, used modern technology (a typewriter) to send his letters to large numbers of targets.

Advance Fee Fraud Scams Since the 1970s

Now let's move forward again to the 1970s and 1980s, when this type of scam first started appearing out of Nigeria. The largely oil-based economy in Nigeria was in decline. Some Nigerian graduates decided to take advantage of this situation to make a bit of money. Typically, they would contact US businessmen, sending them letters or even using the latest technology—at that time, fax or telex—to offer the intended victim favorable oil deals in exchange for a financial advance. Since the mid-1990s, advance fee fraud has flourished with the widespread use of first email and then social networking along with email-harvesting software. Now you don't even have to pay the price of a stamp to send out your attack.[4] Early electronic iterations of this scam involved preposterous stories with even worse spelling and grammar, often involving Nigerian royalty. Recent versions are more believable because now they seemingly come in from friends who we naturally want to help. Targets receive a message from their "friend" via email or social network, giving them an added incentive to forward on the cash advance, such as the London mugging message in the upcoming sidebar.

One of the reasons we fall for advance fee fraud scams again and again is because they are delivered via different mechanisms. Advance fee fraudsters move with the times, taking advantage of new technology: typewriters allowed them to replicate their letters more quickly and thus target more people; email made it quicker and easier still. Airmail allowed fraudsters to target people internationally. The publication of printed newspapers and then television and the Internet kept fraudsters and their targets up to date with current events, giving them the stories they needed to make their scams more believable, using events as varied as Hurricane Katrina or the Paris Concorde plane crash, referred to in Chapter 3, as their backdrop.

What kind of advance fee fraud scam will come next? It depends on what new technology we adopt. In January 2014, security firm Proofpoint discovered a web attack that compromised smart gadgets, using them to route spam. Over a two-week

---

[4]Technically, fraudsters often used counterfeit stamps to post their 419 letters in the 1980s, which resulted in the seizure of the letters by the postal authorities.

The London Mugging

Fraudsters seem to send scams like the London mugging out pretty randomly to a recipient's email address or social networking account. A little bit of research would make the scam a lot more successful. For example, if you knew the person you were impersonating was actually in London, the scam would be a lot more believable. Basically, you need some location data on your targets. You may be able to get this from their social networking accounts—do they use TripIt on LinkedIn, for example?

Here's one version of the scam email (grammar and spelling as per the original email):

Oh my God i am sorry i didn't inform you about my traveling to London, UK. It as been a very sad and bad moment for me, the present condition that I found myself is very hard for me to explain. I am really stranded i am in some kind of deep mess right now, I came down here to London, UK for a short resort got mugged at gun point last night at the park of the hotel where i lodged. All cash, credit cards and cell were stolen, I've been to the U.S embassy and the Police here but they're not helping issues at all, Our flight leaves today and I'm having problems settling the hotel bills, passport, documents and other valuable things were kept on my way to the Hotel am staying,

I am facing a hard time here because I have no money on me. I am now owning a hotel bill and they wanted me to pay the bill soon or else they will have to seize my bag and hand me over to the Hotel Management. I need this help from you urgently to help me back home, I need you to help me with the hotel bill and i will also need to feed and help myself back home so please can you help me with a sum of 1720Pounds to sort out my problems here? I need this help so much and on time because i am in a terrible and tight situation here, I don't even have money to feed myself anymore

period, more than 750,000 malicious emails were sent from everyday consumer gadgets, including multimedia centers, televisions, and at least one refrigerator! Who knows how the scam will be delivered in the future and how the story will be updated to move with the times?

New Technology, New Targets, New Delivery

New technology gives us new things to target as well as innovative ways to deliver attacks. We've seen it with social networks, and we've seen it with the cloud. We will undoubtedly see it with whatever technology comes next, whether it's the ultraconnected Internet of Things or the increasing use of biometrics. Here's an interesting exercise: whenever you hear about a new piece of technology, consider how it could be used or targeted by social engineers. Two of my favorite examples have been a laser camera that takes photos around corners and remote-controllable cockroaches. How could social engineers take advantage of these particular technologies?

Seeing Around Corners

In 2010, research scientists at MIT launched a laser camera that takes photos around corners.[5] The research team believes it has practical uses in search-and-rescue operations and robot vision. According to the team's research paper, potential applications include "search and rescue planning in hazardous conditions, collision avoidance for cars, and robots in industrial environments... medical imaging that could allow endoscopes to view around obstacles inside the human body."

From a security point of view, wouldn't something like this be perfect for remote shoulder surfing? (See Figure 11-2.) You could set up a laser camera around the corner from an ATM and record users' PIN numbers. Or you could use it as part of a physical social engineering attack to let you know if the coast was clear to continue through the building. Of course, as of 2010, the camera was the size of a room and only took stills but you never know what the future holds.

Remote Controllable Cockroaches

In 2013, following a successfully funded Kickstarter campaign, a company called Backyard Brains launched the RoboRoach, an electric backpack that fits onto a cockroach and allows a person to control the cockroach's movements through a smartphone app, pictured in Figure 11-3. The raison d'être for the RoboRoach is to teach people about neurotechnology and electronics. The RoboRoach has been marketed as the world's first commercially available cyborg. It is available for under $100 at https://backyardbrains.com/products/roboroach.

So how could a social engineer use a RoboRoach as part of a social engineering attack? People don't really like cockroaches and are often scared of them. A malicious social engineer could purchase a hoard of RoboRoaches and release them into a building, prompting the exit of its occupants, perhaps. Or he could follow up the invasion by pretending to be from a pest control company. Maybe he could skip the social engineering altogether and attach a tiny camera or microphone to the cockroach to, literally, bug the building. There are plenty of options available to a social engineer with a sufficiently malicious mindset! Of course, you could drop the cockroaches entirely and embrace nanobot technology for your reconnaissance needs, such as the US Air Force's Bugbot Nano Drone technology or the British Army's Black Hornet Nano unmanned aerial vehicle, although it would need to be some serious social engineering with a massive budget.

Biometrics

Although biometrics such as fingerprint and iris scanners have been around for a while, they are increasingly being incorporated into everyday technology such as smartphones and tablets. The iPhone 5S fingerprint scanner, Touch ID, was hacked just days after its release using a duplicate fingerprint. Users leave biometric data such as fingerprints everywhere. A social engineer could easily follow her intended

---

[5]CORNAR: Looking Around Corners Using Femto-Photography, http://web.media.mit.edu/~raskar/cornar/.

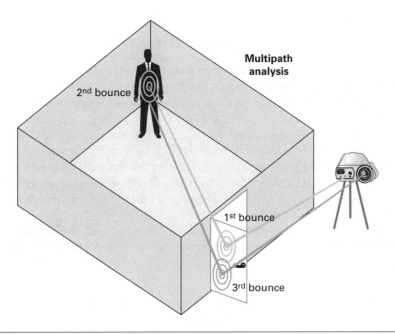

FIGURE 11-2   The camera works by emitting short pulses and analyzing multibounce reflection from the door. (Source: http://web.media.mit.edu/~raskar/cornar/)

FIGURE 11-3   The RoboRoach (Source: https://backyardbrains.com/products/roboroach)

victim for a while and lift some fingerprints—maybe from his desk, a glass he has drunk out of, or his cellphone screen. Or she could use social engineering to trick her intended victim into inadvertently giving her a copy of his fingerprint.

If someone can duplicate your fingerprint, iris, or other biometric data, then you are in trouble. Security researchers at the Universidad Autónoma de Madrid (UAM)[6] have already created synthetic irises that can defeat eye-scanning security systems. Many different options are available for defeating fingerprint scanners, some of which I describe later in this section.

---

[6]http://media.blackhat.com/bh-us-12/Briefings/Galbally/BH_US_12_Galbally_Iris_Reconstruction_WP.pdf.

Acoustic Kitty

Operation "Acoustic Kitty" was a joint project between the CIA's Office of Technical Services and the Office of Research and Development in the 1960s, during the height of the Cold War. The aim of the project, thought to have cost over $25 million, was to turn a living cat into a surveillance machine that could record the conversations of foreign officials. In an hour-long procedure, the cat was surgically altered to have a radio transmitter installed at the base of its skull, a microphone in its ear canal, a thin wire antenna that was woven through its tail and even had some batteries fitted. It turned out that cats aren't very trainable. Operatives found that the cat would get distracted when it was hungry, so they fitted another wire to override this. On its first test outing, the cat was driven to a park and tasked with recording the conversation of two men sitting on a park bench. As it crossed the road, the cat was hit by a taxi and died. Documents relating to Acoustic Kitty were declassified in 2001.

However, from the perpetrator's point of view, possibly the trickiest part of duplicating biometric data is getting a copy of someone's fingerprint, iris, or other biometric data without the person realizing it. You have two options[7]: you can steal the data (for fingerprints, chop off the user's finger[8] or lift his fingerprint from an object he has been in contact with), or use social engineering to get a copy of the fingerprint. If you decide to go down the social engineering route, you have two options once again, assuming you won't be able to trick your victim into actually chopping off and handing over his digit. First, you social engineer your target individual into scanning or copying his fingerprint directly. A malicious individual could use these following scenarios:

- Pretend to be a bouncer or security at a pub or nightclub, or even get a job as security. Bring a fingerprint scanner. Require people to scan their fingerprints to be allowed entry. Some pubs and nightclubs in the UK and Australia have actually started doing this, supposedly in an effort to reduce underage drinking and control alcohol-related violence. Individuals bring their driver's license or passport to the venue and have it verified. So they don't have to keep bringing their documents out with them, the venues give customers the option of registering their fingerprints, so they can just use fingerprint scanners in the future to gain entry. Privacy groups are up in arms. So as a social engineering scenario, this is not so far-fetched after all.

---

[7]There is potentially a third and quite futuristic option, which involves using stem-cell technology for social engineering purposes. You might convince someone to duplicate his finger, even if he wouldn't chop it off for you. Obviously, this scenario is very futuristic at the moment, but not entirely unimaginable.

[8]Although many fingerprint scanners require some level of "pulse," a malicious individual could potentially get around this by wearing a fake fingerprint on top of his finger, so he would have a print and a pulse.

- Impersonate a police officer (which is illegal in most countries). Tell the target individual that he is under arrest for a suspected crime, and you need his fingerprint to prove whether he is guilty.

Alternatively, you could social engineer your target individual into handling a particular object that you can then retrieve his fingerprint from. Nonporous, smooth surfaces such as plastic, glass, or varnished exteriors are easiest to lift fingerprints from using the traditional powder-and-brush technique followed by lifting tape or, alternatively, by simply scanning or photographing the print. Here are several social engineering scenarios that could be used to trick the target into leaving his fingerprints on a shiny surface:

- Buy him a drink and keep the glass he uses.
- Show him some photos. (My photos are covered in fingerprints...)
- Ask him to fill in a survey on an iPad.
- In many countries around the world, if you are sitting in a café in a public area, beggars will place an object (usually a little trinket) on your table. A few minutes later, they will pass by to see if you want to purchase the object. Most people say no and hand it back. Almost everyone picks it up to inspect it. Either they haven't come across this situation before and are wondering why someone has given them something free of charge, or they just can't resist picking up the object. So...pretend you are a beggar, place an object on your target's table (preferably something shiny that will hold fingerprints well) and hopefully collect it from him full of lovely fresh fingerprints.
- Throw a plastic ball at your target's head. Unless he is visually impaired or has really slow reflexes, he is bound to catch it. Even if he doesn't, chances are he will pick it up.[9]

The television show *MythBusters* has a really good episode ("The Myth That Fingerprint Locks Cannot Be Foiled Is Busted") in which one of the team members is tricked into handing over his fingerprint when another member asks him to copy a stack of CDs. The shiny surface of a CD is a perfect medium for collecting and gathering fingerprints. The other team members then dust off the CD, scan the guy's fingerprint, print it on to acetate, and make gel prints. They log into the guy's laptop and open the fingerprint door locks. To top it off, they also use a photocopy of the guy's fingerprint, lick it, and use it to open the door lock!

It will certainly be interesting to see what hacks people come up with to bypass other biometric scanners as they become more popular—and how social engineering may be used by malicious individuals in this process.

---

[9]Please let me know if you ever try this!

How the Biometrics Hacking Team at Chaos Computing Club Hacked Apple's Touch ID

What you will need: an iPhone, a scanner, a pen knife, graphite spray, wood glue. Oh yeah, and a fingerprint. Use your best social engineering skills to get this.

To digitize the fingerprint:

1. Photograph or scan a fingerprint of the iPhone's owner using a resolution of 2400 dots per inch.
2. Convert the image to black and white, invert it, and mirror it.

To make a fingerprint mold:

1. Print the image to tracing paper at 1200 dpi.
2. Expose the print out on photo-sensitive PCB material.
3. Develop and etch the PCB.

To make a dummy fingerprint:

1. Apply a thin coat of graphite spray to the mold. Graphite spray is powdered graphite in the form of an aerosol spray, sometimes used for lubricating locks. In this instance, applying the graphite makes removing the dummy fingerprint easier and gives an improved capacitive response – (the spray is electrically conductive).
2. Smear a thin film of wood glue into the mold and wait for it to dry.
3. Carefully remove the dummy print.
4. Use the dummy print to authenticate to your fingerprint scanner.

A video demonstrating this process is available at www.heise.de/video/artikel/iPhone-5s-Touch-ID-hack-in-detail-1966044.html.

There are several easier ways to bypass fingerprint scanners, but they are not as reliable. These methods include using high-resolution photocopies of the fingerprint and even using putty to defeat the scanners.

The Internet of Things

The *Internet of Things (IoT)* or *Thingternet* is where the physical world intersects with the Internet, where physical objects contain embedded technology and have the ability to communicate. It's widely regarded as the next step in the evolution of the Internet. Some of the intelligent products we have seen to date include smart-building technologies, such as intelligent heating systems and smart lighting; precision farming applications, such as ground sensors that monitor crop conditions and adjust how each part of a field is farmed; and healthcare applications such as microcameras that travel the human digestive tract and pinpoint the source of illness. But we ain't seen nothing yet. As component costs come down, connectivity is expected to become a standard feature in many products—some of which we have not even dreamed of at the time of writing this book. The IoT is expected to increase almost thirtyfold from 0.9 billion units installed in 2009 to 26 billion units installed in 2020, according to research from Gartner,[10] which they claim will far exceed the growth of other connected devices. Social engineers will have a lot more targets.

We've already seen technical attacks against smart televisions, smart medical equipment, and even baby monitors. Devices no one really considered to be vulnerable, simply because they hadn't thought about it before, will suddenly become targets for attackers as they become IP-based. Your phone, your fridge, your TV, even your bed, could turn out to be viable targets. Malicious individuals could disrupt your daily routine by hacking these devices, using traditional hacking techniques or social engineering. They could turn off your alarm clock remotely so you are late for work or miss that all-important job interview, change the temperature of your fridge so your food goes bad, or, even worse, only allow you to watch *Downton Abbey on* your TV.

Three Social Engineering Attacks for an IP-Connected Bed

Even our beds are getting smart. Sleep Number's "superbed," launched at CES 2014, has embedded (excuse the pun) monitoring technology to monitor and hopefully improve the user's sleep. It monitors the body's movements, can identify who is sleeping on it, and can alter the firmness of the bed on the fly. It even claims to help stop snoring by gently moving the guilty party up and down the bed to open the sleeper's airways without disrupting his or her slumber. It presents a couple of potentially interesting scenarios for a malicious social engineer:

- Disrupt the owner's sleep by hacking into the bed and making it shake or making it too hot or cold. Contact the bed's owner, pretending to represent the bed manufacturer. Explain that a number of people have reported faults with their beds and ask if the owner has experienced anything unusual. Offer to come to the house to fix the problem (then rob the owner). Alternatively, ask the owner to download the fix from your "special website." Maybe you could even convince him to provide credit card details to pay for an ongoing monitoring service, a bit like the bogus Microsoft calls that so many of us currently receive.
- If you can gain access to the data collected by the intelligent bed, you can figure out when the owner is sleeping. A new twist for websites such as pleaserobme.com might be ruasleep.com that shows when people are sleeping. Sleeptime could potentially be a better time for attackers to break into not only your house, but also your online accounts as you won't notice until you wake up. If they have data on your sleeping patterns, they will probably know how long their window of opportunity is.
- To social engineer the bed manufacturer, rather than the bed owner, call the manufacturer. Tell them you are a customer who is having problems with a bed. The app doesn't seem to be recording your sleep data properly. Offer to send them a "screenshot" showing the problem.

---

[10]www.gartner.com/newsroom/id/2636073

Imagine the devastation that a denial-of-service or ransomware attack along the lines of CryptoLocker would cause on the Internet of Things. It could keep you out of your house, let alone your computer, unless you paid the ransom. A lockout attack like this could even become a business model for groups like Weight Watchers; they could sporadically lock members out of their fridges and cupboards—talk about guerilla weight-loss tactics! These attacks are obviously technical in nature, but like CryptoLocker, could be propagated or monetized using social engineering.

The IoT promises to enhance our lives, changing the way we do business and even improve our health. To do this, it constantly monitors us, gathering vast amounts of information, which means many more organizations are going to have access to all kinds of data about us, creating many more potential targets for malicious social engineers. Instead of social engineering a particular individual for his or her data, social engineers can try to social engineer the companies that hold the data as well. A similar situation occurred with the cloud, when staff at cloud service providers suddenly became targets. Organizations that hold personal data give social engineers more people to target as well as more people to impersonate.

It will be interesting to see what gets classified as sensitive data on the IoT. Are your eating patterns sensitive? An attacker could potentially use your eating patterns to poison your food or trick you into eating something you are allergic to. Many of us are guilty of blindly following technology; just look at how many people have had accidents or even died from blindly following their satellite navigation, or GPS, instructions. If we were to rely on our refrigerators to tell us what was safe to eat, we could fall into the same trap. Thus seemingly innocuous data could potentially become sensitive and, therefore, a target for hackers and social engineers. From a social engineering point of view, this increased connectivity across all aspects of our lives also means profiling potential targets will be easier than ever before.

Easier Profiling, More Believable Attacks

Social engineering attacks have become more sophisticated and more targeted than they used to be, and this trend is set to continue as we become increasingly connected across different aspects of our lives. The more information that is available about each individual, the easier it is to profile that person and to design a social engineering attack that is personalized, believable, and therefore much more likely to succeed. In the early 2000s, social networking started the trend of sharing information. Back then, we had to actively push information out to the social networks, publishing it about ourselves for the most part. And we still do it. But now technology is increasingly tracking our habits.

Social Networks

Social networking changed the face of social engineering. Social networks provide a huge attack surface, network upon network of potential victims. Social engineers can easily pick targets and even automate their target selection, potentially by setting up botnets to gather email addresses for phishing or phone numbers for vishing or smishing. Do a search on "lost my phone" on any social network, and you will get a ton of phone numbers as users ask their friends to let them know their phone numbers, as in the example shown in Figure 11-4. People publish their email addresses and phone numbers on social networking sites all the time. Now it's trivial to find victims and create a believable attack based on their profile information.

Social engineering attacks are really easy to perpetrate on social networks. They have a low barrier entry point—if attackers can't be bothered or don't have the skills to hack someone's social media account, they can set up a fake profile and copy an existing attack. Social networks operate on a trust model, but there is very little real authentication. Few people validate that the person who has contacted them really is who he or she claims to be, making it easy to impersonate people or set up fake profiles. Look at the case of Robin Sage (from Chapter 2). Impersonation in the real world is much higher risk from the point of view of a criminal. It's more expensive (think of the set up costs, such as purchasing costumes, hiring venues, etc.) and much easier to get caught. In the future, we might see more people using fake names and aliases, not only to perpetrate fraud, but also as a cover to protect themselves.

Individuals aren't the only ones using social networking these days. Many organizations maintain a profile on social networking sites. Hacking an individual's social networking accounts, often using some form of social engineering, is increasingly commonplace. Hacking an organization's social networking accounts can have a huge

FIGURE 11-4   Friends of this user were more than happy to post their phone numbers for all to see.

Breaking: Two Explosions in the White House and Barack Obama is injured

↩ Reply ⇄ Retweet ★ Favorite ••• More

FIGURE 11-5   The Tweet posted by the hacked @AP Twitter account

impact. In 2013, the Dow Jones index fell 150 points in three minutes, briefly wiping out $136.5 billion, when the Associated Press Twitter account was hacked and a fake tweet announced that there had been two explosions at the White House, as shown in Figure 11-5.

There has been a bit of a backlash against the pervasiveness of social media. Every now and again, a celebrity shuts down his or her account. We hear media reports that users are quitting social networking sites for various reasons. Some users view them as a waste of time; some see them as too much effort; others quit because their favorite celebrity has stopped using the site. A seemingly small number of people quit due to privacy concerns. Although social media does have its flaws, it looks like it is here to stay in one form or another, so we need to be aware of the security risks it brings.

The Cloud

The cloud has given attackers new infrastructure and individuals to target or impersonate. Individuals and businesses alike have turned to the cloud for cheap and easy data storage. Therefore, to access this data, social engineers can target either the

---

TagMeNot

Sometimes, no matter what you do to prevent it, someone ends up tagging your photo online. If you don't want your photos to be tagged or recognized by facial recognition software, one option to consider is TagMeNot at www.tagmenot.info. TagMeNot is a free opt-out technology for pictures taken in public places. It provides you with a QR code that links to the TagMeNot.info website, which clearly states that you don't want your picture to be published online unless all details are erased, blurred, or pixilated. The practical applications currently listed on the website include

- Placing the QR code on the outside of your building to let Google Street View and MS Streetside know you are opting out.
- Wearing a QR code on your person to help avoid tagging on social networks.
- Displaying a TagMeNot QR code to state that any pictures of you have to be blurred prior to publication online.

individual or business, or alternatively target staff at whatever cloud service provider their target is using. The Matt Honan social engineering attack described in Chapter 2 is a textbook example of a social engineering attack involving the cloud. Matt himself wasn't directly social engineered, but Amazon and Apple were, and Matt was still the victim. The leaked photos of several Hollywood celebrities in 2011 was a result of the hacker targeting their cloud-based email accounts and using social engineering techniques to trick his targets into sending intimate photos, as per the upcoming sidebar.

Since cloud computing was introduced, more organizations than ever before have embraced the idea of working remotely. The cloud allows their employees to access data from anywhere. Naturally, this means employees can be compromised from anywhere. Social engineers and thieves may target staff not only in the workplace, but also anywhere else they work from, at home, in the coffee shop, or in the airport lounge. From a social engineer's point of view, it may be easier to con people who are used to dealing with their colleagues or clients remotely, and who, in some cases, have never met their colleagues. Impersonating someone your victim has never met or had any voice communication with is much easier.

The cloud has also provided many new social engineering tools for both ethical and malicious social engineers alike, once again providing new mechanisms for delivering attacks. Tools such as TraceSecurity's Phishing Simulator harness the power of the cloud to deliver phishing tests. Some cloud-based tools can be used to detect social engineering attacks, such as Google Safe Browsing API and Webroot's Real-time AntiPhishing API.

> **Tip** Cloud computing has a lot to offer. More and more businesses are turning to the cloud for data storage. However not all cloud providers are equal when it comes to security. Don't forget to check your cloud service provider's security policies.

Wearable Tech

Take a look around you and check if anyone is sporting any wearable technology. It may be on their wrists, clothing, or eyewear. Smart watches, fitness trackers, and digitally enhanced clothing are all gaining in popularity. Other interesting applications include clothing that responds to Tweets (check out EroGear's high heels that can stream live Twitter feeds) and even a solar bikini. Analysts from Juniper Research predict that the market for wearable tech will hit $19 billion by 2018.[11] That's a lot of scope for social engineering and other security-related attacks.

Wearable tech serves many practical (or sometimes aesthetic) functions. It also constantly gathers information about the wearer, profiling her habits and measuring and analyzing her data on the go. With wearable tech, your data always accompanies you, monitoring you wherever you go and improving certain areas of your life (your fitness level, your health, your viewing experience, for example). In many cases, there is a social aspect to the technology as well; it encourages people to share their data. For example, many of the fitness bands such as Fitbit allow wearers to compete with other wearers. Malicious individuals who can access the information gathered by

---

[11] www.juniperresearch.com/reports/Smart_Wearable_Devices

The Hollywood Hacker

The so-called Hollywood Hacker, Christopher Chaney, hacked into the cloud-based email accounts of several Hollywood stars, including Christina Aguilera, Scarlett Johansson, and Mila Kunis, and posted intimate photographs of them online. According to court documents and official testimony, Chaney hacked online accounts at AOL, Apple, Google, and Yahoo!

He started by targeting Simone Haroche, a celebrity stylist. He clicked the "Forgot Your Password" link on Apple's MobileMe login page (this service later became iCloud) and entered Haroche's email address. The system asked for Haroche's date of birth along with several security questions, the answers for which were easily researched online, before resetting the password to one of Chaney's choosing. With access to Haroche's MobileMe account, Chaney had access to her private emails and contact list, which included many Hollywood celebrities.

He used Haroche's email account to send a message to Christina Aguilera. The message asked the pop star to send some photos of herself wearing "very little clothing"—a believable request from a stylist. Aguilera complied. Chaney published the pictures online and proceeded to run a series of similar nude celebrity scams, targeting Scarlett Johansson and Mila Kunis, among others. In 2011, Chaney logged into Johansson's email account and sent a message to the actress's friend who possessed some infamous pictures of her. In addition to celebrity photos and gossip, Chaney obtained details of business contracts, unpublished movie scripts, and social security numbers.

Chaney set Haroche's account to forward incoming emails to a dummy email address under his control, so he could continue to monitor the stylist's account even after she regained access to it.

Chaney was sentenced to ten years in prison in December 2012.

wearable tech can learn a lot about the wearer. Information garnered in this way could potentially help to further a social engineering attack.

For now, wearable tech is still quite a novelty. Almost everyone finds it exciting or useful. I can imagine a social engineering scenario where the attacker sends some wearable tech to her target, who is pleased to receive it and puts it on, allowing the attacker to track the target's movements or habits. Wearable tech could also serve as a good prize to incentivize potential targets to enter a competition or complete a survey.

Some wearable tech may allow wearers to access data on the go. For organizations, wearable tech may make their staff more productive, just as the introduction of cell phones and laptops did. But as with cell phones and laptops, wearable tech will introduce a host of security considerations for organizations that adopt it. For example, how will organizations control logical access to their data and networks via wearable tech? Then there is the physical security aspect. If an employee is using Google Glass, for example, to access company information, and he loses his glasses or has them

The Solar Bikini

New York designer Andrew Schneider has invented a solar-powered bikini that can charge a smartphone or media player while its wearer catches some rays. The bikini has a series of photovoltaic film sewn together with conductive thread, terminating in a USB port where the wearer can charge her devices. Don't worry guys—a male version is in production and might even be available by the time this book is published! The male version, called the iDrink, has a greater surface area and, therefore, more output voltage. This extra voltage will be put to good use in the form of a beer cooler! The bikinis are available on www.solarcoterie.com. Imagine the possibilities for hackers and social engineers alike as our swimwear becomes smarter...

(Image from http://andrewjs.com/solarbikini.html)

stolen, or the data is stolen from storage media (*I filmed my lunch but accidentally leaked a corporate report*), what does it mean for the organization? How often have you lost a pair of glasses or sunglasses—just put them down somewhere and then walked away? Gadgets to help prevent you losing your glasses will become increasingly important, down to the glasses chains people use to hang their glasses around their neck when not in use. Such eyewear will probably be quite valuable, especially if you can access sensitive information through it, so the glass strings or chains would have to be reinforced so thieves couldn't just cut right through or snatch and grab them.

The ultimate in wearable tech from a social engineer's point of view would be a Harry Potter–style invisibility cloak. Scientists have made several attempts to develop such a cloak and have made great progress. In 2013, scientists at the University of Texas designed an invisibility device that can hide objects at a range of light frequencies[12] (although it does make them more visible at certain frequencies). It would be great to do a physical social engineering test with an invisibility cloak! From a security professional's point of view, we need to think about how future technology could be misused and find ways to implement controls to detect unauthorized individuals in invisibility cloaks. You couldn't rely on staff challenging intruders if they can't even see them!

Countering Surveillance

New York–based artist Adam Harvey has several projects that explore the impact of surveillance technologies on society. A number of these projects focus on how we can counter surveillance technologies using makeup or fashion.

Harvey's CV Dazzle project combines makeup and hair styling (or other modifications) to thwart face-detection software. The name comes from two sources: "CV" is a common abbreviation for computer vision, and "Dazzle" was a type of camouflage used in the First World War that protected warships from submarine attacks. CV Dazzle uses eye-catching patterns and colors (which look like something Lady Gaga might wear) that alter the contrast and spatial relationship of key facial features, thus rendering the face unrecognizable to face-detection systems. Although CV Dazzle users stick out in a crowd, because of their crazy makeup or styling, they remain undetected by face-detection systems. Face detection is the first step in facial-recognition systems, and by preventing the software from detecting the presence of any face at all, CV Dazzle can reduce the probability of a face being recognized. According to Harvey, the CV Dazzle method has successfully thwarted the facial-recognition software used by Facebook, Picasa, and Flickr.

Creating a CV Dazzle look is all about challenging the assumptions of what a typical face looks like and thus confusing the face-detection process so the probability of detecting a face is greatly reduced. Some of the key steps in this process involve

- Creating asymmetry in the person's face, as face-detection systems expect symmetry between both sides of the face
- Concealing key facial features, such as the nose bridge, lips, and ocular region under the eye so face-detection software does not pick up on them
- Using tonal inverse, that is, light colors on dark skin and dark colors on light skin. Face-detection software uses skin tone to detect a face so this can help to confuse the software.

---

[12] Pai-Yen Chen, Christos Argyropoulos, and Andrea Alù, "Broadening the Cloaking Bandwidth with Non-Foster Metasurfaces," *Physical Review Letters* 111, 23 (2013).

FIGURE 11-6   A CV Dazzle look designed by Adam Harvey (Source: http://ahprojects.com/projects/cv-dazzle)

Figure 11-6 shows one of the CV Dazzle looks that has been used to successfully thwart face detection. There are online tutorials available on how to create your own CV Dazzle look, including Jillian Mayer's YouTube tutorial on how to hide from cameras: www.youtube.com/watch?v = kGGnnp43uNM.

Another of Harvey's projects, Stealth Wear, is fashion that uses counter-surveillance technology. The range includes some "anti-drone" wear to thwart thermal imaging by reducing the wearer's thermal signature, the XX T-Shirt, which protects the wearer from X-ray radiation (for example, in body scanners), and the OFF Pocket, which is a cellphone cover that blocks all incoming and outgoing phone signals.

At the time of writing, Harvey's next project, "How to be DNA-Ambiguous," involves DNA spoofing, which will investigate how you can scramble genetic material so it cannot be used for surveillance. As part of this project, he has come up with some DIY techniques for evading genetic surveillance, which involve things like sharing hair brushes so they have hair strands belonging to different individuals, chewing other people's chewed chewing gum, and even gluing someone else's fingernails on top of your own.

You can read more about Harvey's fascinating projects at www.ahprojects.com and purchase Stealth Wear clothing at www.privacygiftshop.com. You never know when Harvey's projects may come in useful on a social engineering test!

Implanted Tech

Going one step further than wearable tech is the concept of implanted tech. When technology that we incorporate into our bodies becomes networked, like the Internet of Things, it brings a host of security concerns into play. From a social engineer's point of view, it could be even better than wearable tech for profiling a target.

In 2006, a Cypriot-Australian performance artist by the name of Stelarc had a third ear surgically implanted into his left arm, as shown in Figure 11-7. The ear has a microphone in it that connects to a Bluetooth transmitter and transmits the audio over the Internet (usually to galleries that are displaying his work). What if Stelarc does telephone banking or makes a credit card purchase over the phone while he is transmitting? Anyone tuned into his arm ear can presumably overhear this information. The options for a social engineer or identity thief looking to steal his details or identity are staggering.

Even more so than wearable tech, implanted tech tracks the user 24/7. How do you turn it off? Can you set it so it doesn't record the *really* sensitive bits? In the future, our data will accompany us everywhere all the time. It will undoubtedly improve many aspects of our lives, but we must be alert to the security implications that such futuristic technology will bring.

This constant connectivity, whether it's through social networking, the Internet of Things, wearable tech, or even implanted tech, means profiling potential targets is easy. We live in a society where surveillance is taken for granted by the majority of people. We expect our every move to be recorded. We may even be knowingly recording our own movements for various reasons. The term "Quantified Self" was proposed by *Wired Magazine* editors Gary Wolf and Kevin Kelly in 2007 as "a collaboration of users and toolmakers who share an interest in self knowledge through self-tracking." Although the Quantified Self, in theory, involves *self*-tracking, there may also be *other people*-tracking by various groups or individuals. Al Gore, the former US vice president, called the situation a "stalker economy," but he could have just as

FIGURE 11-7　Stelarc's Ear on Arm project (Source: http://stelarc.org/?catID=20242)

Stop the Cyborgs

Some groups such as Stop the Cyborgs have launched campaigns against the increasingly prevalent use of wearable tech and the constant surveillance that it brings. The "Stop The Cyborgs" movement (www.stopthecyborgs.org) was born out of a concern for privacy when it comes to wearable technology. From the website:

> "Stop The Cyborgs" was founded in response to the combination of wearable technology with "big data." The aim of the movement is to stop a future in which privacy is impossible and where the iron cage of surveillance, calculation, and control pervades every aspect of life.

easily have described it as a "social engineering economy," with all the opportunities it brings for social engineering attacks.

Because we are knowingly or unknowingly sharing more data, there are more tools to analyze and make sense of this information. Social engineers have access to tools to profile their targets, such as Cree.py or Maltego. Developers are sure to create tools to analyze the vast amounts of data created by the IoT and wearable or implanted tech. Such tools will allow social engineers to more quickly create believable, personalized social engineering attacks that are harder to detect.

In years to come, who knows—maybe there will be a market for buying and selling information garnered from the IoT and wearable/implanted tech, like the credit card and identity theft markets today. You might buy a profile that says John plays tennis at St. Peter's on Tuesday between 2 and 5 P.M. and eats at Wagamama directly after. Maybe you could buy an analysis that lists all the people with heart problems that go to a certain doctor. The more information that is collected, the more opportunities the social engineer has.

Final Thoughts

Whatever the future holds for social engineering, it is sure to be interesting. We have only seen the tip of the iceberg to date. Up to now, social engineering attacks have been, for the most part, rather pedestrian and, in many cases, easy to detect. This basic level of social engineering will always exist, and someone, somewhere will fall for it. But most of us are wise to these basic attacks now. Social engineering is about to get exciting, however! We will see far more imaginative but believable attacks in the future, delivered in new and innovative ways.

Those of us in the information security industry need to take measures to prevent social engineering attacks from being successful. Reading this book and keeping up to date with social engineering news will help you to become aware of the kinds of tools and techniques that social engineers use. This awareness is the first step in defending against malicious social engineering attacks. Performing a social engineering test is another great way to do this. So my final prediction for the future of social engineering, for better or for worse, is there is going to be a lot more ethical social engineering testing.

Social engineering will always work. On some level. At least some of the time. Make sure you are prepared.

Index

Numbers

A

Q